PROGRESSIVE EDUCATION

Revisioning and Reframing Ontario's Public Schools, 1919–1942

THEODORE MICHAEL CHRISTOU

Progressive Education

Revisioning and Reframing Ontario's Public Schools, 1919–1942

UNIVERSITY OF TORONTO PRESS
Toronto Buffalo London

© University of Toronto Press 2012
Toronto Buffalo London
www.utppublishing.com
Printed in Canada

ISBN 978-1-4426-4542-4

Printed on acid-free, 100% post-consumer recycled paper with
vegetable-based inks.

Library and Archives Canada Cataloguing in Publication

Christou, Theodore Michael, 1978–
Progressive education : revisioning and reframing Ontario's public
schools, 1919–1942 / Theodore Michael Christou.

Includes bibliographical references and index.
ISBN 978-1-4426-4542-4

1. Progressive education – Ontario – History.   2. Public Schools –
Ontario – History – 20th century.   I. Title

LA418.O6C48 2012   370.9713   C2012-904189-0

This book has been published with the help of a grant from the Canadian
Federation for the Humanities and Social Sciences, through the Awards to
Scholarly Publications Program, using funds provided by the Social Sci-
ences and Humanities Research Council of Canada.

University of Toronto Press acknowledges the financial assistance to its
publishing program of the Canada Council for the Arts and the Ontario
Arts Council.

 Canada Council   Conseil des Arts
for the Arts   du Canada
 ONTARIO ARTS COUNCIL
CONSEIL DES ARTS DE L'ONTARIO

University of Toronto Press acknowledges the financial support of the
Government of Canada through the Canada Book Fund for its publishing
activities.

For the namesakes, and for the muse.

Contents

viii   Contents

Preface

This book arose from a need to develop an inclusive model for describing the historical meanings of progressive education, which is a historical movement and ideology that has fascinated educationists for most of the twentieth century. Various historians have argued that progressive education has been the seminal force for reform in the twentieth century. Others have blamed it for all the ills plaguing contemporary schooling. Still others, frustrated by the many debates about and differing definitions of progressive education in the literature, have declared the term meaningless. This book examines one era – Ontario after the First World War – during which progressivist thinking transformed the rhetoric and the structure of schooling. It examines reformist thinking during a time of social, political, and economic progress. The world at that time seemed transformed, modern, and new, yet education seemed woefully out of touch with social reality. A progressive society appeared to demand progressivist schools that could actively relate learning to the real world.

These themes remain fresh: progressive education continues to be examined in academic studies of North American education. The present study seeks to describe the particular themes and subjects of progressivist schooling in Ontario, where the entire landscape of public education – including the curriculum and avenues to post-secondary study – was transformed over a twenty-year span. It examines the rhetoric of reform that was published between 1919 and 1942 in two widely distributed and accessible journals in Ontario: *The School* and *The Canadian School Journal*. These sources, which have rarely been used or cited by historians, brought together a variety of educationists in the province, including teachers, school board representatives, members of the Department of Education, inspectors, and the staff of teacher training institutions, and were forums for exploring new and progressive educational ideas. Various conceptions and interpretations of what progressive education would entail were published side by side, in parallel.

The model developed and described here organizes Ontario's progressivist rhetoric and thought into three themes, or domains: active learning, individualized instruction, and the linking of schools to contemporary society. These themes are not monolithic; at the time, Ontario's educationists offered various interpretations of what, for instance, active learning actually entailed. This book will describe three distinct interpretations of each progressivist theme. The first progressivist orientation was primarily concerned with child study and developmental psychology; the second, with social efficiency and industrial order; the third, with social meliorism and cooperation. Hence, I draw not only on three different domains of progressivist rhetoric, but also on three distinct orientations to reform. What emerges is a description of how different progressivists understood and represented Ontario's transforming schools, in a context affected by the forces of modernity, world war, and economic depression.

Acknowledgments

This manuscript has received careful, comprehensive, and thorough feedback from a number of colleagues and friends to whom I am greatly in debt. First, thanks are due to Dr Rosa Bruno-Jofré, who adopted me as a son and whose patience and guidance serve as testaments to the friendship and care that are at the heart of scholarly associations. From the first stages on, the careful and diligent suggestions and mentorship of Dr Ian McKay helped shape and contour this project. I am further grateful to Dr Eva Krugly-Smolska for her numerous readings of this manuscript, her keen eye for detail, and her kindness. Further thanks are due to Dr Elizabeth Smythe, Dr Jeff Brison, Dr Marguerite Van Die, Dr Skip Hills, and Dr Scott Johnston for their suggestions, which helped transform a doctoral dissertation into a book manuscript. Len Husband at the University of Toronto Press has encouraged me, guided me, and shielded me through this process; I am grateful to him for his patience and for his expertise. For their assistance through the final stages of translating my manuscript into this book, I thank Frances Mundy, Matthew Kudelka, Shoshana Wasser, as well as the other good people working fastidiously at the University of Toronto Press.

I wish to acknowledge the generous funding of several organizations, institutions, and councils. Archival work is dreadfully expensive. These sources include the Social Sciences and Humanities Research Council of Canada (SSHRC), various Queen's University awards, including the Martin Schiralli Fellowship, the William C. Leggett Fellowship, the Walter F. Light Fellowship, Graduate Student Awards, and the Kent Haworth Archival Research Fellowship from York University. I also thank the Canadian Federation of Humanities and Social Sciences for extending this project the generous Aid to Scholarly Publishing Program (ASPP) grant, which made publication of this book possible.

It is essential to acknowledge, albeit in broad strokes, my colleagues – the faculty, graduate students, librarians and archivists, and support staff – at both Queen's University and the University of New Brunswick, who lent their support to these research efforts. I would be remiss in not including the names of a few individuals whose mentorship has been invaluable throughout my life in the academy (Dr Alan Sears, Dr Ann Sherman, Dr Kieran Egan, Dr William Pinar, Dr Richard Volpe, and Dr Helen Raptis). The Toronto District School Board gave me my first big shot at professional education, for which I will be forever grateful. My students always taught me more about education than I could ever teach them.

Thanks most of all to my dear wife (Aglaia), to my parents (Theodora and Michael, whose names I carry), and to my sisters, Pantelitsa and Stavrini. Thanks to the grace of God and the power of prayer. Thanks for an overabundance of love that has always steadied my sometimes-faltering heart.

PROGRESSIVE EDUCATION

Revisioning and Reframing Ontario's Public Schools,
1919–1942

Introduction: What Was Progressive Education?

Today we live in a complex civilization which it is necessary to understand in order to be adjusted to it. Schools are the means by which we accomplish this period of adjustment.*

As a classroom teacher in Toronto, Ontario, I was accused of being a *progressive* on three different occasions. On the first occasion, I was leading the students in my sixth grade class in a redesign of our classroom layout. We had been learning about perimeter and area. We catalogued items and furniture in the class – carpets, desks, filing cabinets, and so on – recorded measurements for these, and designed new layouts for the space. These models were then applied, and each student's measurements and designs were put to the test via a practical rearrangement of the classroom. We had fun, and a colleague accused me of being a progressive for following through with this plan.

On the second occasion, I permitted my students to jump out of the classroom windows. It was all very orderly. The classroom was a portable, and the windows were, perhaps, two-and-a-half feet off the ground. It was a beautiful spring day, following a particularly harsh winter, and the sun was shining in through the windows at us. The students were looking wistfully out at nature's glory, and I took pity on them for sitting so quietly in the rectangular tin can of a classroom that had been allotted to us that year. 'You'd like to jump out of the windows into the sunshine, wouldn't you?' I asked. They did, so I lined them up in orderly fashion. One by one, gingerly and cautiously, they

---

* 'Educational News,' *The Canadian School Journal* (November 1933): 403.

stepped up onto the window frame, tucked their heads down, and hopped out. Then we went back to studying math, or whatever subject was scheduled at the time. That afternoon, a parent, having heard of the miniature expedition during lunch hour, asked to speak with me. I expected that I would have to justify what I had done; rather – which was worse – I was called progressive.

On the third occasion, a student teacher completing her internship under my supervision described my assessment strategies as progressive. This was surprising, as I had taken heat from some of my colleagues for not grading as rigidly and as rigorously as they expected of me. I permitted students to redo assignments as many times as they wished. Instead of emphasizing grades, I wrote comments that explained how my students were able to demonstrate their understanding of concepts or skills. My goal in this was to combat learned helplessness of the sort that manifested itself when students told me, for example, 'Mr Christou, I can't do math.' When I asked why they could not *do* math – or speech arts, or whatever it was they felt unable to participate in adequately – the response from students was something like: 'I've always had Cs in math.' I did not understand how anything that I was doing was particularly progressive.

For that matter, *everything* seemed to be called progressive. Who wants to be a *regressive* teacher? What administrator would implement a *regressive* reform policy in the school? Apparently, everything from trying to understand students' need to be outside the classroom, to permitting them opportunities to apply their learning or even show their learning in different ways, was deemed *progressive*. If everything was progressive, the term had no utility and was, therefore, meaningless.

I began reading in the history of education to try to understand how this term had become so tangled. The more I read, the less I understood about the concept. The more I studied the history of education, the more I wondered why my teacher education program had not included a formal component exploring educational history. My colleagues and I – even my administration and the school board superintendents – all drew a blank on this subject. Why did schools look the way they did? Why do we describe things as we do? How can I and the teacher next door to me think so very differently about the same things, such as assessment? I wondered how things had become so messed up.

Two years later I began doctoral studies at Queen's University in Kingston, Ontario. It had never been my ambition to pursue a PhD, but the opportunity to study the history of education in Ontario more formally was one that I seized. My focus was on the problem of 'progressive education.' I wanted to know what that term meant at the moment of its birth in the province. How was it understood, and how was it described? Unravelling the question historically led me to the interwar period. After the First World War, in the wake of dramatic social, economic, and political changes in Ontario, the rhetoric of progressive education took root and began to spread throughout the province. The war had transformed the world, and schools no longer seemed suitable for the modern age. Progressive education would be required for a progressive age. We are following to this day the wake of that progressive movement; and in the clarion calls for twenty-first-century schools that echo through contemporary school districts and faculties of education, I can hear the progressive ethos rejuvenated. At the root of '21C' – the catch term now popular among educationists in several provinces when they refer to the cultivation of skills that will be necessary in the coming century – is the progressivists' insistence that schools adjust to modern life, which is fraught with radically accelerated technological and social change.

As an educator, I have had the privilege of teaching in early childhood, public, private, and post-secondary institutions. The *progressive* label always puzzled me, not least because I was uncertain what that term meant. What kind of progressive was I, and to what ends was I progressing? Conversely, what might a *regressive* approach to education look like? The literature on progressive education was equally baffling to me as I began this research, for it seemed to identify manifold and even contradictory beliefs and practices with the progressive camp. The present book thus evolved into an effort on my part to provide an inclusive framework for describing the dominant themes of progressive education. Within this inclusive model, various orientations to and interpretations of progressivist themes could then be compared and contrasted.

As you will see, how progressivist ideas were interpreted in the context varied. The progressivist educators described herein seemed to be working out the meanings of progressive education, even as they advocated them. Here it is worth quoting from an editorial published in the 1930s: 'The meaning of progressive education, as the term is used in recent educational writings, is not easy to define. It is in the nature of the word that the types of educational activity to which it is applied should continually vary.'[1] The first progressivist orientation that I describe was concerned primarily with child study and developmental psychology;

the second, with social efficiency and industrial order; the third, with social meliorism and cooperation. Thus, my analysis will be drawing not only on three different domains of progressivist rhetoric but also on three distinct orientations to reform. What emerges, I hope, will be a description of how various progressivists understood and represented Ontario's transforming schools.

Throughout this book, the term *progressivist* will be used to describe a specific educational stance toward educational reform in Ontario. *Progressivist* is a descriptor for the language and ideas of progressive education; it refers to arguments that schools need to provide individualized instruction, opportunities for active learning, and knowledge or experiences related to contemporary life outside the schools. The term relates to matters of pedagogy and rhetoric, not political or ideological trends of progressivism writ large in provincial or national contexts.

This study draws primarily on editorials and articles published in two journals that were widely distributed between 1919 and 1942, *The School* and *The Canadian School Journal*. These journals' editorials presented progressivist visions for school reform, which I examined many decades later in order to describe what Ontario's educationists considered the aims and objectives of progressive education. The sources are discussed at length in chapter 2 of this book. By *educationists*, I am referring to the broad spectrum of stakeholders in education, including – but not limited to – teachers, administrators, professors of education, school inspectors, and officials in the Department of Education.

The central research questions in this manuscript inquire into the qualitatively different understandings of progressive education between 1919 and 1942. Specifically, I ask: What did progressive education *mean* to Ontario's educational community in this period?[2] The central themes, or domains, that I investigate – active learning, individualized instruction, and linking schools with society – and the distinct orientations that interpreted these domains – child study, social efficiency, and social meliorism – will be discussed at length. The thesis here is that the progressivist rhetoric in Ontario's educational journals between 1919 and 1942 needs to be described both in terms of common themes, or domains, and in terms of distinct orientations that interpreted these themes in various ways.

With regard to progressivism in Ontario's education system, the rhetoric clusters around three themes: (a) a concern for active learning, (b) a preoccupation with individualized instruction, and (c) the desire to link schools with contemporary society. These can be thought of as frames for understanding the common concerns of progressivist educationists. They emerged from three critiques of traditional schooling that progressivists set out to address: (a) passive learning, defined by reliance on memorization and examination, (b) an overemphasis on teaching the curriculum at the expense of the individual learner's interests and abilities, and (c) a traditional curriculum that had been established to transmit knowledge valued in the past rather than information relevant to the present. In many respects, John Dewey's contention that progressivists had defined their aims in terms that were oppositional to an alternative educational approach, which they described as 'traditional,' were accurate in the Canadian context: 'Mankind likes to think in terms of extreme opposites,' he wrote. 'It is given to formulating its beliefs in terms of *Either-Ors* ... At present, the opposition, so far as practical affairs of the school are concerned, tends to take the form of contrast between traditional and progressive education.'[3]

In the present context, the distinct orientations to the three progressivist domains are also threefold: (a) child study and developmental psychology, (b) social efficiency, and (c) social meliorism. I argue that describing progressive education in any particular historical context requires us to frame both the domain of progressivist thought and the orientation to this domain – or, the various ways that aspects of progressive education were interpreted.

Chapter 1 of this book examines Ontario's interwar history (1919–42) – the social, economic, and political changes experienced by the province – and relates these to the system of schooling that existed in Ontario at the time that the progressivist articles I examine were being published. The separate schools, the Department of Education, the curriculum revisions, and the expansion of educational opportunity are all discussed. Chapter 1 is intended as a general overview of Ontario's school system at the time, with the aim of providing a context for the educationists' progressivist discourse.

Chapter 2 begins by describing the historical sources examined and explaining their importance to this study and to the province's educational community at the time. The chapter then explores various approaches to the study of progressive education. What do the educational journals reveal about the qualitatively different understandings of progressive education in Ontario?

Chapters 3, 4, and 5 – the core of this study – discuss in depth the themes of progressive education as well as their various interpretations. Each examines one of the three domains of progressivist texts that I have identified: active learning, individualized instruction, and the linking of schools to the realities of contemporary life. Each of these chapters in turn has three sections, which correspond to distinct progressivist orientations: child study, social efficiency, and social meliorism. The sections describe how various types of progressivist articles depicted the aims and means of school reforms in Ontario between 1919 and 1942.

Chapter 6 examines the decline in the emphasis on humanistic and classical educational aims within the sources. It also considers the critiques of progressivist reforms of Ontario's education emanating from the established, traditional paradigm for schooling. Receiving special attention is the humanists' advocacy of school libraries as havens for canonical texts and classical works of literature. In this book, notwithstanding the broad associations of terms such as the *humanities* and *humanistic study*, the term *humanist* is used as a foil to the progressivist position. The humanists' defence of the classical curriculum – principally, that it developed intellect and trained mental faculties – lost its dominance at the rhetorical level; that said, the humanists also believed that at least libraries, which preserved traditional educational ideals, would remain closely associated with schools. This book views the humanistic arguments as the principal critiques of progressivist discourse in the source journals.

Chapter 7 opens by examining Ontario's 1937 curriculum reforms, characterizing these revisions as an attempt to weave various progressivist concerns – including health, social studies, and cooperative activity – into a broad and comprehensive vision for the province's schools. The same chapter considers some of the effects of the Second World War on Ontario's progressivist rhetoric, beginning with the swell of arguments defending democracy and promoting active citizenship. The early 1940s, like the entire interwar period, demanded that Ontario's citizens respond to what George Tomkins referred to as the 'problems of economic recession, political confusion, sectional conflict ... and fears of Americanization.'[4] Progressive education would be linked to the shifting needs of contemporary life, as defined by educationists at the time.

1 Ontario's Educational Context in the Interwar Period

It is, then, the responsibility of educators of every grade and rank, from the primary school to the university, to acquaint themselves with the facts of the present day world, and if possible, to determine a philosophy adequate for the construction of that new society which may emerge from the present chaos.[*]

This chapter explores continuity and change with regard to such matters as teacher education, curriculum reform, school organization, federations, and the professionalization of teaching in Ontario. Insofar as political and socio-economic factors in Canadian and Ontario society affected education, these will also be discussed. The expansion of education in the province is reviewed, and emergent themes, including child study, health, and social efficiency, are introduced.

We begin in 1919. The years following the First World War in Ontario exposed the influence of progressivist educational ideas in the province.[1] In the interwar years, progressive rhetoric and reforms would flourish across the country. John Herd Thompson and Allen Seager write that 'the 1920s saw a flowering of the movement for "progressive" education in Canada.'[2] By the early 1930s these influences on educational discourse were being felt in all Canadian provinces.[3] By 1919 the social and economic effects of a sudden and dramatic increase in immigration and urbanization had taken hold across Canada; in Robert Patterson's words, 'after World War I, Canadians entered a new

---

[*] Joseph McCulley, 'Education in a Changing Society,' *The Canadian School Journal* (February 1932): 60.

era, characterized by industrialization, urbanization and increasing emphasis on democratic development.'[4] Tom Mitchell writes that after the First World War, middle-class Canadians projected a national identity 'by casting the post-war order in a particular idiom of nationalism informed by a common Canadianism rooted in Anglo-conformity and a citizenship framed in notions of service, obedience, obligation and fidelity to the state.'[5]

The Second World War also provoked great change across the country, influencing notions of citizenship as well as education's role in shaping a polity.[6] The Great Depression of the 1930s, which nurtured the belief that educational reform could bring about economic and social change, also falls within the scope of this study.[7] Notwithstanding two recessions in the decade following the First World War, Ontario's economy had benefited immensely from exporting its vast northern mineral and timber reserves.[8] The auto plants and steel mills in the Golden Horseshoe stretching from Hamilton to Oshawa and in the province's southwest also fed Ontario's economic boom.[9] The development of efficient hydroelectric power decreased the province's dependence on imported coal and reinforced its status as an industrial powerhouse.[10]

Ideas about modernity and progress transformed society in the interwar years.[11] Kieran Egan paints in striking colours a social landscape that was being changed by rapid growth in population largely due to immigration, industrial expansion, universal schooling, and the growing influence of the theory of evolution:

> As your train carries you on, at a speed and with a comfort unimaginable to any traveler before you in history, you recognize that the physical and social changes you see are reflected in, or are products of, a ferment of new ideas. The number and novelty of those new ideas is disruptive on a scale never before experienced. The result creates anxiety in those who see the foundations of their old intellectual world being threatened but is exhilarating to progressive minds.[12]

Education had often been viewed as out of touch with life's ever-evolving realities. But now it was also seen as a force for remedying ills, preparing for the future, and enabling upcoming generations to deal with the modern world.[13] A new, progressive education was required for a modern, progressive world.[14]

Soldiers returning from the war found their homes and worlds being transformed. Many of their wives and sisters had left home or entered the workplace. These women were gaining the right to vote in the federal elections, lobbying for temperance and the prohibition of alcohol, and becoming active citizens.[15] Moreover, the postwar industrial crisis meant that many veterans found themselves unemployed upon returning home, while others were unable to work because of injuries and disabilities they had suffered in the war.[16] This provoked a sharp increase in strike activity as well as 'demands for social justice and decent living conditions.'[17]

The urbanization of Canada that had begun at the turn of the twentieth century continued unabated. Municipalities wrestled with rising unemployment, an influx of newcomers, and the need to plan urban growth.[18] Rural people – 40 per cent of Ontario's population as late as 1921 – saw their world vanishing and their world view under attack and began to unite and fight for their values in the political sphere.[19] The United Farmers of Ontario swept into power at Queen's Park in 1919, buoyed by the rural vote.[20] Faced with deteriorating work conditions, labour groups began to unite, and strike activity rose dramatically in the years following the war.[21] The All-Canadian Congress of Labour, the Canadian Federation of Labour, the Trades and Labor Congress of Canada, the Workers' Unity League, and the Congress of Industrial Organizations were, along with individual unions, active during this period in Ontario and across Canada.[22]

Many of these changes were undertaken in the name of progress, and reformers across Canada were 'trying to provide more adequately for the present and future' in contexts that had altered significantly since 1914.[23] There were many reform causes, but those of the farm communities were among the most influential in the immediate postwar period; in fact, 'their concerns constituted the core of the Progressive movement in Canada.'[24] A new progressive coalition led by E.C. Drury comprising members of the United Farmers of Ontario (UFO) and the Independent Labour Party (ILP) won fifty-five seats in the 1919 provincial election.[25] This coalition largely represented labour and farmer interest groups, but a growing intellectual elite in the country was also interested in social and political policy reform.[26] In the words of Robert S. Patterson, the UFO felt that 'the old national political parties were ... allies of the commercial, industrial, and financial interests that were taking unfair advantage of the farm population.'[27]

In the early 1920s the strength of rural reform interests made itself felt with the success of the Progressive Party, which 'won sixty-five seats to become second in strength to the Liberals. But the success was short-lived in the federal arena; their representation dropped to twenty-four in the 1926 election.'[28] The Progressives failed to entrench themselves in federal politics, or in Ontario politics; this was evident in their failure to establish any substantial economic reforms. Dissatisfaction with political representation and economic policies was not limited to the rural electorate; unrest was 'apparent among other segments of the population. Women struggled for and gained new strength through suffrage. The labour population was the centre of a still greater uneasiness.'[29] This contributed to a growing tendency among working-class Ontarians to seek broader change through the ballot box.[30] Parliamentary activity – seemingly a more useful approach to reaching for a new and better society than direct labour unrest – increased in Ontario immediately after the First World War; yet ethnic, local, and occupational differences made broad-based political reform movements difficult to build.[31]

Strikes, demographic changes, immigration, political dissatisfaction, and rapid industrialization had altered the world view of Ontarians. As Patterson notes: 'Strikes were frequent. A proposed national strike was not launched, but in Winnipeg in 1919 a city-wide strike vividly indicated how conditions had changed.'[32] Economic breakdowns – most obviously the Great Depression that began in 1929 – 'convinced many Canadians that basic changes were inevitable ... Many of the changes considered in the twenties were implemented in the thirties.'[33] Progress would have to be made if social policies and government were to respond to the realities of life.

This broader push for progress affected various government policies, which together signalled a rejection of laissez-faire government. Many of these new policies affected welfare and the public good more broadly; they included unemployment insurance, which was first attempted at the national level in 1940; and, during the Depression, the running of budgetary deficits in order to fund public works projects that would provide jobs and stimulate economic recovery.[34] Similarly, in education, progressive reforms signalled changes in the relations between government and the citizenry.[35] Schools, like society, could be reformed and made 'progressive'; they needed to educate citizens for the realities of the modern world, not the Victorian one.[36]

Brian Titley has suggested that progressive education – with its concern for child study, individualized instruction, and active learning – emerged from and is 'clearly linked with two related reformist movements that gripped North America early in this century: progressivism and the social gospel.'[37] In his assessment, both progressives and social gospellers were concerned about changes wrought by modernity, industrialism, immigration, and fear of social instability; they were driven by a strong sense of middle-class Christian morality to reduce conflict, foster community, and build social responsibility.[38] Robert Patterson, reflecting on the vastness of Canada, its internal diversity, the uniqueness of each province's system of schools, and the multidimensional aspects of progressive education, is more hesitant to delineate the causes and effects of the movement.[39] He is certain, though, that progressive education affected Canadian schooling in a profound way:

> Its principles and beliefs gained prominence in the rhetoric and writing of school officials, political leaders and social reformers. Throughout Canada, especially in the 30-year time span between the outbreak of World War I and the end of World War II, advocates of school reform relied heavily on the message of progressive education in their efforts to effect change. Curriculum reforms occurred in virtually every province, and the so-called new education became visible in the methodology and purposes of the schools of the nation.[40]

Patterson's observation that the reform movement expanded slowly and cautiously, culminating in the late 1930s, confirms my reading of Ontario's educational journals. As will be seen in the following chapters, the most common and consistent refrain in those sources is an acute awareness of the changes wrought by modernity on the province, together with a call for educationists to narrow the gap between schools and society.

In 1928 an editorial in *Canadian School Board Journal* commented on that refrain, which was already being widely discussed in periodicals and at educational conferences.[41] In response to the needs of the modern world, the article noted, educational aims were shifting: 'A perusal of the printed volume of Proceedings from year to year would show the bearing the discussions, resolutions and addresses of the various sections have had in adapting the educational system of the province to meet modern needs.'[42] That same year, *The Canadian School Journal* reported labour leader Thomas Moore's pronouncement at the Ontario Educational Association Conference that 'educational systems must necessarily undergo changes to enable the youth to meet the demands of modern complex civilization.'[43]

Progressive schools, it was argued, should respond to a fast-changing world. Telephones, electric motors, refrigerators, streetcars, telephones, films, automobiles, paved highways, airplanes, and radio all were evidence that society was growing increasingly complex; schools designed to relate to past societal needs were now out of touch.[44] Throughout the interwar years, the rhythmic thumping of the theme of modernity was constant. It lent impetus to the progressivists' demands for educational reform and – at least in the sources examined here – was so relentless as to be commonplace. Even in 1942, when Canadians were fully engaged in the Second World War, the calls for a new order in touch with modern times persisted – so much so that Professor R.J. McCracken of McMaster University felt compelled to comment on the 'striking parallel between what is being said now about post-war aims and what was being said from 1914–1918.'[45] Between the end of the First World War and the beginning of the Second, arguments that life must be refashioned for modern times had become slogans – yet substantial changes, particularly in schooling, were still being awaited.[46]

This interest in aligning schools to a changing, progressive society had a particular significance for immigrant populations in Ontario. Education was crucial if society hoped to assimilate new Canadians into the dominant model of citizenship propagated by the British Empire and the Commonwealth. Bringing schools and society into closer alignment would promote democracy and thereby combat communism or socialism; it would also underscore the importance of English-language fluency and help students (as well as immigrant adults) adjust efficiently to the requirements of industrial capitalism. Rosa Bruno-Jofré has written that after the First World War 'schooling was identified as the main agency to develop unity of thought, teach English to the new immigrants, educate them in Canadian ways, and generally to make them proper members of the national polity.'[47] This position would only gain strength from the social unrest of the interwar years.

After the First World War, successive educational authorities identified the expansion of schooling – and of educational opportunity more generally – as an important aim for the province. R.H. Grant, the Minister of Education, reported in 1919 that 'the awakened interest in the training of youth is one of the few beneficial legacies of the War, and there is little doubt that the people of Ontario will prove themselves equal to the educational problems that confront them.'[48] By 1923, Ontarians could 'scarcely pick up a newspaper published in any part of the Province without reading an account of the opening of some new educational institution.'[49] The railway car schools, which started in operation on 26 September 1926, were one creative way of expanding educational opportunity.[50] G. Howard Ferguson's discussion of the province's 'School Cars for Isolated People' would depict the program as an unmitigated success.[51]

Ferguson would describe how these schools on wheels were outfitted with a basic classroom as well as cooking and sleeping accommodations for the teacher. They were moved along the transcontinental railway system by CNR engines, stopping for short periods in small hamlets along the way. The teacher would provide direct instruction for several weeks before distributing assignments to students of varying ages and moving on to the next stop. On the return trip, the teacher would evaluate students' learning and provide further instruction. Ferguson recounted that 'two boys, living far from the railway line, journeyed forty miles to the car, set up an old tent in mid-winter, thatched it with balsam boughs and lived in it while the car was near.'[52]

Many railway car students were immigrants from Europe, and their instruction included not just English skills but Canadian citizenship as well.[53] In 1927 the Department of Education launched a review of the railway car school program, which reported back that 95 per cent of learners were non-English and that 'the School Car has become their social centre. It is exercising a wholesome Canadianizing influence. Parents and pupils are making contact with Canadian history, ideals, modes of life and government.'[54]

Providing a democratic alternative to Bolshevism through education was often cited by the Minister of Education as a purpose of the schools on wheels.[55] At the core of English Canadian national identity was the notion of Anglo-conformity, which immigrants were always negotiating and resisting in various ways.[56] This notion refers to the assimilation of new Canadians – including children – to British mores and behaviour.[57] Well over three million people had immigrated to Canada since 1894, including many European farmers and labourers.[58] Industries such as forestry and mining had drawn them to Canada with the promise of work.[59] The need to integrate these newcomers was strong. V.K. Greer, Chief Inspector of Public and Separate Schools, would report in 1933 that the railway cars served the purpose of 'weaving the homes into the fabric of the social and national order. The parents are profiting almost equally with the child. At the inauguration of the service 90 percent of them were non-British; today 90 percent are naturalized citizens of Canada.'[60]

Adult education and citizenship training were extended via the railway car schools to northern Ontario. In urban centres, also, adult schooling was directed at immigrant Canadians as a way of teaching English language and citizenship.[61] The broad goal of extended adult education programs was to provide 'the labouring classes with liberal education designed to fit them for their role as citizens.'[62] Anglo-conformity dominated conceptions of citizenship, albeit masked by the rhetoric of democratic citizenship and international cooperation. W.L. Grant of Queen's University remarked that even when the adult learners were involved in technical or vocational training or retraining, the 'alliance between labour and learning is not technical training, nor even technical education. Its aim is social education, a training in citizenship; it is liberal, not technical, education.'[63]

Also important to Ontario's education system in the early interwar period was the introduction and rapid expansion of correspondence courses. Like the railway car schools, these courses depended largely on self-directed and self-motivated learners. By the start of the 1930s, Ontario, as well as 'Nova Scotia, and the four western provinces were successfully using correspondence courses to reach students in areas without organized school districts. The initial emphasis was upon elementary education.'[64] To qualify for correspondence schooling, a student had to (a) live in a remote part of his or her province, where there was no access to an educational institution; (b) be unable to travel to a school for the winter months because of severe conditions and isolation of residence; or (c) have a physical ailment that prevented travel to school, despite the mental ability to progress through the program.[65] In Ontario, the first correspondence courses began in 1926; by the Second World War, 2,500 students were enrolled in the program.[66] The Department of Education boasted that many graduates of the correspondence system had been able to pass their high school examinations; many did so more quickly than students in the traditional program.[67]

The extension of schooling also led to the formation of auxiliary classes for the developmentally delayed. Separate classes for slow learners were actually introduced in 1910. These classes were expanded in 1921, when special programs were designed for learners with physical and mental impairments, including speech impediments.[68] These classes were a direct result of the rise of a mental testing movement, which itself was part of an important development in Ontario education during the interwar period – namely, the rise of scientific management and planning of the school system. A prominent figure in the developing field of experimental psychology and mental testing was Peter

Sandiford of the Ontario College of Education. He had been a graduate student of Edward Thorndike, a major player in the progressive education movement in the United States, at Columbia University.

According to Robert Patterson, Sandiford was one of the 'educational experts in a variety of specialized areas [who] made recommendations based upon what they felt were sound research techniques and findings.'[69] John Dewey's work is associated with the pedagogically progressive (or child-centred education) camp; Thorndike's contributions are more closely linked to the administratively progressive (or mass education) camp exemplified by the rising science of educational testing and by the growth and centralized authority of large bureaucratic school districts.[70] Sandiford, like Thorndike, was drawn to the more scientific and administrative side of progressive education. J.G. Althouse, Dean of the Ontario College of Education, remembered Sandiford as someone who almost single-handedly 'secured funds to establish the first university department of educational research in the Dominion.'[71] Indeed, by securing funds from the Carnegie Corporation of New York, he was able to establish a Department of Educational Research at the Ontario College of Education, the first of its kind in Canada, which 'laid the foundations for a range of standardized group intelligence and achievement tests that were to dominate the field and exert considerable influence on educational practice in Ontario and in other provinces for many years.'[72] According to W.G. Fleming, Sandiford's research department would spearhead work in educational test development and standardized ability testing throughout the 1930s and early 1940s.[73]

In 1919 a provincial report requested compulsory medical examinations for students that would identify those with a mental age below their actual age, to identify learners requiring auxiliary education. The Department of Education referred to these students, who were set apart by their IQ, as mentally handicapped, retarded, or feeble-minded.[74] In 1929, Inspector of Auxiliary Classes H.E. Amoss reported that the Department of Education would be using the term *direct learners* as a less offensive designation.[75] By that point, there were more than two hundred auxiliary classes in the province, attended by 2,500 students.[76]

Another form of expansion in the Ontario school system related to educational programs and infrastructure. Beginning in 1911, a series of federal industrial, vocational, and technical education acts provided financial support to new programs in the province's public schools.[77] Manual and vocational training, as well as household and domestic science courses, underwent an expansion throughout the 1920s. Though the provinces had jurisdiction over education, the Dominion government passed the Technical Education Act immediately after the First World War. It appropriated '$10 million for any form of vocational, technical, or industrial education which would promote industrial development or enhance the lives and/or contributions of the workers.'[78] Secondary school curricula were revised in Ontario, to take advantage of the monies this legislation made available to expand courses and to overhaul facilities for vocational and technical education. By 1932, some 27,000 students were in vocational schools; by the time the act 'expired in 1929 only Ontario had utilized much of the available monies.'[79] The act was renewed three times, each time for five years, ending in 1944.

Child study and child health emerged as dominant themes around this time. Frank T. Sharpe, General Secretary for the Big Brother Movement in Toronto, contended that 'teachers should be more like gardeners than mechanics. Knowledge of the forces of life adjustment shows us where we may improve the conditions for growth. As a gardener gives water, controls insect pests, lifts a stone around which a young plant is trying to grow, so should we study each of your young charges, plan and direct them for the very best that life has to offer.'[80]

Child study, which emphasized mental hygiene, social adjustment, and developmental psychology, emerged as a field of study in the interwar years. Its advocates argued that health and the holistic study of children should be at the centre of Ontario's schooling. Dr William E. Blatz and Helen MacMurchy Bott, two prominent early figures in the movement who were based in the University of Toronto's Institute of Child Study (ICS), stressed that 'the main emphasis in the technique we have to offer will, therefore, be upon prevention rather than cure, to grasp certain principles, which can be utilized to facilitate the normal adjustment process.'[81]

William E. Blatz, a developmental psychologist, was the founding director of the ICS and the public face of the child study movement.[82] It has been said that he 'guided the hands that rocked the cradles of a whole generation of Canadian children. From the mid-1920s to the mid-1950s, Blatz was Canada's own world-renowned expert on raising children.'[83] Blatz, a prolific writer and speaker, was intent on carving out a distinct terrain – institutionally, methodologically, and rhetorically – for child study. The ICS would have a seminal influence on developmental psychology in Ontario's education system, by drawing increased attention to the field (see chapters 3, 4, and 5 of this book).[84] The ICS was launched by a grant from the Laura Rockefeller Memorial Foundation. When Blatz was named its director in 1925, it was named the St George's School for Child Study.[85]

Parents, school medical inspectors, and the province's Division of Child Hygiene also emphasized physical and mental health.[86] The healthy growth and development of children depended on sanitary schools, clean homes, appropriate levels of exercise, and a healthy diet.[87] Instructional information regarding the resources and benefits of preventive medicine was disseminated through booklets, advertisements, and parent education seminars.[88] The child health lobby would launch four principal campaigns: for more intensive local health administration; for the expenditure of more money on health work; for better cooperation from the medical profession; and for increased efforts in health education.[89] As Frederick Minkler from the Ontario College of Education noted, 'physiological needs – health and happiness – are the first concern of the progressive school.'[90]

Minkler, noting the child study movement's concern for educational reform, explained that 'progressive education demands a most comprehensive programme of health at all times. Indeed, the progressive programme must include mental hygiene.'[91] The child study researchers promoted in-school health examinations as well as surveys of buildings and educational practices. By the late 1930s, however, the emphasis had turned to preventive discipline as well as to health as a curriculum subject.[92] To disseminate the message to parents and teachers that educationists needed to put the child's health and development before anything else, a number of initiatives were undertaken. These included the launching of a magazine, *Understanding the Child*, for teachers, as well as the publication of a manual for teachers and a bibliographic service to assist them 'in understanding the nature of child development and the problems frequently encountered in the classroom.'[93]

Without question, the promotion of physical health, welfare, and disease prevention affected school programming (health and physical education), school construction (open yards and playgrounds for exercise outdoors), and administration (school health and medical inspections).[94] Howard Ferguson, the Minister of Education, boldly declared in 1929 that 'the year 1930 will take its place in the list of years marked by progressive measures in education on account of the change in inspection alone.'[95] Heightened concerns about inspection and health examinations would persist throughout the interwar years. This would be reflected, for example, in campaigns launched by organizations such as the Canadian Dental Hygiene Council, the Health League of Canada, and the Ontario Society for Crippled Children. These groups would lobby for healthy teeth and medical check-ups and work to eradicate diseases such as typhoid, diphtheria, and tuberculosis.[96] The child study movement's supporters in Ontario, like their American couterparts, emphatically supported physical exercise and extolled the virtues of nature and fresh clean air.[97]

George S. Henry, who followed Howard Ferguson as Ontario premier and Minister of Education, argued in his 1932 *Annual Report* that reforms to school timetables could free up more time for children to get outdoors for play and exercise by providing for 'so-called homework to be done in school.'[98] The same year, the province's high school inspectors reported that great progress had been made in Ontario's schools with regard to health and child study. Spacious rooms, improved lighting, extracurricular activities, auditoriums, gymnasiums, physical education classes, and health study were proof of this progress; the 'question of the physical well-being of the pupils in relation to their mental alertness is an important one, and teachers are wisely giving considerable attention to it.'[99]

Health education was increasingly viewed as an matter of grave national importance.[100] Physical and health education was intended to develop habits and attitudes that would serve as the basis of a healthy life.[101] In 1930 the Deputy Minister of Health secured, from the Rockefeller Foundation travelling scholarship, funds for the Director of Health Education, who would visit teacher training institutions and schools in Ontario to lecture on health education. In addition to this, a joint committee sponsored by the Ministers of Health and Education was organized in 1936 to develop a manual on health teaching, to distribute health teaching aids to educators, and to find ways to provide added instruction in secondary schools on health education, among other tasks.[102]

Besides child study and health, *efficiency* as an educational aim would be an influential and persistent theme throughout the interwar years in Ontario.[103] In Peter Baskerville's assessment, an industrial ethos infused all of Ontario society, so 'the ideals of the factory – such as the efficiency pursued through time-and-motion studies by the American engineer Frederick Winslow Taylor – invaded the home.'[104] Elimination of educational waste – be it defined in terms of educational costs or in terms of curricular congestion – could be facilitated by the principles of efficient management as had been promoted by and perfected by industry.[105]

'Education should be considered a business,' explained secondary school teacher H.M. Cooke. Costs, he argued, could be reduced without impairing standards: 'Idealists, humanists, radicals, and labour unions have been one in the spending of the taxpayers' money, the result being our huge overhead of today. Appraisal of our position calls for action. The advice of trained business economists should be obtained and followed before our educational costs get out of hand.'[106] The pupil, a ward of Ontario's system of schooling, needed to be trained for useful employment.[107]

Society's needs and structures had altered. In the view of many educationists, such as George F. Rogers, Ontario's Chief Director of Education and later Deputy Minister of Education, planning and management was as necessary in educational matters as it was in industry, where progress was largely controlled, directed, and efficient.[108] In educational contexts, a *Canadian School Journal* editorial explained, it was important to help 'pupils whose characters are developing, not only to make it possible for each student to discover his proper place in the educational scheme, but to direct him into it as soon as his aptitudes and capacities are known with reasonable accuracy (and that is surprisingly early).'[109] Efficiency, the hallmark of success in industry and business, could be promoted in schools. Progress in education required efficiency, which in turn demanded management. In 1940, an editorial in *The School* expressed the same sentiments in more dramatic terms. Canada, it argued, had entered 'the scientific age. In government, industry, and even retail business, experimentation, study, and planning are the order of the day ... So in education – the day of haphazard idiosyncrasies in the little red schoolhouse is gone.'[110]

By the end of the interwar period, the efficiency movement as a 'progressive' lobby had achieved significant gains. In the eleven reports submitted in 1940 by Departments of Education to provincial governments across Canada, as well as to then independent Newfoundland, marked tendencies were already clear. 'Educational progress' was most predominately marked by two domains: 'vocational and practical subjects [and] trades schools.'[111] Two issues 'gaining ground' for Canadian educationists were larger administrative units and increased vocational guidance.[112]

Ontario in the interwar years saw a surge of educational foundations and organizations, both public and private. Robert Patterson observes that between 1916 and 1920, 'teachers in British Columbia, Saskatchewan, Alberta, Manitoba, New Brunswick, and Ontario established provincial organizations.'[113] In July 1920, at the Calgary Public Library, these provincial organizations forged a national coalition, the Canadian Teachers' Federation, with the mandate 'to provide machinery by which the various provincial and territories [sic] organizations could be kept in touch with one another, and through which mutual assistance could be quickly and readily given.'[114]

Ontario's teachers joined the national coalition of four provinces that formed the Canadian Teachers' Federation. But at the provincial level, they were 'organized in a manner unique among Canadian provinces, with recognition given to the four distinguishing features of level, sex, religion, and language.'[115] Differences between the federations notwithstanding, all of Ontario's teacher organizations were 'concerned with the protection and welfare of their members, giving continuous attention to salaries, job security, superannuation, and other such matters.'[116] The various teachers' federations in the province were as follows: the Federation of Women Teachers' Associations of Ontario, the Ontario Public School Men Teachers' Federation, the Ontario Secondary School Teachers' Federation, the Ontario English Catholic Teachers' Association, and L'Association des Enseignants Franco-Ontariens.

Parent groups also began forming across the country into various home and school associations. The first 'was established by Mrs. A. C. Courtice in Toronto in March 1916. The Ontario provincial organization came into existence in 1919.'[117] Representatives of these organizations developed a strong presence in the source journals throughout the period being studied. By 1926, interest groups such as these were common across the country, but they were systematically organized only in Ontario and British Columbia. Their aims and purposes included these: the promotion of cooperation among stakeholders in educational matters; inquiry into educational problems; and the development of a healthy Canadian citizenry.[118] In Ontario, the Home and School Council was legally constituted in 1933, after which the managing board of directors grew rapidly within a few short years, from 9 to 115 members. This paralleled a growing concern for linking the province's schools to contemporary social problems.[119]

Child study and child health advocates also founded organizations to support their causes. 'Mergers are the order of the day,' announced the newly founded Association for Childhood Education (ACE) in *Educational Research Bulletin*. Everywhere, it noted, 'educational institutions are joining to form larger more powerful combines.'[120] The International Kindergarten Union disbanded in order to join the association, and the

National Council of Primary Education merged with it to create a more formidable union – one that could combine the interests of the nursery school, the kindergarten, and the primary teacher. The ACE stated explicitly that its greater size could make its lobbying on educational policy more potent, 'promoting progressive nursery school, kindergarten, and primary work throughout this country.'[121]

Interwar Ontario enjoyed growth and development in all aspects of social, economic, and educational life. But the Great Depression would dramatically alter every aspect of life in the province. In 1930, Premier Howard Ferguson stepped down to assume the post of Canadian High Commissioner to London.[122] George S. Henry, his successor, assumed leadership of the province just as Ontario was entering the worst and, as it turned out, longest economic crisis in its history.[123] Like his predecessor, Henry would hold on to the education portfolio, remaining minister of that department until his party's political collapse at the polls in 1934. Henry's first and second annual reports to the province on behalf of the Department of Education optimistically pointed to progress being made in the schools in the midst of the province's economic storm. In fact, he reported that 'the check to material prosperity which displayed itself during 1930, but which is hoped to be a temporary depression only, produced no visible effect upon the schools.'[124] In 1932 he reported that in the previous year, 'education in Ontario has continued to make its usual progress, in that the conditions of the schools, the supply of teachers, and the attendance of pupils are alike satisfactory, in spite of the financial stringency and the pressing need of a prudent economy.'[125] Peter Baskerville has observed that the Depression did not bottom out in Ontario until the latter part of 1933; in the years that immediately followed, the province's Department of Education would be, by necessity, less concerned with progress than with maintaining acceptable efficiency.[126]

Municipalities and local school boards suffered for lack of funding.[127] The decreases in government support were complicated by ballooning unemployment and by financial distress among families. Taxes, a principal source of funding for schools, often could not be collected. The ratepayers were unable to make up for the shortfalls in provincial funding; they were also often unable to keep themselves out of bankruptcy.[128] Building projects were suspended. School repairs, unless utterly essential, were halted. Equipment was no longer readily purchased for the new science labs, the domestic science classes, and the manual training shops. New textbooks became rarities, and the growth of school libraries was stunted. Hardest hit were rural schools and those in small urban centres.[129]

Attendance figures in Ontario's secondary schools, which had been growing steadily since the Adolescent School Attendance Act of 1919, continued to do so.[130] Many students who could have left school at the age of sixteen did not. Others who might have assumed part-time employment went to school full time.[131] Throughout the 1920s, retention rates in Ontario's secondary schools 'were higher for boys than for girls; this is attributed to male-oriented school programs, traditional societal expectations, and job availability ... Retention rates were much higher in academic programs.'[132] This has been attributed to the new vocational programs and to the limited availability of jobs during the Depression years.[133] Charles Phillips noted that between 1921 and 1948, the number of students in secondary schools rose from 84,000 to 278,000, while elementary school enrolment actually declined.[134] In his assessment, the trend could be attributed to 'greater wealth, smaller families, less need for immediate wage earning, more need in business for educated employees, fewer jobs in depression years, new secondary school courses of utilitarian value, more consideration of pupils' interests and needs, and the cumulative effect of a growing appreciation of the value of education in successively better-educated generations.'[135]

According to Robert Stamp, with unemployment rates skyrocketing, the job markets were glutted with trained and mature adults.[136] These individuals were now forced to take the lower-paying and entry-level jobs that adolescents would normally have assumed. As a result, the modern technical institutes and the one-room schoolhouses were filled to capacity. Class sizes in some schools swelled to fifty or more. At the same time, by 1934, provincial funding to schools had actually plummeted by one-third.[137]

The actual burden of doing more work in education for less pay fell upon the teachers. Dramatic salary reductions rocked the profession. In the 1932–3 school year, nearly $250,000 less was paid to teachers in the province.[138] As George S. Henry put it, 'one effect of the above situation is that the teachers have readily accepted greater responsibility and additional duties. Their financial sacrifices have been of great assistance to municipal authorities.'[139] The following year, cutbacks doubled, nearing half a million dollars.[140] This translated into a decrease of between 5 and 33 per cent per teacher, depending on the school district.[141] On average, male teachers lost $353 each; female teachers, $281.[142] The difference can be explained by the fact that female teachers' salaries before the pay cuts were less on average than those of their male counterparts. In reporting these cuts, V.K. Greer explained that Ontarians' dwindling incomes necessitated tax relief. Assuaging the teachers, he posited that 'no body of people has accepted the loss of income more graciously and with less open complaint than the teachers. They responded with their best work.'[143]

Despite the presence of three strong teachers' federations in the province at the time, Ontario's public educators appear to have accepted these losses with relative quiescence.[144] This speaks to the depressed and singularly devastating conditions throughout the province. Teachers who held on to their jobs, even after the pay cuts, fared relatively well compared to Ontarians employed in agriculture and industry.[145] Furthermore, there had never before been such an oversupply of trained and qualified teachers. Between 1927 and 1933 the number of teachers who earned permanent teaching certificates in the province rose from 133 to 519.[146] No one's job, it appeared, was safe.

The teachers' federations did not initiate strikes or labour unrest, but they were far from passive. They mounted a public relations campaign to promote education as an investment in the future. The federations' bulletins made frequent reference to the importance of keeping educational matters in the public eye and drawing ratepayers into the schools.[147] Education Weeks were established and became an important part of teachers' campaigns to reach out to parents and draw ratepayers into the schools.[148] Extracurricular activities, including fairs, clubs, and sports teams, became important ways to connect education with community.[149] School and society forged an iterative relationship.

Relating the education system to the needs and interests of society had a different connotation in Ontario's separate Roman Catholic schools. According to Premier Mitchell Hepburn's biographer, the separate school issue was an ongoing political dilemma for provincial governments.[150] Yet education as a political issue was not much discussed in the source journals. Perhaps because of the sometimes politically charged atmosphere surrounding separate schools – in particular regarding funding and administration – discussion of the separate school issue was muted. Based on a reading of *The School* and *The Canadian School Journal*, one would have very little understanding of the tensions and complexities that bedevilled separate schools.

Between the turn of the century and the 1930s the number of pupils who annually attended separate schools more than doubled, reaching 100,000.[151] This trend 'increased the separate school proportion of the total elementary population from 10 to 17 percent.'[152] This was partly due to the overall growth of Ontario's population. More significant, though, to the spread and growth of separate schools was Premier Ferguson's repeal of the controversial Regulation 17 in 1928. That regulation, which had been enacted in 1912 when Ferguson was a backbencher in the provincial government of James Whitney, had restricted French-language instruction after the first year of schooling and prohibited French instruction after grade four.[153]

Regulation 17 had been supported by many Protestants, but it caused dissent both internally and with the neighbouring province of Quebec.[154] Ferguson's modifications to Regulation 17 improved relations between the provinces and facilitated negotiations with Quebec Premier Louis-Alexandre Taschereau over trade and the development of hydroelectric power, mining, and the pulp and paper industry in the largely rural north.[155] Yet as Robert Stamp observes, separate school attendance 'was largely urban – 76 percent as opposed to 56 percent in the public school system – due to the historic and continuing urban destinations of Roman Catholic immigrants.'[156]

It was not until 1929, the year following the repeal of Regulation 17, that doubts concerning the 'constitutional rights of Roman Catholic separate school boards to operate secondary schools' were removed by the Judicial Committee of the Imperial Privy Council in London, England.[157] Further to that landmark, the Act to Amend the Assessment Act, passed in 1936 and surrounded by a fair deal of controversy, was 'the first really significant financial and legislative concession since the Scott Act of 1863.'[158] The Scott Act (long title: An Act to Restore to Roman Catholics in Upper Canada Certain Rights in Respect to Separate Schools) enabled constituencies to establish separate schools in each ward. More than seven decades later, the 1936 act required that a proportion of taxes 'be divided according to ownership or assessment, but not according to attendance; separate school boards were still denied access to public utility taxes.'[159]

Following a political maelstrom and the defeat of a Liberal candidate in a 1936 by-election in the district of East Hastings, Premier Hepburn announced that he would support the repeal of this controversial act.[160] At this point, at the end of 1935, Ontario's separate school population stood at 77,928 pupils.[161] Having won re-election in the province, Hepburn found ways to secure financial assistance for the separate schools via provincial equalization grants. In so doing, he held fairly true to his 1934 campaign promise that Catholic education 'should be maintained at a level of efficiency equal to that of the public schools.'[162] Consequently, 'by 1938, the total money committed to provincial school grants surpassed pre-Depression highs; by 1941 it doubled, rising from 10 to 20 per cent of the provincial share of total education costs.'[163]

During the Depression, economic affairs had returned the separate school debates to the forefront of the political arena with an intensity similar to that of the 1880s, when, as Robert Stamp remarks, the Liberal government of Sir Oliver Mowat staked out a middle position between Catholic spokesmen 'calling for full control of Catholic Schools on the model of Quebec's dual confessional system' and 'equally militant Protestant opponents who sought the total abolition of separate schools.'[164] Ultimately, the constitutional status of separate secondary schools was accepted, and Catholic interests were now pushing for improvement in this status. The Catholic Taxpayers' Association (CTA), formed in 1932, 'campaigned for a permanent, legislated settlement rather than one dependent on the whims of future governments.'[165] It lobbied persistently for a guaranteed share of the local proportion of public utility taxes.[166] The CTA and the complicated realities of Ontario's separate school system played an important role in smothering any attempts to decentralize provincial education and move it 'to municipal control, for neither public nor separate school ratepayers were willing to hand over control of their schools to city councils which in all likelihood would include both Protestant and Catholic aldermen.'[167]

Beyond the separate school system, Ontario maintained a small but robust network of private schools. With the notable exception of Joseph McCulley, Headmaster of Pickering College, stakeholders in Ontario's private school system contributed little to the two educational journals that circulated widely in the province.[168] W.G. Fleming noted that Canadian private schools never garnered the same proportion of students as did those in Great Britain, the United States, and Australia: 'In 1921 one pupil attended a private elementary or secondary school for every twenty-three who attended publicly controlled day schools; in 1948 the ratio was one to twenty-two.'[169] Part of the reason for this relatively small proportion of students attending private schools relates to the Roman Catholic system's classification as public. This distinguished Ontario's schools from those of, say, the United States, 'where parochial schools are private.'[170]

The Department of Education was significantly transformed throughout the interwar years. Robin S. Harris's *Quiet Evolution* is perhaps the most detailed account of the developments that influenced schooling in Ontario over the period examined in this book.[171] Harris writes that in 1919 the position of Superintendent of Education was abolished after the death of John Seath, who as Superintendent of Education had dominated Ontario's education scene.[172] The superintendent's position had been created to 'afford the Department the constant assistance of professional experience and knowledge disassociated from the full administrative control which remains in the hands of the responsible Minister.' Ultimately, this had led to a strong concentration of authority within the Department.[173] After the First World War, the superintendent's responsibilities were delegated to a number of department heads, including an Inspector of Public Libraries, a Registrar, an Inspector of Manual Training and Household Science, a Chief Public and Separate School Inspector, a Director of Industrial and Technical Education, an Inspector of Elementary Agricultural Education, a Director of Professional (Teacher) Training, an Inspector of Auxiliary Classes, and, lastly, a Provincial School Attendance Officer. The last three positions were established in 1919; the others had existed, with varying responsibilities, as far back as 1882.[174]

The shuffling of positions and titles over the next twenty-five years generated a fair amount of confusion in the department. This prompted George Drew, the new premier and Minister of Education, to revert in 1943 to the 1906 departmental organization.[175] Harris's description of this shuffling is best recounted verbatim:

> In 1923, the Superintendent's position was revived again, this time under the title of Chief Director. The appointee was F. W. Merchant ... Merchant reached retirement age in 1930, but continued for four years as Chief Adviser to the Minister. George F. Rogers was appointed Chief Director in his place in 1930 but with the accession of the Hepburn Government in 1934 reverted to High School Inspector ... He was replaced by Duncan McArthur, until then a professor of history at Queen's University, who a few months later also became Chief Director. Then in 1940, to make matters even more confusing, McArthur was appointed Minister of Education, and Rogers came back as Deputy Minister.[176]

In the midst of all the shifting within the department, a number of significant structural changes were made within the school system at the secondary level. In 1921, following the recommendations of the Royal Commission on University Financing in Ontario, the six years of secondary schooling in the province were reduced to five. This limited upper school to one year and effectively did away with an entrenched distinction between honour junior matriculation and senior matriculation.[177] The status of grade thirteen, which had been parallel to the first year of four-year Bachelor of Arts programs in universities, was elevated, ultimately becoming the only route to university.

To summarize, between 1919 and 1942, Ontario's educationists concerned themselves with how schools could respond to and prepare students for a province that was undergoing a multitude of changes. The two world wars, along with the Great Depression and the effects of rapid industrialism, immigration, and urbanization, made Ontarians increasingly attentive to the changing circumstances and realities of contemporary life. Progressivist educators saw the schools as out of touch with the modern world. Various scientific approaches to educational reform, including developmental psychology, child study, health promotion, and social science, were increasingly associated with the aims and means of progressivist schooling. In a fast-changing social context, many progressive administrators and schools viewed scientific management and control as a reasonable approach. Educational organizations such as teachers' federations and home and school associations were founded in order to represent and lobby for particular interests in Ontario's schools.

Most stakeholders in Ontario's separate schools – including the Catholic public system and the network of private institutions – were not necessarily part of the same discourse community as representatives of the English public schools. Even so, the province maintained a small but robust separate system. The Department of Education underwent significant changes, while Ontario's schools expanded their mandate and scope. Adult education programs, correspondence courses, and auxiliary programs were some of the means for extending the educational franchise to more citizens. In the following chapter, the primary sources for this study, *The School* and *The Canadian School Journal*, will be considered. Chapter 2 will also explore the problems inherent in defining, analysing, and approaching progressivist discourse in education.

2 Approaching Progressive Education

What was the progressive movement? This deceptively simple question, posed in different ways, holds prominent rank among the many controversies which have consumed historians' patient energies, spawned a flurry of monographs and articles, and confused several generations of students.*

As the tides of reform rose and swelled, what opinions were held by educationists regarding progressive education in Ontario? The two sources of principal interest to this book were both educational journals in Ontario. *The School* and *The Canadian School Journal* had an audience and a discursive community of a relatively broad range of Ontario's educationists. Though they had different publishers, the similarities between the two journals far outweighed the differences. Indeed, editorial pieces published in one source were often reproduced in the other several issues later. Journals such as these were not published solely in Ontario. *The Western School Journal* is a notable publication of like kind.[1] In the United States as well, educational journals were important venues for news, opinion, and longer articles by educational leaders and intellectuals. John Dewey's 'My Pedagogic Creed,' for example, was first published in the *School Journal*, which was published by the University of Chicago and had a readership similar to that of the Ontario periodicals.[2]

Robert Stamp and Robert Gidney have cited the two Ontario jour-

---

* Peter G. Filene, 'An Obituary for "The Progressive Movement,"' *American Quarterly* 22, no. 1 (Spring 1970): 20.

nals is their work; except for that, neither journal has received much attention even though both were widely read in Ontario. This is not surprising when we consider how difficult it is to find complete sets of these journals. Both *The School* and *The Canadian School Journal* are listed in the library catalogues at many of Ontario's university libraries, but many of these catalogues are – or, were, at the time of my research – out of date. On occasion, I travelled several hours to a library only to find that the dates in the catalogue did not match what was actually present in the library. For instance, my discovery of the *Canadian School Journal* collection was purely by chance; according to the library catalogue at OISE/University of Toronto, that journal did not exist for the years in question; yet when I looked, the storage facility held nearly every issue and volume. Any historian who aspires to use these journals systematically will require patience as well as the assistance of highly skilled librarians.

Both journals published articles, news items, and editorials relating to education in Ontario, other provinces, and – occasionally – other countries. These were staples of both publications. It was the editorials that interested me the most, for it was in them that I encountered the most sustained discussions of progressive education. Both periodicals also published letters from subscribers, book reviews, advertisements for educational supplies, and reports on government legislation; and both covered the proceedings of educational conferences.

Each was published monthly. *The Canadian School Journal* produced eight issues a year, *The School* ten (see Appendix C for circulation figures). Between 1930 and 1940, each journal reached at least 5,000 readers per year.[3] Each sent a copy of every issue to every school board and district in the province, and to every student in a teacher training program, as well as to individual subscribers. Both, it is worth noting, also had a fairly strong aversion to political discussions. Pelham Mulvany's assessment of another, expired, educational journal published in Toronto with a similar name, *The Canada School Journal*, serves as an appropriate description of the sources being discussed here: 'The general tone of the journal is decidedly liberal; it does not meddle with party politics, but confines itself strictly to educational issues.'[4]

The Canadian School Journal was the official organ of the Ontario Educational Association (OEA), which W.G. Fleming described as a broadly based educational association 'concerned with a wide variety of issues cutting across educational levels.'[5] For the various educational organizations that were founded after the First World War, affiliation with the OEA was an advantage.[6] Fleming describes several categories of membership in the OEA, and his description indicates who the readers of *The Canadian School Journal* most likely were.[7] Associate members, who were students registered in one of Ontario's teacher training institutions, were exempt from all fees. Ordinary members, who belonged to one of the OEA's sections, paid annual fees. These sections, each of which could adopt a constitution and elect its own officers, comprised four departments: Elementary, College and Secondary, Supervising and Training, and Trustees.[8] Corporate members – those educational associations or federations affiliated with the OEA, which included the Ontario Federation of Home and School Associations – also paid annual membership fees.[9]

E.C. Guillet's centennial history of the association, *In the Cause of Education*, is the most detailed source on the OEA, covering the century between 1861 and 1960. Guillet discusses the association's involvement in the province's educational affairs, moving chronologically.[10] Besides publishing *The Canadian School Journal*, the OEA organized an annual educational convention that reached all stakeholders in Ontario's educational system, including teachers, officials in the Department of Education, school inspectors, academics, and lecturers from abroad – a scope broader than what we see today, even on the national level. The conventions were held during the summer holidays so that more educators could participate as stakeholders in the province's educational system. 'The prestige of the O.E.A. appears to have been very high,' W.G. Fleming remarks, for 'among the speakers of current or later prominence were university presidents, cabinet ministers, premiers, Prime Minister R. B. Bennett, and ... the Governor-General, Lord Tweedsmuir.'[11]

These conventions shed some light on the mission of *The Canadian School Journal*. The proceedings of the OEA conventions were published in the source journal, and much space was devoted to articles that discussed or editorialized about speeches and developments at the annual sessions. It was important to encourage Ontario's educational community to read and contribute to the journal, given that, as Guillet notes, 'the problems of selecting, condensing, and editing articles and other materials' were numerous.[12] The OEA had been founded in 1892 through the union of the Ontario Teachers' Association and the Public and High School Trustees' Association of Ontario.[13] In 1921 it drafted a constitution under the name of the Ontario School Trustees' and Ratepayers' Association (OSTRA). Thus OSTRA now represented the taxpayers and school board trustees and involved them in disseminating ideas that were also those of *The Canadian School Journal.*

The source journal was launched in 1921 as *The Ontario School Board Journal* with the following two aims:

1 To co-operate with the Trustees and Ratepayers to secure the best interests of Ontario Schools and Scholars.
2 To keep the readers of the Journal informed upon subjects connected with the welfare of the School and the Scholar, considered particularly from the viewpoint of Trustees and Ratepayers.[14]

The principal concerns of both the journal and OSTRA were these: high school and collegiate institute fees; methods of financial support for public and high schools; assessments in schools; holidays; grant payments; the character and usefulness of the curriculum; amalgamation of school boards; election of trustees; teachers' contracts; school attendance; health supervision; and school building and equipment.[15] Between 1921 and 1923 the *Ontario School Board Journal* was published monthly, with each issue typically under thirty pages. During those years, it did not include advertisements, and its circulation numbers are not reported. The journal reported on conventions, educational issues of interest, and legislation, and printed letters from ratepayers. It was printed in Port Perry with the support of Samuel Farmer, publisher of the *Port Perry Star.* Even when the official publisher, the OSTRA, was listed at 1104 Bay Street in Toronto, the journal continued to be printed in Port Perry.[16]

In 1923, two years after its founding, the journal was renamed *The Canadian School Journal,* reflecting a desire to broaden the publication's mandate so as to encompass the concerns of all members of the OEA and OSTRA, as well as teacher trainees and members of various school boards. To address the needs of rural school boards, it would now provide 'graded lists of books considered suitable for school libraries, which helped to remedy the inability of many trustees to make appropriate choices. Books on the list were recommended by the Department of Education or by an inspector.'[17] The total cost of resources listed was ten dollars, which was seen as the minimum expenditure for the proper maintenance of libraries. Directly applicable articles like these were published beside those discussions of educational progress that were of most significance to my research. In June 1927 the objectives of the OEA and its official organ, *The Canadian School Journal,* were characterized as twofold: advancing the interests of the teaching profession, and promoting the cause of education in Ontario.[18] Its concern with progressive education explicitly addressed the need to adapt provincial education to modern needs.[19]

The Canadian School Journal was much more compact than *The School*, mainly because it did not publish sample lesson plans, instructional articles addressing particular school subjects, teaching aids, or model classroom assessments. Because it devoted much less space to advertising, most of its issues were under thirty-five pages.[20] It did not pay for articles. Contributions were 'invited on any topic of real educational value' to Ontarians; that said, the journal's content and tone were very close to the positions espoused by the Department of Education.[21] Its content included reprinted conference speeches, minutes from school board meetings, letters from individual taxpayers, and occasional contributions from educational organizations outside the OEA; many of the contributors were state employees.[22] *The Canadian School Journal* would remain the official organ of the OEA until 1968, when it merged with the journal *Argus* and was renamed *Ontario Education*.

The School also had a heavy practical component. This is because it was published through the Ontario College of Education at the University of Toronto, the main institution for secondary school teacher education in the province. Thus it was obligated to provide its readers with instructional materials and references that they could use in classrooms. *The School* featured sample lessons, examinations, and tests, as well as reviews of resources, along with editorial notes and news items. Contributors to this journal included educators, administrators, school inspectors, academics, and various other stakeholders in education.[23]

Every month, noted Charles E. Phillips, 'apart from the advertising and paid announcements there were about one hundred and twenty-five pages, or fifty thousand words to be edited.'[24] The issues varied in length from 80 to 120 pages, including advertisements.[25] Less than 10 per cent of the content related to the study at hand; interpretations of progressivist ideas were mostly confined to editorials, news and current events, items of interest, and, occasionally, general articles espousing progressivist teaching methods for a particular discipline or subject. Less than 1 per cent of these articles could be described as humanist or critical of progressivist ideas.[26]

The periodical was distributed to all school boards and organizations in the province. Each copy was sold for twenty cents; a personal annual subscription could be purchased for $1.50 per year. By 1941 'the Gov-

ernment of Ontario purchased subscriptions for all teachers-in-training
and the Government of Manitoba had for a second year purchased
1,800 subscriptions to the elementary edition.'[27] The School's practical, classroom-oriented emphasis was so important that in the 1935–6
school year, following the death of the periodical's editor, Professor
W.E. Macpherson, it was divided into two editions. Elementary and
secondary school volumes were published concurrently, containing
level-appropriate educational resources while maintaining, as Charles
E. Phillips observes, 'about fifty pages of common interest, including
news, editorials, and articles of a general professional character ... this
significantly increased the appeal of The School to teachers.'[28]

The School was published monthly, from September through June,
throughout the years that are the focus of this study. Its articles covered
a vast range of topics, from sample lessons on art written by elementary
school teachers to profound meditations on citizenship and schooling
written by the Minister of Education. The School, which was committed to developing a forum for disseminating educational developments
and ideas, as well as for the professional development of teachers,
provides a fascinating window onto the changing ways in which educational thinking has been mediated in Ontario. In the context of this
study, however, expertise in educational affairs was certainly more
centralized than the many opinions of people contributing articles to
The School. For forty-five years after the closing of Faculties of Education in Kingston and Toronto in 1920, the Ontario College of Education
'was the sole institution in the province preparing secondary school
teachers and it was directly funded and controlled by the Ministry of
Education.'[29]

Considering the Ontario College of Education's funding sources and
management, its expressed aversion to discussing politics is under-
standable. The School's content did not always align with the reforms
advocated by the Department of Education, but the language expressing any criticisms was always moderate and the outlook cautiously
optimistic. It thus came as a shock to Charles Phillips when his first
editorial in The School, published during the 1940–1 year, caused an
uproar. Phillips's editorial, 'Declaration of Faith,' propounded a meliorist progressivist thesis that was summarized in the sentence, 'This is the
philosophy of liberal democracy and the new education to which we
ascribe.' At the staff meeting that followed the editorial's publication,
four or five of Phillips's colleagues called for his dismissal.[30]

To Phillips's critics, the journal was a pedagogical forum, not a politi-

cal one.[31] The above example indicates the extent to which openly oppositional discourses were deemed to exceed the periodical's mandate.[32]
Phillips would learn that as editor, while he could choose the journal's
content and positions, this came with the proviso that it sell enough
subscriptions to remain in business.[33] And, as already noted, it was the
Department of Education that paid for the bulk of subscriptions.[34] In
the end, budget constraints and 'the high cost of materials and labour'
led to the decision to stop publication of *The School*, which had been in
press since 1912, after the 1947–48 school year.[35] By then, it had been an
influential voice for forty-five years.

Progressive education has become a tangled term. The problem of progressive education, for this study's purposes, amounts to a problem
of defining and understanding the field of investigation. Progressive
education, as an educational movement, has been proven, rejected, cor-
ralled, set adrift, and denied by various educational historians over
the past century.[36] More recently, many educationists have turned the
problem into a global one by asking how the educational philosophy of
notable progressives such as John Dewey has been adopted, received,
and interpreted in different contexts.[37] My concerns rest predominately
with the context of Ontario.

Ontario's progressivist rhetoric reveals opposing and conflicting
visions for reform. It was precisely this lack of clarity regarding the
meanings and interpretations of progressive education that drew me
to the work of Herbert Kliebard, whose study of school reforms in the
United States led him to the following conclusion regarding the progressive education movement:

> In the end, I came to believe that the term was not only vacuous but mis-
> chievous. It is not just the word 'progressive' that I thought was inappro-
> priate but the implication that something deserving a single name existed
> and that something could be identified and described if we only tried. My
> initial puzzlement turned to scepticism, my scepticism to indignation and
> finally to bemusement.[38]

Certainly, confusion regarding what *progressive education* means is
nothing new, and a review of the literature reinforces the hypothesis
that the lack of clarity has emerged from the wide variety of historical
approaches and definitions.[39] One of the earliest and most significant
reflections on progressive education was John Dewey's *Experience and
Education* (1938). That text was written in response to what Dewey felt

were narrow misinterpretations of his writings, which had attempted to describe a more comprehensive theory of experience. Dewey in his book analysed both traditional and progressive education and demonstrated fundamental flaws at each extreme. As Joseph Schwab would note, much 'of what has been said by and for educators in the name of Dewey has consisted of distorted shadows and blurred images of the original doctrine-epitomes, diverse in content and tending to oppose or exclude one another.'[40] In his editorial introduction to *Experience and Education*, Alfred Hall-Quest insisted that 'neither the old nor the new education is adequate. Each is miseducative because neither of them applies the principles of a carefully developed philosophy of experience.'[41]

According to Dewey, 'traditional' education lacked a holistic conception of the learner, focused instruction on content, and disregarded process. Yet by the same token, progressive schools had been too reactive, focusing on educational activity and process without adequately stressing disciplinary content knowledge. In so doing, they had incorrectly developed 'opposition between the idea that education is development from within and that it is formation from without.'[42] This opposition 'so far as practical affairs of the school are concerned, tends to take the form of contrast between traditional and progressive education.'[43]

For Dewey, the 'traditional'/'progressive' dichotomy in schools was problematic:

> The general philosophy of the new education may be sound, and yet the difference in abstract principles will not decide the way in which the moral and intellectual preference involved shall be worked out in practice. There is always the danger in a new movement that in rejecting the aims and methods of that which it would supplant, it may develop its principles negatively rather than positively and constructively.[44]

Progressive educators who had proceeded according to this principle of continuity had neglected questions central to the pedagogical project, including these:

> What is the place and meaning of subject-matter and of organization *within* experience? How does subject-matter function? Is there anything inherent in experience which tends towards progressive organization of its contents? What results follow when the materials of experience are not progressively organized?[45]

According to Dewey, then, educational experiences were the basis of learning but were individually, not inherently, meaningful. That is, they were not necessarily educative for everyone. The pedagogical value of experiences was determined by their effects on the individual learner's present and future, as well as by the degree to which they enabled the learner to contribute positively to society. Dewey challenged progressivists to be more critical of their own pedagogical principles and claims. He worried that progressive education was in danger of becoming 'as dogmatic as ever was the traditional education which it reacted against.'[46]

For Kliebard, circumnavigating the indistinct shores of what progressive education meant began with charting how earlier historians had first approached those same shores.[47] One such approach might best be described as strictly celebratory.[48] The history of education, accordingly, was one of increasing sophistication, complexity, and improvement. Time passed, schooling evolved, and progress was made. From this perspective, progress in education amounted to improvement over time. Such histories typically justified or rationalized the present state of affairs and envisioned the present as a culminating point. This approach is best characterized by Ellwood Cubberley's *Public Education in the United States* (1919).[49] Cubberley's approach set the tone for four decades of educational historiography.[50]

From Cubberley's perspective, education, the hallmark and the triumph of democracy, was ever improving. This improvement, he argued, was intertwined with the betterment of American society. For Cubberley, the education system was both the result of progress and the key to *future* progress. One of his guiding principles was the search for connections between past and present policies or problems in education. His institutional, celebratory history was intended to instil pride in the profession for teachers and those involved in teacher preparation.[51] Yet when the field of view was narrowed to matters of relevance to educators, educational history grew increasingly *irrelevant* to other historians. In addition, Cubberley clung to the idea that he could develop a 'science' of education that could accurately depict the past, despite the obvious anachronism of this view.[52]

A wave of reform in the 1960s swept away the celebratory and instrumentalist historiographies associated with Cubberley's work. Bernard Bailyn's *Education in the Forming of American Society* (1960) outlined a very different approach to the historical analysis of progress in education. This orientation generally approached education in terms much broader than those that limited themselves to schooling and saw it as the broad process of social and cultural transmission.[53] Bailyn's approach brought educational history closer to social and cultural history. The same can be said of Lawrence Cremin's *The Transformation of the School: Progressivism in American Education, 1876–1957*.[54]

Cremin's approach broadened the scope of educational history. It characterized progressive education as the convergence of three trends. The first of these related to the expansion of school curricula and programs. The second considered the application of scientific principles to school organization, administration, and management. The third involved greater tailoring of instruction to individual learners or groups of students.[55] These trends were broadly situated in the movement toward the professionalization of teaching and the creation of a modern educational superstructure, which preceded the interwar period and continues today. That movement is too broad and diverse to discuss in depth here, but it involves questions of teacher education, professional knowledge, certification, the feminization of teaching (primarily in the elementary system), unionization, salary, tenure, and regulation.[56]

A different approach to progressive education has involved developing a working definition that narrows the field of description to certain terms – terms that are sometimes delimiting. This approach excludes or marginalizes reforms that do not fit the criteria established by the historian. Arthur Zilversmit, for example, has argued that progressive education meant only certain core values, including the meeting of individual students' needs and the establishing of nurturing pedagogical environments.[57] He identified a limited set of progressive ideals: the beliefs that learning should be active, individualized, child-centred, and holistic, in the sense that instruction should involve more than content. John Dewey, Francis Parker, and William Heard Kilpatrick were truly progressive according to these narrow definitional parameters; other, conflicting reform initiatives, such as the mental testing and efficiency movements, were declared pedagogically regressive and repressive and were left out of the analysis. By this definition, vocational education, manual training, scientific management of schools, and mental testing were not aspects of progressive education. The constraints of this position, while they enable historians to probe certain ideas, are highly problematic in my view. Overly narrow definitions of progressive education have added to the conceptual confusion regarding what progressive education *is*. If each account sets its own parameters as to what is progressive, the entire field of study has become normatively constructed.

Certainly, defining what progressive education can mean is necessary in order to tighten the focus of analysis and to allow detailed explications of particular orientations; but at the same time, doing so excludes much of the slipperiness and complexity of the past by removing one orientation from the very messy context in which it was embedded. Dewey is at the forefront of Zilversmit's analysis of progressive education, at the expense of major figures in pedagogical history such as Edward Thorndike. This reading seems especially narrow in light of previous studies by the many historians who view Thorndike's impact and approach to educational progress as profound and wide-ranging. Ellen Lagemann's oft-quoted statement that 'one cannot understand the history of education in the United States during the twentieth century unless one realizes that Edward L. Thorndike won and John Dewey lost' makes this point quite clearly.[58] The point here is that the criteria historians have used to define progressive education have resulted in the highlighting of different reactions to traditional education.[59]

David Tyack, who differentiates between administrative and pedagogical progressives, seems to have approached the field with the aim of demarcating differences within the progressive movement without excluding elements that do not fit very narrow parameters.[60] His approach had the effect of hyphenating progressives, by including them within the broader framework of progressivist concerns while differentiating different clusters of concerns. According to Tyack the 'administrative' progressives succeeded at reforming schools and policy. Their influence over actual pedagogical reforms dwarfed that of the pedagogical progressives.[61] There are two criteria at play here: 'The first indication of success comes when and if the policy is translated into a concrete program of action and the second when the policy is weighed in terms of the extent to which it actually succeeded in accomplishing the stated purpose.'[62] Tyack, then, assessed progressive education according to criteria that would enable him to identify a relatively coherent ideology enacted by particular individuals.[63]

Tyack's approach, which divides progressivists according to their area of interest – administrative or pedagogical – seems to say little about their actual orientation toward those domains.[64] According to David Labaree, 'the heart of the tale is the struggle for control of American education in the early twentieth century between two factions of the movement for progressive education.'[65] The developmentalists, both Tyack and Labaree argue, were divided between those two groups. In other words, they were principally concerned with either classroom practice or administrative matters: 'the conservative and social efficiency groups fit more or less within the administrative category and the liberal and social reconstructionist groups fit roughly within the pedagogical, with child development straddling the two.'[66]

The orientations discussed above have in common a concern for discerning whether, and to what extent, progressive education actually affected classrooms and systems of schooling.[67] In a related sense, other historians have taken for granted progressive education's impact on education and have focused on unearthing elements of it that remain embedded in contemporary schools.[68] The work of Daniel Levine represented a different approach from this, one that considers varying interpretations of progressive education and that tries to address the historical problem of coexistent definitions defining the field.

Levine argued that in light of these coexistent complexities and the relativity within the field, progressive education was a misleading and (it follows) useless concept.[69] Likewise, Peter Filene questioned whether the progressive movement could be considered a movement at all since it lacked a coherent program, ideology, or membership.[70] To replace the vision of a unified or consistent ideological movement, he offered the model of 'shifting coalitions' of reformers who mobilized on different issues according to their particular interests.[71] Filene's position established grounds on which the ambiguities and complexities related to progressive education could be explained. In his view, the kinds of thinking that had led to narrow definitions of progressive education had to give way to a realization that educational reforms can best be understood in terms of shifting coalitions of interests.[72]

James Fraser, Julia Wrigley, and William Reese, evidently following Levine's and Filene's critiques of a singular progressive education movement, identified multiple progressive subgroups in their historical examinations of educational reform in the United States.[73] Among them, these three historians identified and explored ten progressive subgroups – social gospellers, populist parties, socialist groups, labour unions, parent associations, women's organizations, school administrators, middle-class municipal reformers, militant teachers, and curriculum reformers.[74] Raymond Williams's *The Long Revolution* (1975), in a European context, was another example of this approach. Williams argued that the nineteenth-century curriculum in British schools was a compromise among three competing perspectives: the public educators, the industrial trainers, and the old humanists.[75] A final example of this approach is Kieran Egan's *Getting It Wrong from the Beginning: Our Progressivist Inheritance from Herbert Spencer, John Dewey, and Jean Piaget* (2002), which explicitly addresses conflicting progressivist visions implicated in education. Each, he argues, represents a fundamentally different world view and as a consequence undermines rather than shores up the others.[76]

Other historians, dealing at length with the tensions and ambiguities involved in education, have constructed critical or revisionist accounts of progressive education. Many, in the spirit of Lawrence Cremin, have situated educational reform discourse in relation to larger social and political orientations that have affected schooling. The works of Edward Krug, Michael Katz, Samuel Bowles and Herbert Gintis, and Joel Spring are examples of educational histories of reform and progress; all have viewed the field more broadly, often exposing economic, social, and political elements previously ignored in educational history.[77] These historians, the so-called radical revisionists, have all questioned the ideological and political roots of educational progress.[78] Their studies have even offered Marxist (in the case of Katz, Bowles, and Gintis) and anarchist (in the case of Spring) explorations of progressive education.

The final historical approach of note to be considered is that of Klie-bard, who sets out to debunk claims that any unified progressive education movement existed in the United States. The progressive era, he argues, was an age of criticism and debate directed at the established order of schooling. Like Filene, who once declared that '"the progressive movement" never existed,' Kliebard sees the field of progressives as populated by shifting coalitions of interest groups, each competing for influence over school reforms.[79] He argues that the very term *progressive education* begs a question: 'I was frankly puzzled by what was meant by the innumerable references I had seen to progressive education. The more I studied this the more it seemed ... that the term encompassed such a broad range, not just of different, but of contradictory, ideas on education as to be meaningless.'[80]

Kliebard has identified three distinct and divergent progressive interest groups embroiled in a struggle for the curriculum and school policy, each advocating a particular reform aim: efficiency, social reconstruction, or developmental psychology. He writes that the developmentalist interest group held an almost romantic faith in nature and in the unfolding stages of child development. The developmentalists traced their 'ancestry as far back as Comenius, most prominently to

Rousseau, and then to the work of Pestalozzi and Froebel.'[81] Pedagogically, the orientation, which was geared principally toward the scientific and psychological understanding of human development, had as its central principle a striving 'first of all to keep out of nature's way.'[82] The social efficiency advocates, for their part, saw scientific management of schools as the best means to reform schools and make them more progressive. 'Of the varied and sometimes frenetic responses to industrialism and to the consequent transformation of American social institutions,' Kliebard notes, 'there was one that emerged clearly dominant both as a social ideal and as an educational doctrine. It was social efficiency.'[83] The third interest group that Kliebard considers in relation to progressive education is the social meliorists, whose zeal for confronting social injustice in society through educational reforms reached its zenith during the Great Depression.[84]

Kliebard argues that the social meliorists, the developmentalists, and the efficiency advocates represented fundamentally distinct interests and as such should not be seen now as belonging to one movement. While this may not in itself sound controversial, what sharply differentiates Kliebard from his predecessors is the daring conclusion he draws from his analysis: absent any cohesive vision for reform among the interest groups he examines, and in light of the confusion fostered by competing definitions of progressive education, he dismisses the entire concept of progressive education as meaningless, dangerous, and null and void.[85]

Kliebard's challenge to historians is a serious one. If progressive education meant, as Kliebard posited, many different things to many different people, and if – furthering the point – many of these meanings represented fundamentally different things, then a big bag category may be meritless. In Kliebard's assessment, progressive education was 'a loose, largely unarticulated, and not very tidy compromise' of divergent aims and interests.[86] The present study is largely interested in addressing Kliebard's challenge by isolating the progressivist language in the journals and probing it for its meanings within the parameters of common themes, or domains.[87]

The articles published in the educational journals, particularly the editorials, demonstrate attempts by Ontario's educationists to work out the meanings of progressive education. Those editorials, which were widely distributed in the province, reveal what the new education meant to educators at the time. They advocated changes to the province's system of schooling, and they did so under the banner of progressive education. Charles Phillips has noted a fundamental difference between an educational publication that provided educators with 'ready-made busy work and other aides' and those primarily concerned with the exploration of 'ideas for the improvement of education.'[88] Both *The School* and *The Canadian School Journal* were forums where educationists could put forward visions for progressive educational reform. With regard to the editorial content, there was very little to distinguish the two journals; each presented a progressivist vision for Ontario's schools. The tone and language, likewise, consistently strove for what Phillips referred to as 'the rather high intellectual level appropriate' for educationists.[89] The most notable difference between the two journals had to do not with the editorial content or opinions but rather with the intended audience: *The School* was mainly for educators and teacher candidates, *The Canadian School Journal* for administrators and trustees.[90] The editorials, and to some extent the speeches made at educational conventions and later reprinted in the journals, are the key sources for this exploration of progressivist discourse in Ontario.[91] Kliebard, in his study of American progressive history, dismissed the discourse and writings of progressive educationists as mere rhetoric 'not … influencing the course of events.'[92]

The present study is primarily interested in the language used by progressivists in its own right, independent of any pragmatic tests of its causes and effects. Sol Cohen, likewise, has argued that the language of progressive education is itself a useful source for uncovering historical meanings. In his words, a study of progressivist rhetoric

> is not about claims of truth: that there *really* was a 'progressive education' or that there wasn't. A category or concept like progressive education is just an instrument. The questions are: Does it still illuminate? Is it still useful? My answer to both questions is in the affirmative. To accept Kliebard's position would mean the end of an important historiographical discussion.[93]

In this last point, Cohen is saying that if, in fact, Kliebard's claim concerning the vacuity of progressive education were correct, there would be no point in continuing to explore the topic. Cohen's appeal to explore the meanings of progressivist discourse, however, steers the discussion away from instrumentalist concerns of cause and effect in order to focus on the meanings embedded in the extant language. He takes up the call of John L. Rury, who takes for granted that progressive education existed but who claims that its history has not yet been written, largely because it has been greatly concerned with the transformations of schools.[94]

There are a number of further reasons why this study concentrates exclusively on progressivist language. The first reason relates to what David Labaree calls 'the four levels of school reform,' which is a nested model for conceptualizing educational reforms.[95] Each has its own actors, media, and discursive community. He refers to the top level – the one where most reform efforts begin and typically end – as the level of rhetoric.[96] This research addresses precisely this tier, where progressivists make 'statements of principle, educational visions, rationales for change, frameworks for representing that change, and norms for reconstructed educational practice.'[97] The actors at this level, as well as their primary media – which Labaree describes as enabling a broad range of educationists to contribute and interact – match the context and sources of my study with relative accuracy.[98]

The last note in reference to this nested model is that histories addressing the level of educational rhetoric can typically say little about reforms at other levels – for example, those of enacted practice.[99] Labaree's caveat was foreshadowed by Rosa Bruno-Jofré's qualification that 'historically there has always been a gap between educational aims and policies in the form of statements, documents of various sorts, curricula, and what actually happened in schools.'[100] These statements make it clear that my focus on the rhetorical meanings of progressive education in Ontario's educational journals has certain limitations. It is outside the scope of this book to find material evidence of classroom practice or policy being transformed along progressive lines, and it is not possible to fully explain why particular explanations are undertaken and how those evolve over time. The aim here, to reiterate, is to explore distinct orientations to progressive education published in two of Ontario's educational periodicals between 1919 and 1942.

This book is not a tale of fierce struggles for the curriculum, fought by warring interest groups that were commandeered by public intellectuals engaged in debate.[101] Ontario's educational journals were not particularly conducive to debate. High drama, if it existed at all, is sparsely reported in the present book. The periodicals presented parallel views, not firestorms and debates.[102] Progressivists used these forums largely to lay out their reformist visions and to critique and deride humanists and their outmoded, so-called traditional, visions of schooling. Polemical exchanges between progressivists were not featured in the source journals and are not the concern of this study.

If prominent intellectuals or interest groups did publish articles, these were not accentuated over those of other educationists who shared the space in any particular issue. Ontario's educational journals' main concerns included the presentation and dissemination of ideas.[103] No homegrown George Counts emerges from the sources to lead meliorist brigades, and no local David Snedden becomes the voice of social efficiency in the province.[104] According to Kliebard, the period of progressive reforms in the United States amounted to an epic battle fought on the terrain of the curriculum. In Ontario, by contrast, the educational journals provided parallel opinions on educational progress, with little combativeness or polemic. So in this study, I give greater regard to similarities and differences between progressivist orientations than I do to individual educationists' politics or personalities.[105]

Progressive educators, for all their differences in orientation, were held together by four common perspectives, which operated as 'ideational glue.'[106] The first – and it was overarching – was a critique of the traditional humanist curriculum.[107] It was the humanists' key concepts and subjects – faculty psychology, mental discipline, and the classics – that were critiqued most often by progressivists. The other three common interests among progressive educators dovetailed with the first; it was on those grounds that progressivists deemed the traditional schools to be unsuitable.[108]

According to the progressivist sources, the humanistic curriculum emphasized passive forms of learning, including rote memorization; it subjugated the individual learner to often out-of-date subject matter; and it was out of touch with knowledge relating to real life. Thus the journal articles that I have identified as progressivist express concern for active learning, for individualized instruction, and for relating the schools more closely to society. Establishing this unifying framework for exploring progressive educational discourse allows for a more accurate and subtle understanding of the diverse and sometimes conflicting perspectives within it.

I define the first of these orientations, child study, in relation to the emerging field of developmental psychology. This element of progressivist reform was concerned mostly with fostering individualization and self-fulfilment through Ontario's schools. Students could, from this progressivist orientation, be understood on their own terms and nurtured to develop into self-directed, moral citizens. Second, I define social efficiency as an ideal closely related to the fields of experimental psychology and industrial management. This thread of progressivist reform was concerned with social planning and management. Accordingly, students' interests and abilities required careful study in order for specific courses of training and study to be developed so that each individual would be best prepared for his or her vocational and social niche. Lastly, social meliorism was a network of ideas related to the idea of social justice. Social meliorism was a course of progressivist reform concerned with fostering participatory citizenship and equity in society. Students could, from the perspective of this orientation, engage with social problems and inequities in order to learn ways of critically considering their own situations and striving for a more equitable world. The following three chapters consider these differing progressivist orientations with respect to three domains of progressive education: active learning, individualizing instruction, and developing the relationship between schools and modern society.

3 Progressive as Active Learning: Critiques of Rote Scholarship in School

Some few years ago I was looking about the school supply stores in the city, trying to find desks and chairs which seemed thoroughly suitable from all points of view – artistic, hygienic, and educational – to the needs of the children. We had a good deal of difficulty in finding what we needed, and finally one dealer, more intelligent than the rest, made this remark: 'I am afraid we have not what you want. You want something at which the children may work; these are all for listening.' That tells the story of the traditional education.*

This chapter is concerned with active learning, one of three domains of progressivist texts in Ontario's educational journals. Three different progressive orientations – child study, social efficiency, and social meliorism – will be used as lenses to examine the complexities associated with active learning.[1] Progressive educationists in Ontario argued that the traditional curriculum placed the learner in the essentially passive role of rote memorizer and regurgitator of facts.[2] Progressivist texts in Ontario's journals were critical of passive, rote learning.[3] As will be shown, these critiques were often presented in mocking or sarcastic texts that ridiculed the province's traditional curriculum for treating students as passive receptacles for academic content. In this chapter, I divide these critiques into three groups, each representing a different orientation toward progressive education. Each orientation – child study, social efficiency, and social meliorism – presents essen-

---

* John Dewey, *The School and Society* (Chicago, IL: University of Chicago Press, 1907), 47–8.

tially different concerns and aims with respect to the progressivist aim of increasing the active participation of students in learning.

Child Study and Developmental Psychology

Pedagogically, the child study orientation was geared principally toward the scientific and psychological understanding of stages of growth and qualitative development. G. Stanley Hall best summarized its central principle: 'first of all to keep out of nature's way.'[4] Educational activity was described as essential for the healthy development of mind and body.[5] The child, like a plant or flower, would grow and develop through natural stages; the educator needed to understand these in order to foster (and avoid impeding) healthy growth.[6]

The practical experience of early child study advocates in Ontario, such as William E. Blatz, was rooted in the rehabilitation programs for traumatized and wounded soldiers returning from the First World War.[7] The principles of child study were, in large part,

> an outgrowth of the re-education methods and psychological principles that were developed for the muscle-function training of crippled veterans at the University of Toronto during 1916–1919, namely, that patient must not remain passive and psychologically dependent, but must become a participant learner, if he is to master his present limitations and thus be able to meet later situations with confidence.[8]

With respect to the study and education of children, ascertaining the stage of the learner's development and the complexity of the tasks involved was simpler, yet the emphasis on active self-direction and the progressive achievement of small goals was the same.[9]

With veterans, rehabilitation entailed slow progress toward an often physical objective. With children, the objective of progressive education was successful adjustment into the next stage of human development. The perception was that all learning was experiential.[10] The learner's active engagement with tasks suitable to his or her stage of development promoted both health and happiness; in Blatz's words, 'if all reading, grammar, mathematics and other academic subjects were removed from the school time-table, and drawing, modeling, craftwork, music and dancing substituted, we should have in the next generation not more intelligent but happier adults.'[11] The most natural way to educate children, he argued, was through creative and expressive activity.

The nursery and laboratory schools that were integral to child study were described as 'outgrowths ... they came into being at the same time when the human sciences were beginning to speculate upon the significance of childhood for human adjustment.'[12] These schools allowed researchers to form developmental hypotheses of real children as they actively engaged in pedagogically progressive activities with their peers. In constructing such environments, Blatz appealed to his experiences at the University of Chicago and to the model laboratory school developed there by Dewey. The children 'worked on a loom and baked bread. There were school trips to the harbour, to art galleries, and to the train station. A newspaper was launched.'[13] These ideas, commonplace today, were a far cry from the seatwork and rote learning that characterized the traditional classrooms in Toronto at the time.[14]

Today's educators know that education must aim to be developmentally appropriate, but it was in the context of interwar progressive rhetoric that these ideas were first teased out in Ontario. Child study texts promoted the idea that special activities needed to be developed for dealing with a child at each stage of his or her evolution. Each stage of development had its own pedagogical activities and challenges. Overall, and regardless of age, children needed to enjoy what Blatz referred to as 'an atmosphere of freedom, self-dependence, regulated habits, adequate social contacts – and of serenity. The latter is the sine qua non of any well-conducted Nursery School.'[15]

Educational experiences were all about active engagement with situations that promoted and provoked new knowledge. An address by Professor N.S. MacDonald to the Kindergarten Section of the OEA in 1928, reprinted in the *Canadian School Board Journal*, made it clear that activities should engage a child's present stage of development, not some future aim. The article presenting MacDonald's ideas noted that the foundations of child study were the belief that 'education is a process of growth rather than instruction' and the conviction that 'present interests rather than future needs should determine the method and material of instruction.'[16] In order to adjust to his or her stage of development, a child required developmentally appropriate learning experiences.[17] Children's total personalities developed only as they learned – in other words, as they encountered developmentally appropriate experiences with which they could interact. For educationists concerned with child study, action was primary in progressive education, and content was only a secondary consideration.[18] The best learning experiences were responsive to the developmental level of each child, and this in turn required that appropriate skills, interests, and habits be considered.[19]

The goal of the teacher, then, was to understand the child's stage of development. With that in mind, an evolving educational plan needed to be constructed that could guide the learner's activities through increasingly complex stages. Here, the learning situation 'was defined simply but dynamically as the response whereby the child seeks to meet his needs within his environment.'[20] Success in a learning situation required effort and reflection on the student's part. It followed that the teacher's role was to construct situations that directed the learner's natural energies and instincts toward educational aims. An article in *The School* reviewing the guiding principles of active learning as embodied in Alberta's 1922 school reforms depicted the following principles (among others) as admirable:

> 1. Learning is not something that a child *gets*, but something that he [*sic*] *does* ... 2. The school programme must respond meaningfully and purposefully to the child's call for things to do, by setting up goals for the child's activity as well as objectives for the teacher ... 3. The natural way of learning used by children in their play life may be adopted by the school, and re-directed to educational objectives.[21]

The Alberta activity program – a model of 'the new curriculum' based on research on progress and development – was described as fostering cooperative activities among teachers, pupils, parents, and school boards.[22]

A key concern of child study progressivist texts was the sociability and social activity of children. T.A. Brough expressed this in the following way: 'A democratic state should be composed of citizens able to play their part and to make new adjustments in an evolving and progressive social order ... The best social experience at the own age-level is the best preparation for the child's later life.'[23] Sociability, like other behaviours and subjects for learning, would progress rapidly as long as there were meaningful learning experiences to promote that growth. Social development, then, was viewed as motivated by active learning and experience.[24] The teacher, having set out an experiential program of learning for the students, thereafter needed to observe these carefully and assume a supervisory role with a minimum of interference in the learner's free social play.[25]

The progressive, experiential curriculum promoted by articles concerned with child study was seen as largely directed toward the development of habits. These habits were in turn described in terms of experiences that provoked individual development, which would persist throughout life.[26] William E. Blatz, contributing to *The School*, explained this aim by describing how successful experiences in solving problems, social or otherwise, would lead the child to develop confidence that solutions can be attained through the exercise of intelligent judgments.[27] Furthermore, active learning encouraged children to take responsibility for their own behaviour and, in cooperative situations, to work with peers to overcome obstacles. Blatz explained this in terms of learning to evaluate the consequences of one's own actions, which involved two implications of education: 'First of all, to *recognize consequences*, which assumes an intelligent appraisal of actual experience; secondly, to develop an attitude toward consequences either of acceptance or avoidance ... The second factor is independent of intelligence and knowledge as such and is concerned primarily with the arrangements for the individual's social and physical adjustment.'[28]

Teachers might, according to Blatz, be charged with arranging experiences and guiding development, but learning was an active process that persisted throughout life. It was driven by children's native curiosity and adaptability. 'Learning is an instinct,' Blatz argued, 'because of the fundamental needs he [*sic*] will strive for satisfaction. Among his needs is the appetite of change which, for its satisfaction, requires new experiences.'[29]

Especially at the Institute of Child Study, one implication of the belief that children's learning was a dynamic and active process was the associated belief that children needed practice solving problems, social and otherwise, using the '"art of non-conformity," or so-called creative endeavour.'[30] When children experienced working cooperatively, or how to 'conform,' they learned to believe in others; when children learned to be creative and independent, however, or to 'nonconform,' they learned to have more trust in their own abilities.[31] The teacher, as guide, had to develop both independence and dependence through a balance of cooperative and independent learning experiences. This demanded of the adult a dynamic rather than a purely passive role, involving the discovery of ways to support and encourage children to choose goals and to support various paths toward their accomplishments.

For the child study progressivists, then, it was important 'not to instruct, but to provoke.'[32] Learning could provoke many feelings, but boredom was among the worst.[33] Problems were seen as òften arising from boredom or disinterest on the part of students, stemming from a lack of imagination on the part of teachers concerning how to develop meaningful learning experiences. Blatz often made this last argument in relation to his underlying functionalist conviction that knowledge is meaningful only when it is used.[34] Throughout the period being examined here, active learning was commonly emphasized, as was practical activity that kept children pleasantly occupied and engaged at all costs.[35]

Progressive education inevitably excited learners and aroused their native interests.[36] Quelling mischievous activities in students was a matter of proactively preparing activities for them that were attractive, interesting, and purposeful.[37] Without practical work and activity in the classroom, children would find learning 'meaningless, dull, and tiresome.'[38] Gordon Young, Inspector of Public Schools in Kemptville, Ontario, explained that curricula such as those entrenched in Ontario had enforced a passive subjugation to content without regard for individual interest. Such frameworks not only quelled motivation but also strongly hindered individual progress.[39] A progressive curriculum, by contrast, provoked enthusiasm and excitement for learning because it permitted the individual to pursue interesting experiences. Once students were freed to pursue learning activities related to their own aims and personal concerns, they could plan their lives and prepare appropriately. J.D. Griffin, a psychology professor at the University of Toronto, countered the view that students needed vocational guidance and structure in order to enter appropriate career paths by explaining that students who had had such opportunities to pursue meaningful experiences would already have developed the 'ability to choose a vocation ... quite naturally.'[40]

Experiential learning, like developmental appropriateness, can be traced back to progressivist child study advocates. Ontario-born Donalda Dickie, one of Alberta's foremost progressivist voices, developed and advocated an enterprise method of learning that integrated concern for child study with developmentally active learning experiences.[41] For her, the '"progressive" type' of school would develop the gifts and personality of each student, while acknowledging that 'the individual cannot be isolated from the group.'[42] A progressive, enterprising school necessarily emphasized learning activities to develop 'co-operative achievement of a social purpose that the teacher presents to the class with a view to having them use it as an exercise in intelligent social behaviour.'[43]

Enterprises involved the analysis and identification of a social problem, guided discovery of some solution, and the cooperative application of that solution.[44] Ideally, the subject matter of an enterprise engaged a learner's developmental stage and provided 'a good range of contacts, experiences, and activities.'[45] The activities intentionally blended topics of study with the actual lives of students.[46] School work was intended to be intimately related to the actual development of learners' abilities and to involve students in active inquiry.[47]

Social Efficiency and Adjustment to Industry

Progressivist articles considered in this section as representing the social efficiency orientation to school reforms promoted active learning that trained students to develop specific vocational skills. Many of the authors of these texts had links to vocational training or guidance, industry, and school administration. Throughout the interwar years, critiques of a general, humanistic education often hinged on the notion that transfer of training was impossible.[48] A skill learned in one particular context was not necessarily transferable to another – indeed, this might not even be possible. This thesis was first presented in the 1890s by researchers such as William James at Harvard University. It was echoed in Canada by progressivist C.C. Goldring, who wrote on this question explicitly in an article written for *Toronto Saturday Night*, which was reprinted in *The Canadian School Journal* in 1935.[49]

Goldring had been appointed the Director of the Toronto Board of Education in 1933 at the age of thirty-three. He described 'the transfer problem' as emanating from scientific evidence that 'transfer of training usually takes place only when the situations are similar. It will be generally agreed that the conditions of business differ radically from the conditions of school.'[50] For efficiency's sake, schools needed to engage students in learning activities that were particular, precise, and specialized; this would train them for their future vocational lives.[51]

Stating this point with abundant clarity was Ontario's Minister of Public Welfare, W.G. Martin, who in 1932 announced to the Trustees' and Ratepayers' Department of the OEA that 'we are no longer satisfied with a system of general education ... The work of training the boy of to-day must follow along some particular line instead of fashioning our youth in a common group.'[52] Educational activities needed to be designed efficiently so that they might 'take the boy of school age and seek to fit and equip him for some special and definite avocation or calling.'[53] This was, Martin argued, an 'age of specialization.'[54]

In other words, educational reforms of a truly progressivist orientation would help students adapt efficiently to Ontario's new industrial order. Robert Stamp describes Goldring as 'flirting in the 1930s with what was called "progressive education."'[55] What Stamp does not consider is that Martin's 1932 article in *The Canadian School Journal* reveals a particular orientation to progressive education. Goldring is expressing a distinctly social efficiency progressivist reading of the school's responsibility to the established industrial order: 'Since it is certain that all the mature members of a society will die, it is obvious that the conservation of a society depends upon rearing the new-born members in such a way that they will appropriate its functions and sustain its values.'[56] Furthermore, since 'school graduates will look for positions in business, it is important for the school people to have some knowledge of the viewpoint and requirements of the employers in industry.'[57] Goldring's message to progressivists was that educational activities should prepare students to adjust to the extant social order, not to reconstruct it.

This active adjustment to industrial demands entailed training students to conform in personality, not merely in skill. A. M. Laird and J.E. Durrant reported in *The School* that they had, like others in the Department of Education, undertaken a thorough occupational survey in order to take note of particular skills and habits required by different professions.[58] Their work, funded by the Ontario Training College for Technical Teachers, had two aims: 'The first was to learn something definite about the industries, commerce, and major occupations in the city. The second was to analyze this information in its relation to secondary education and the kinds of courses required.'[59] The logic behind these surveys was quite straightforward: if educators were to develop educational activities that could train students to perform specialized tasks or manifest particular character traits, these needed to be identified as behavioural objectives.[60]

By 1935 report cards in Toronto schools were assessing students' progress toward developing particular, desirable personality characteristics. These, in the words of Goldring, provided 'a record of progress in some of the qualities of a good citizen. The development of personal qualities is as important as a good standing in the subject of study.'[61] A good citizen, then, was one whose activities facilitated his or her adjustment to the established order.

Active citizenship for a progressive society, for example, required that schools train students directly in all those characteristics that would foster conservative obedience to the state order, including these:

1 Respect for authority – (a) Parental; (b) Positional.
2 Industry – (a) Thoroughness in work done; (b) Time not wasted.
3 Thrift – (a) Regular savings; (b) Avoidance of waste.
4 Courtesy – (a) Recognition of the rights of others; (b) Politeness, good manners.
5 Integrity – (a) Honesty, Truthfulness; (b) Trustworthiness.
6 Care for property – (a) Private; (b) Public.
7 Tidiness – (a) Personal; (b) Environmental.
8 Contribution to the public good – (a) Cooperation; (b) Initiative, suggestiveness.
9 Self-control – (a) Actions; (b) Feelings.
10 Courage – (a) Physical; (b) Moral.[62]

Efficiency-oriented progressivist texts argued that these could not be learned by independently and quietly sitting in classrooms focused on reading and writing tasks; personality, like skill, required active training.[63]

The educational journals reported the benefits and successes of several progressivist programs that had been established in Ontario's schools in order to train students actively and specifically in the habits of mind consistent with a social efficiency viewpoint.[64] Programs such as Manual Training, Domestic Science, and Technical Education were introduced into the province's curriculum, and the Penny Bank program was specifically designed to teach children the value of regular savings, thrift habits, and business practice.

Educator J.R. Littleproud, whose list of traits defining good citizenship was just noted, was Ontario's Chief Penny Bank inspector. His 1934 article in *The Canadian School Journal*, which also provided a thorough historical survey of the Penny Banking program, equated students' participation in the program with citizenship education: 'As a civic institution, the public school can justify its existence to-day only by the type of citizen it produces.'[65] Littleproud was not shy in proposing that educational activity in a progressivist context had as its ultimate goal the production of efficient citizens: 'Recent years have witnessed a revolution in the field of pedagogy as far-reaching as any revolution ever effected [*sic*] in the political affairs of mankind or in the industrial world. There has come a new viewpoint in the minds of educators, a new objective for the schools, a new test of the school's efficiency.'[66] A young child participating in a project and activity promoting frugality would become a mature citizen of the province with experience handling his or her finances.[67]

According to Littleproud, under the terms of the federal Penny Bank Act of 1904, which had the cooperation of local chartered banks, the Penny Bank of Toronto had been organized in 1905.[68] It had begun taking deposits as of 1 May 1905, and by the end of that school year, it had enrolled 42 schools in the provincial capital, with a combined balance of $50,400. By the start of the First World War, 187 schools in 48 different cities were involved in Penny Banking, with a total balance of an astonishing $395,000.[69] This progressive program for active learning that correlated to real life was maintained throughout the Depression, actually expanding during that period to 470 schools in 124 cities, serving as custodian for $1,200,000 belonging to the children of the province.[70]

Progressivist rhetoric concerned with social efficiency also touted the importance of active learning in education, only it emphasized that this activity needed to be purposeful and useful. The traditional, entrenched curriculum was inefficient not only because it focused on content unrelated to life but also because the method of instruction did not relate to purposeful and useful activity. As Reverend C.R. Durrant said in his address at the 1934 OEA convention, a new and progressive school system would 'train for living. Many things we have regarded as fads, frills and fancies, will be looked upon as necessities in the new day approaching.'[71]

Charles F. Deeley, an Ontario educator, would interpret educational training for living in terms that related it to classroom instruction through projects. 'The new curriculum has given a very marked impetus to individual or class projects in both the public school and lower school grades,' he explained.[72] Calling out to his colleagues in *The School*, Deeley summarized very effectively the efficiency concern for making all classroom activity both useful and purposeful: 'Teachers, let us evaluate our project before the activity is begun by two criteria: first, the knowledge which such an undertaking will convey to our pupils; second its value in the light of the time and labour which the work will entail.'[73] The article expressed two common progressivist preoccupations in journal articles concerned with school planning: usefulness and efficiency. Lessons were supposed to concentrate activity as efficiently as possible in terms of the time and effort invested by both teacher and student.

An active program of schooling that promoted utility and efficiency was often represented as one that would be of greater interest to learners than a curriculum inculcating academic knowledge and habits. Learning that was strictly academic was a remnant of Ontario's past, when only a privileged elite could pursue higher learning. In the modern world, an editorial in *The School* explained, a progressive system was one that allowed for the fact that 'high schools enrol upwards of three-fourths of the young people of high school age.'[74] A fair proportion of those students, the argument continued, had neither the inclination nor the ability to pursue academic studies. These students deserved the right to pursue studies actively that would prepare them best for their future vocational lives by providing precise and adequate training.[75] Such training was necessarily active, participatory, and directed toward realistic aims. Any course that did not actively engage students in practical work relating to life missed the mark. If history, for example, was treated as 'merely a matter of memorizing sequences of past events, its study might better be abandoned. Its chief purpose is training pupils to appreciate the significance of current happenings and to understand the nature of historical cause and effect.'[76] Mere memorization of textbooks was, in a progressivist context, inadequate learning.

Interwar Ontario's progressive push sowed the seeds for the contemporary emphasis on school administration and order. Progressivist articles concerned with educational efficiency dealt mainly with administrative issues, including the management and control of testing systems, school organization, and finance. Yet the microcosm of the classroom and the operations of public school teachers were not ignored by efficiency progressivists. S.B. Sinclair, for instance, a school trustee in rural Ontario, published an article in *The Canadian School Journal* arguing that for a school board to be efficient, 'the first step in the wise selection of a teacher is to determine, in a general way, the special kind of teacher required.'[77] The hiring of teachers required prudence, and a number of factors were crucial to the development and cultivation of useful, efficient citizens. Just as students learned desirable skills and habits through activity, teachers should actively intervene in student affairs, particularly with regard to discipline.

Among the principal problems of education, explained George Rogers, was the presence of teachers who were poor disciplinarians: 'If we are serious in our desire for economy, we may have to change the organization of many of our schools. Teachers will have to perfect a technique for handling larger classes.'[78] Rogers, writing in 1933, at a time when ballooning enrolments during the Depression stretched the province's educational infrastructure to its limits, believed that no efficient organization of schools could be sustained if teachers were inefficient managers of classrooms. Particularly in the case of vocational schools and technical training institutions, where 'there are a number of large boys who are behaviour problems, a teacher who is known to be a good disciplinarian is better than one who has no experience.'[79] An efficient teacher minimized distractions and kept students on task for a maximum time.

Furthermore, since the transferability of training between contexts was, at best, debatable from this perspective, the efficient teacher also required specific and efficient training. Particularly for technical and vocational schooling, courses were set up during the summer, in the evenings, and in the normal schools for the preparation of teachers in different domains of training. Rogers argued that in terms of academic and professional training, 'the candidate who holds a first class certificate and certificates for successful courses in Agriculture, Household Science, Music, Drawing, Physical Culture, Auxiliary Class work, two years Normal School training etc. is sure to do better work as the result of superior preparation.'[80] More training and increased specialization were imperative for the promotion of progressive teachers, who could use input from school inspectors, school principals, administrators, and peers to improve the efficiency with which they fulfilled their teaching duties.

Conference and conversion appear as themes in the progressivist rhetoric. There was an almost missionary element to certain progressivist texts, some of which argued strenuously for the conversion of educationists holding other views. In a 1932 editorial in *The Canadian School Journal*, for example, the following sentiment was expressed: 'Too many of us forget that we must win those who do not see eye to eye with us. In fact all our convention and association effort is really directed to winning the active co-operation of those who are either opposed to certain ideas, which we consider progressive; or are indifferent upon the matter.'[81] The same editorial took aim at unnamed but alternative progressivist visions for school reform that did not consider the promotion of efficiency paramount. There were, it acknowledged, alternative orientations to progressive education; these, in effect, decreased the efficiency of progressivist aims.

This appeal is notable because it highlights another dimension of activity within progressive education – namely, that of progressivists themselves. The publication of editorial articles and of lesson plans or news reports bearing relevance to progressivist themes represented, in itself, active engagement with progressive education. Progressivists not only promoted active learning within learning situations but also actively engaged in writing about and conferencing on progressive education. Furthermore, if the cause of progressive education were to be furthered in the most efficient way, it would happen through some form of agreement and active cooperation.

The same editorial of 1932 invited progressivists to confer about their problems and discuss the best course for school reform.[82] From the efficiency perspective, the greatest test of any measure was a utilitarian and pragmatic one: it was 'the test of its value.'[83] Social efficiency claims to value would always be strongest because these were based on surveys of the realities of vocational life – surveys that had consulted with business leaders to ascertain their particular demands for the schools. W.E. Gordon, manager of the Robert Simpson Eastern Company, having defined a modern school as one that taught students the personal qualities that would ensure their success in business life, explained to Ontario's educational community that 'the progressive, intelligent graduate of to-day … is the industrial leader of to-morrow.'[84]

Research into educational costs and expenditures was another dimension of what progressivist interests saw as active engagement with schools. Contemporary educationists find such studies commonplace today, but Ontario's educators first experienced the transformative effects of these in the interwar years. Throughout 1937, *The Canadian School Journal* in particular provided space where leaders of business and industry could present their concerns to Ontario's educationists. A common theme taken up by these leaders was the desirable characteristics and skills that school graduates should have upon entering the workplace. Progressive schools were not wasteful ones, and it was imperative to 'discover, if possible, where we are wasting effort and money.'[85] Efficiency-minded progressivists often published the reports of these investigations and related them to contemporary concerns.[86] The Ontario Secondary School Teachers' Federation, for example, aimed to discover 'where eliminations, combinations, and reconstructions can be made, that will at the same time relieve the burden and increase the effectiveness' of Ontario's high school programs.[87] This advocacy of school efficiency had the effect of making expenditure control an overarching administrative concern; in the words of one edi-torial, it 'accentuated the movement for reducing educational costs.'[88]

More than any other factor, the Depression strengthened efficiency progressivists' pleas for the financial and institutional restructuring of schools. Yet this rhetoric was widespread and was not restricted to the Depression years. In 1928, for example, when the Department of Edu-cation was in the throes of expansion and developing building plans – which would soon be halted by the Depression – a number of arti-cles were published advocating an overhaul of school boards, fund-ing mechanisms, regulations, and administration.[89] At a time when the world was viewed as increasingly modern, specialized, and scientific, claims were being made that education was out of touch with the new spirit of scientific planning and efficiency.[90] It was often suggested that at a time when all of society was changing, school administration had remained relatively static. According to an editorial in *The Canadian School Journal*, 'the same administrative machine we set up sixty years ago, some of it nearly one hundred years ago ... [now] works badly.'[91] Another editorial in the same journal four months earlier had stated: 'In the transition from the more cultural period of our system to the intensely practical, the system has, through the enthusiastic efforts and appeals of the many idealists, become so cumbersome as to be a burden to both the teacher and pupil and correspondingly ineffective.'[92] The war against waste required reflection, study, and vigilant action. Wher-ever efficiency could be increased, without increasing costs, progress was being achieved.[93]

Social Meliorism and Engagement with Social Ills

Articles with a social meliorist orientation focused mainly on promot-ing active, reflective, and critical citizenship. By and large, these pro-gressivist texts were concerned with fostering a cooperative rather than an individualistic society. With respect to active learning, this section will discuss meliorist progressivist articles' advocacy for schooling that would engage students with the problems facing contemporary soci-ety and that would show students how to analyse and resolve them. Schools could become spaces where future citizens learned to challenge social injustices and promote greater equality.

The themes of social meliorist progressivist rhetoric included social justice and the need for educational and social change. In both source journals, Joseph McCulley, headmaster of one of Ontario's largest private schools, Pickering College, emerged as a significant advocate of social meliorism.[94] From his perspective, the drive for a progressive system that would support a more just and cooperative world had been prompted by social circumstances that 'arise which cause a general unsettling in the intellectual atmosphere; in this environment creative thinkers find a more satisfactory opportunity to achieve their purpose and change comes about much more rapidly than at other times.'[95] The world had changed dramatically, and it could be changed to reflect a more equitable social order.

New conceptions of life and schooling could never supplant established curricula or doctrines without the active struggle, advocacy, and support of citizens. McCulley thought that the cause of progressive education could rally the support of educationists in times of inequity or injustice because 'any "ism" or "ology" which is sufficiently critical of present conditions or which claims itself as a panacea for the ills of our body politic will find at least its quota of adherents.'[96] Moreover, active citizenship required a critical perspective toward the ideas and circumstances of life so that viewpoints could be debated without blind adherence to any particular doctrine.[97]

Active involvement in terms of promoting social welfare and justice involved more than reading and reflection. Progressivist schools, teachers, and students were represented as those that, instead of confining themselves to within school walls, sought to engage with social problems and issues.[98] 'Don't stand aside and leave it to others,' implored W.G. Martin, an Ontario teacher, 'for the opportunities are at your threshold, in every town and village where you happen to live. The tasks are there and every one of us can play a part, for the race is not necessarily to the swift nor the battle to the strong.'[99] Concern for the common good called on each progressivist to turn his or her gaze to others in society. Each person was considered equally capable of this task, and neither intelligence testing nor auxiliary classes could replace a commitment to active involvement in the reconstruction of society.[100]

The alternative – a strict and narrow efficiency view of progress – was a fundamentally immoral one. Thus, an editorial in *The School* criticized progressivist visions not grounded in social meliorism by equating them with Nazism.[101] Civic cooperation, social justice, and intelligent activity were hallmarks of democracy; by contrast, the Nazis were treating Germans like animals that needed to be trained:

Having no grounds for confidence in the intelligent, self-motivated, cooperative activity of a lion fresh from the jungle, the trainer relies on his own intelligence to gain his own ends and on emotional and physical force to make his animals behave in a manner conducive to such ends. For the application of this method to human beings see *Mein Kampf* by A. Hitler, who bases his social and educational philosophy on Darwinian theory.[102]

More just reforms to Ontario's schools would promote social cooperation over the rule of brute science, enabling each child to 'assume responsibility for his own welfare and the welfare of all.'[103]

Active learning was largely concerned with practising cooperative living. Accordingly, for progressive schools to develop in children an understanding of the benefits of cooperative living and social welfare, they needed to engage them in classroom activities that would build relevant and rewarding experiences. The pupil, explained educator John Cook, 'having been shown the particular value of this principle in the world around him, should be placed in a position where he may take part in the actual demonstration of it.'[104] Cooperative activities directed toward some social purpose or benefits were often cited as ways in which students might gain active experience with the benefits of mutual care and sharing.[105]

R.H. Macklem, for instance, a teacher at Runnymede Collegiate Institute in Toronto, argued that 'community schools' could be founded as models of 'a reciprocal service between school and community.'[106] Community involvement included activities with social benefits, such as the construction of benches for needy organizations and the formation of school choirs that would tour the community and promote goodwill. Schools, Macklem explained, could improve the social welfare of the communities in which they were situated: 'There is a school in every community, but few communities have schools which do more than render a minimum of service to the people.'[107] Furthermore, progressive schools could become social centres – places where students and adults could come together as a group, 'playing and studying, singing and conversing – *together*.'[108]

Activities in education would offer opportunities for Ontario's students to practise the habits of engaged and active citizenship. A democratic and socially just province required active and committed citizens. As F.J. McDonald, Inspector of Separate Schools for Ottawa, explained: 'Unfeeling, apathetic citizenship of people is proving fatal to democracy.'[109] A progressive school was one that fostered active, critical reflection and that promoted cooperative, responsible, and associative living based on the question 'Who is my neighbour?'[110] In resounding Deweyan tones, McDonald argued that a progressive school could play a significant role in 'the improvement of social order' by successfully promoting cooperative 'learning by doing.'[111] 'Doing' cooperative citizenship entailed far more than memorizing facts about government, civics, or morality; it required the habit of living democratically. Progressivists could promote active citizenship in schools by adhering to the following precepts:

(1) That civilization is a co-operative task
(2) That living is a joint responsibility
(3) That the success of the social enterprise depends upon individual effort, sociability and dependability
... These aims are to be constantly held in mind in training our citizens. And the greatest of these is participation.[112]

Ontario's schools could help students become active and moral citizens by promoting those same values through classroom activities. For instance, B.C. Taylor explained, 'if the society is to be successful in revealing democracy, it should train each member in a democratic way.'[113] The formative place for this life was the school, where the lessons of communal work and play were first learned. *The School* reported that the elementary school teachers' federations had sent out to their members a memorandum 'supporting attitudes and teaching methods which will foster democracy as a way of life. Democratic teaching rather than teaching democracy is approved as desirable practice in elementary school.'[114]

Stanley Watson, principal of Toronto's Keele Street Public School, argued that such democratic teaching necessarily emerged from a paradigmatic shift in the roles of teacher and learner.[115] Watson used *The Canadian School Journal* as a forum for his opinions on this, explaining that the teacher was supposed to be a director of student activities and not an imparter of information.[116] A progressive educator, he continued, was concerned neither with the projected training value of educational experiences, nor with the passive absorption of academic facts. 'The modern teacher' guides rather than inculcates, he wrote, because he or she 'no longer thinks of education in terms of knowledge to be acquired and facts to be stored.'[117] A progressive school was being represented here as one that liberated both student and teacher from the tethers that restrained their concern for community, justice, and other social problems.

In 1937, *The Canadian School Journal* reproduced the text of a lecture that Duncan McArthur presented to the OEA, in which he described these restraints as detrimental to the essential elements of democratic life.[118] This was the same year that the Department of Education would introduce its revised *Programme of Studies*, and the article presented McArthur at his rhetorical best. In strong meliorist tones, he outlined a progressivist vision for Ontario's schools in which 'children must be freed from any authoritative concepts or any blind worship of tradition or the status quo. In their school days they must have some opportunity to learn how to choose – to choose between opposed alternatives that path which will be for the ultimate good.'[119] For McArthur, the cultivation of a scientific and democratic educational community would help build a better and less prejudiced world. This article, spanning seven pages, was almost epic in both its scope and its energy. In it, McArthur, who would feature prominently in the development and presentation of Ontario's newly minted progressivist curriculum, was striking while the iron was hot. A lengthy citation of the text is merited:

> The school of tomorrow must, above all things, turn out citizens who are capable of facing their very different problems intelligently, courageously and with sympathy for all living beings. In this connection I make a plea for freedom of discussion, even of the most controversial issues in the classroom. The teacher must not be a propagandist but be encouraged to develop in the minds of his pupils the importance of ascertaining all the facts in a given situation, of accepting differences of opinion with tolerance and of making a decision, not on the grounds of personal prejudice but on the basis of the total community good. Education at its best in the intellectual sphere is the doing away with prejudices.[120]

Around the beginning of the Second World War in 1940, a flurry of articles appeared in the journals concerned with preserving the integrity of a democratic attitude toward education.[121]

Between 1940 and 1942, the dominant theme in the sources was the fostering of community and democratic activity in schools. One article, which reproduced a document drafted by an anonymous member of a Board of Education in Ontario, gave robust expression to this theme: 'Our democratic government is only meant for people who can do their own thinking ... liberty and freedom are not gifts from heaven, bestowed on a favoured people, but are the price of an everlasting struggle for justice in high places and low.'[122] McArthur's call for schools to foster opportunities for free discussion and democratic choice became a rallying cry for many progressivist articles in the early 1940s. Democracy was being represented as an ideal to be lived as well as taught.[123]

Social studies as a subject for teaching civics and examining contemporary social issues in Ontario was born in the progressivist, interwar context. Civics courses were often described as one way for progressivists to enable active and experiential training for citizenship. The school curriculum had been overextended and overloaded with courses that were either entirely academic or vocational; meanwhile, the most practical necessity of all – learning about being a critical and reflective citizen of the province – had been neglected. 'It is not possible for all to become carpenters, or dressmakers, or milliners,' explained James Keillor, a teacher at North Toronto Collegiate Institute, but 'all are called upon to assume the duties of citizenship.'[124] In the 'progressive educational journals and in the columns of our daily newspapers,' he continued, 'we read much regarding efforts to adapt the curricula of our public and high schools to the needs of the average Canadian citizen.'[125] A truly progressive school system would focus on the study of society, with the understanding that 'the pupil can learn citizenship only by being an active citizen during his school life.'[126] Most important, in terms of active learning, 'a text-book, if any is used, will be valuable chiefly for reference in seeking more information after class discussion … the chief value of such action lies in the development of habits of right social thought and action.'[127]

'Social studies,' a notion widely adopted in the rhetoric and curricula of schools across Ontario in the 1930s, was closely linked to the social meliorist orientation toward progressive schooling.[128] Prior to the 1930s, explained an editorial in The School, the term had 'been used rather loosely to include history, civics, geography, and economics. Some effort has been made to correlate these subjects, but up to the present they have generally remained quite separate.'[129] Other models of classes typically referred to as fusion courses were essayed – to the dismay of meliorists, because these often consisted of fragments of different subjects without any focus on life's actual social circumstances.[130] The rise of social studies as a significant subject for discussion in the journals during the Depression is not surprising, particularly in light of references to the instability and insecurity that seemingly permeated the age.[131] Advocacy of social studies as a means to actively examine contemporary social problems would lead to the entrenchment of the subject in the Ontario curriculum in 1937.

In the lead-up to the revised *Programme of Studies*, *The School* reported on the *Report of the Commission on the Social Studies* in 1936. Here, at length, it cited Part XIII, 'Curriculum Making in the Social Studies,' which argued that 'the essential task in our schools ... is to aid youth to the fullest practicable understanding of our social order; to a meaningful realization of the ways in which the individual, both pupil and adult, may participate effectively in that order; and to motivate for effective participation.'[132]

Unity in social studies was seen as achievable through the thematic study of various social problems and injustices.[133] Social studies was viewed as a potential domain for studying social life and improving it actively and systematically. Social studies would make for the 'laboratory study of social living. In some substantial sense, this approach means a laboratory study of social living ... Every pupil provides his own singularly complete laboratories; and his laboratories are not artificial – they are real life.'[134] Social studies was represented as a dynamic approach to unifying independent subjects treated as mere 'collections of insignificant facts' and concentrating them on 'the scientific study of the development of the society in which we live.'[135] By engaging a class of students as a community in the study of actual social phenomena, a 'progressive teacher ... of the social sciences will soon develop a scientific method of instruction,' one that treated the students as a miniature scientific community.[136]

Meliorist texts argued for greater inclusivity, especially with respect to the economically disadvantaged. In part, their vision was inspired by adult education. As E.A. Corbett, a strong advocate for adult education and training, reported in 1938, the Canadian Association for Adult Education had been actively lobbying for opportunities for adults to pursue learning, particularly in rural areas.[137] The association stood for the following purposes: '(1) to serve as a clearing-house and maintain a working library; (2) to develop interest by means of publications, radio, and conferences; (3) to suggest methods and to improve the work in adult education.'[138] In part as a result of this sort of lobbying, educational opportunities were extended vigorously throughout the interwar years, even during the Depression, when infrastructure projects were often shelved.[139]

'Adult education is indeed closely bound up with democracy itself,' declared R.S. Lambert of the Canadian Association for Adult Education.[140] He argued that programs for adult learning were based 'on the very principles which make democracy flourish – the development of individual personality, the encouragement of the creative instinct, the rational approach to social and international problems, and a sound balance of duties and responsibilities in citizenship.'[141] Adult education was thus a 'powerful antidote to the evils of propaganda.'[142] Educational reforms needed to incorporate greater debate and discussion, which were vital to democratic citizenship.[143]

Correspondence classes, which provided courses to individuals who were unable to attend school because of geographical distance or physical disability, were represented as valuable extensions of Ontario's educational franchise.[144] Radio broadcasts, slide lectures, agricultural talks, and moving motion picture machines were also advocated by progressivists as worthy investments supporting the 'increasing effort [of schools] ... to reach the most remote parts' of the province that did not have equality of access to education.[145] In an ever-changing world, the development of critical skills and democratic principles in the adult population would further the cause of educational and social progress.

To summarize, themes for considering the various meanings of active learning for progressive educators in Ontario were explored from three different progressivist orientations. First, regarding child study, active learning represented developmentally appropriate tasks for students that stimulated healthy growth and further mental development. Second, regarding social efficiency, active learning involved training in particular skills and habits related to students' projected vocational paths. Thirdly, regarding in the case of social meliorism, active learning engaged students with actual problems in society and was intended to foster active citizenship in a democratic community. In the following chapter, the same three orientations will be used to shed light on the meaning of individualized study for Ontario's progressivists.

4 Progressive as Individualized Instruction: Critiques of Content-Driven Learning

Now the change which is coming into our education is the shifting of the center of gravity. It is a change, a revolution, not unlike that introduced by Copernicus when the astronomical center shifted from the earth to the sun. In this case the child becomes the sun about which the appliances of education revolve; he [sic] is the center about which they are organized.*

This chapter examines the meanings of individualized instruction, a second domain of progressive education explored in Ontario's educational journals. It does so, once again, from three orientations: child study, social efficiency, and social meliorism. Considered from the first orientation, the progressivist concern for educating the individual child was related to the holistic study of each learner's development and instruction and supported enabling individual personalities to unfold over time. From the second orientation, the individual child was seen as having a particular mental aptitude that could be diagnosed objectively and used to develop a channel of study leading to a suitable vocational niche for each student. From the third orientation, the individual was seen as one part of a democratic community, who could be helped to develop a critical intelligence and a concern for social justice.

Child Study and Developmental Psychology

The first progressivist nursery schools and child study centres in Ontario, like the first rehabilitation programs for traumatized First

---

* John Dewey, *The School and Society* (Chicago, IL: University of Chicago Press, 1907), 51.

World War veterans, had been developed as social welfare initiatives with the core ideal of health promotion.[1] In the same way that measurements of physical health, such as weight or blood pressure, were interpreted in terms of certain normal ranges, children's growth and development was viewed as moving through normal, diagnosable stages.[2] In historian Cynthia Commachio's assessment, 'child behaviour became a legitimate area of medical investigation just as child psychology was developing as a distinct field, and there was much inter-borrowing between medicine and psychology.'[3] The developing child unfolded naturally through stages that could be, at least in the abstract, studied and used to generate educational principles. The progressivist concern for child study, borrowing heavily from the medical field's promotion of health, had three overlapping concerns – therapeutics, prophylaxis, and promotion:

> *Therapeutics*, the curing of the sick, is an art.
>
> *Prophylaxis*, or the prevention of disease, is, however, an application of scientific discoveries to human welfare.
>
> *Promotion* of physical health is one of the latest interests in human welfare. To undertake a promotion program, a standard must be approved.[4]

A progressive education was thus seen as one that helped children's development progress through certain normal stages of growth, each with 'its characteristic problems, and the successful adjustment during one stage is the best guarantee of a corresponding success for the individual in the next.'[5] Stages of human development spanned all of human life. At the Institute of Child Study, the following rough demarcations were the basis of developmental assessments: 'The pre-school period, the school age, adolescence, marriage, parenthood, middle life, and old age.'[6] There were stages within these demarcations; for the school age, these roughly corresponded to school grades.

Without such standard measures of normal child development, there could be no useful criteria for measuring or understanding growth. As William Blatz and his colleague Helen MacMurchy Bott explained, '*norms* of development, ascertained for different cross-section levels ... are therefore a kind of shorthand for recording the differences observed at such levels.'[7] Historian Cynthia Commacchio has observed that the normalization of children was motivated mainly by the 'postwar desire to define and promote "normalcy"' and was 'infused with the spirit of industry, with its demands for regularity, repetition, scheduling, systematization, discipline, and productivity.'[8] However, within the progressivist child study orientation, it was often argued that developmental psychology needed to be differentiated from scientific management. Blatz, for instance, was adamant that child study not play second fiddle to the promotion of efficiency and industry: 'Today the nursery school must be looked upon neither as a charitable institution, nor as an expedient for increasing the number of mothers in industry, nor as a convenience for parents, but rather as a necessary adjunct to child care and training ... The nursery school is for neither the privileged nor the underprivileged, but for both. The nursery school is not a luxury, it is a necessity.'[9]

The foundation of the Institute of Child Study was, Blatz believed, an entrenchment of the progressivist concern for education concentrated on the individual child. It was organized in the spirit of John Dewey's laboratory school at the University of Chicago, and it prided itself on being the 'first organization to achieve a truly child-centered philosophy – a philosophy which considers the child's experiences first and cultural expectations second.'[10]

Individualized instruction necessitated holistic study and assessment of children's development and growth; understanding where the individual learner *was* necessitated a general and broad understanding of all children's normal development. On 18 and 19 November 1939, almost a year to the day after the New Education Fellowship drew crowds of educationists to Hamilton, Ontario, the U.S.-based Progressive Education Association (PEA) held its fourth Annual Conference of the International Border Region in Windsor, Ontario.[11] This was the first time the PEA had held a conference on Canadian soil. The event involved forty-five formal addresses and 1,800 registered delegates.[12] Ontario College of Education representative Frederick Minkler wrote a report of the conference for *The School* that spanned six pages and attempted to synthesize his understanding of what progressive education entailed.[13]

The character of progressive education conveyed in Minkler's article was thoroughly grounded in the terms of child study. It envisioned holistic development of individual children as the core element separating progressivist from traditional views of learning. Minkler put forward the following thesis: 'In traditional education, the predominant interest was in intellectual development, and the emphasis was on subject-matter. In the *new education*, the predominant interest is the complete development of the personality, and the emphasis is on the needs of the individual.'[14] The consideration of these needs and their entrenchment as the focus of schooling was seen as what separated progressivists from traditionalists.

A child's needs extended from the physiological to the mental and psychological. None could be neglected; the child needed to be considered holistically.[15] The traditional school was concerned only with mental development, and by positing the transmission of academic knowledge as the pinnacle of educational interest, it neglected the holistic development of children. 'When the child is viewed as a whole,' Minkler explained, 'everything which he [sic] does is of importance in his development.'[16] A child's holistic development could not be facilitated within the narrow parameters laid out by the traditional curriculum.

Child study progressivist depictions of holistic study integrated concerns about the healthy development of children's physical, social, emotional, and intellectual capacities.[17] The aim of progressive education was not to teach academic content; rather, according to Professor S.R. Laycock of the University of Saskatchewan's College of Education, it was 'to see their pupils *grow* ... to see them develop wholesome personalities.'[18] He further argued that progressive school programs necessarily abandoned unsatisfactory attempts 'to confine their efforts to the development of skills in "the three R's," or to cramming their children with facts.'[19] 'The philosophy of modern progressive education,' he continued, 'is to develop persons who are high-grade physically, socially, emotionally, and intellectually.'[20] Child study could not be truly progressivist if its definitions of schooling did not include physical, social, emotional, and intellectual terms. The child was a whole person; he or she would with proper guidance develop into a healthy, well-adjusted, and qualitatively different kind of person – an adult.

The concern for holistic child study was inevitably rooted in the medical and psychological science of the new discipline. Again, it was Laycock who expressed this most cogently, arguing that progressivist educators were those who understood that 'the *whole child comes to school*' and, with that knowledge, were compelled to diagnose healthy development – emotional, physical, intellectual, and psychological.[21] Each of these, within a particular stage of development, operated within a normal range; consequently, baseline measures of what constituted a 'normal child' were useful guidelines for teachers to follow.[22] From this perspective, the task of progressive education was to cultivate different dimensions of the child, whose abilities and knowledge had a great deal of plasticity and resiliency, within normal levels of growth.[23]

The holistic assessment and diagnosis of a learner's development included, then, more than a measure of academic memory garnered from a traditional examination. It also included more than a standardized measure of IQs or aptitudes.[24] Measures *did* matter to child study progressivists; each provided information regarding one aspect of the whole child's development.[25] But *how* IQ data were used to promote further development was of greater interest than whether such tests were administered.[26] Multiple data sources needed to be combined for a balanced view of the child's educational development.[27] A truly progressive education, Blatz explained, 'looks beyond the entrance, beyond the B.A., and, believe it or not, beyond the I.Q.'[28] An education that was overly concerned with intelligence was ultimately too narrow in focus. Blatz concluded his argument with the following thought: 'To sum up: it is possible, through training, to develop in every child, irrespective of I.Q. and inheritance, a social pattern which is recognized as ambitious, persistent, honest, interested, courageous, and humorous. What more can we ask of any educational programme?'[29] Human development and education, from a developmentalist progressivist perspective, ultimately concerned students' holistic progress, not merely their cognitive abilities.

For child study progressivists, freedom, happiness, and psychological well-being were the principal aims of individualized education. They believed that for progressive education to truly concern itself with the holistic development of individuals, it needed to make provision for the learner to pursue personal interests freely.[30] Interest was seen as instinctive, self-direction as the force that could drive children to learn about new and interesting things. In terms of energy, the traditional curriculum was incredibly wasteful in that it applied undue pressure on children to learn academic content that was of little interest to them. With some sarcasm, Blatz commented on how useless it was to force unwilling pupils to submit to external interests:

> Many teachers seem to think that education is based on the laws of thermodynamics. Energy is indestructible. The more energy, the more force. One may envisage the interaction between teacher and pupil as illustrated in the physics text-book by the hydraulic force pump. I will never forget the fascination of that picture. Pressure is exerted in the slender cylinder on the left, and bang! – up goes the elevator on the right. I could never dis-

associate the piston on the left from the teacher in front of the class – and still can't. Now, education is nothing of this sort at all.[31]

Blatz, here, was expressing a concern often voiced by child study progressivists at the time – namely, that the forceful inculcation of knowledge deemed either useful or necessary is problematic. It is not only an image of violence, but also one of oppression.

Child study progressivist texts, then, often referred to the educator's role as entailing guiding and leading, as opposed to teaching. As Frederick Minkler noted, progressivists were different from their traditionalist counterparts in that they were responsive to the innate differences, personalities, and interests of students: 'The traditional school attempts to fit the child into a predetermined mould, to train him to fit into the social order to which he now belongs. The progressive school attempts to guide, with little or no dictation, the development of the child as an individual.'[32] Here, Minkler was expressing a nuanced understanding of how child study progressivists balanced individualism and compulsion.

The 1937 revised *Programme of Studies* indicated clearly how this balance might be maintained.[33] According to Duncan McArthur, who played a formidable role in formulating and explicating the program, the reformed course of study aimed to create 'a central core of subjects to be open to all pupils. These might include English, geography, history and civics, one science, mathematics and a second language.'[34] Students, now free to choose subjects they found interesting and important, would probably extend the very scope of education: 'beyond this group of subjects, options might be offered in a wider range of subjects than is at present available.'[35]

Assessments of Ontario's curriculum reforms published in the journals praised the progressivists' concern for individual freedom and interest. D.S. Woods, Dean of the Faculty of Education at the University of Manitoba, praised the 'new school outlook, conditioned by individual needs rather than by university requirements.'[36] Woods made a positive assessment of curriculum reforms in Ontario, Alberta, B.C., and Manitoba; in his view, a progressivist outlook influenced by an 'increasing knowledge of child growth … is emerging and gradually winning sanction from public opinion and school teacher alike.'[37] The pedagogical ideal was to balance common subjects with individual electives.[38]

Freedom to pursue studies of personal relevance was seen as an important element in motivating students and as a vital ingredient of their ultimate happiness. Professor W.C. Keirstead from the University of New Brunswick expressed this progressivist theme plainly in May 1940. Amid calls for democratic education that could counter the oppressive tendencies of fascist and Nazi youth training, Keirstead argued that the pith of any modern and progressive educational system needed to be concern for the individual learner: 'The person is the centre of all intelligence, of initiative, of discovery, of creative thinking, and therefore the pivot of social progress. The home of all experiences of value, of all happiness, or misery, is the soul of the individual.'[39] Freedom to pursue studies and subjects of interest was not only pedagogically sound practice for child study progressivists, but also essential for health and happiness.

Social adjustment, rather than social conformity, was vital for each individual child. The promotion of a healthy balance between ideas such as freedom and responsibility extended to the perceived relationship that progressive education could promote between the individual and society. Each individual's primary purpose was to lead his or her life responsibly, but no one lived outside society. Keirstead depicted children as the centre of educational activity but still felt that they were required from birth to adjust to their social environment.[40] Within any space or institution, an individual's freedom was subject to particular norms and expectations. A progressivist school concerned with child study should not ask for obedience and conformity. Individual freedoms must be adjusted to and restrained by the realities of social life.[41]

This philosophy was by no means uncontroversial; in 1941, an editorial in *The School* reported on a visit to the Institute of Child Study intended to ascertain how true reports were that its progressivist philosophy was leading to unfettered self-direction: 'For years the city teacup telegraph had been causing eyebrows to rise at the scandalous goings-on among the younger set at 98 St. George Street. The impression was abroad that those four-year-olds were really making the bric-a-brac fly in an orgy of self-activity. No one could safely enter those premises, we thought, unless doubly protected in the armour of the spirit and a suit of medieval form.'[42] Fear of unfettered freedom was always the counterpoint to the terror of oppressive discipline and punishment; balancing the two remained a consistent aim of child study progressivists.

Teacher Fern Holland believed that it was the responsibility of progressivist educationists to facilitate the development of individuals within a social framework. A classroom, like society, imposed pressures and structures that required adjustment and accommodation on the part of students. It was the traditional schools, however, that promoted conformity, not the progressivist ones. Classrooms of the past had imposed 'the kind of education that consists in memorizing facts and dates and theories and delighting the teacher by showing that one has done the memorizing.'[43] Child study, by contrast, led educationists to conclude that individual students needed to develop and retain a distinct sense of self. In Holland's terms, children had to preserve their own 'personalities and identities in spite of all the organized machinery of education could do to them, in an effort to make them conform to a general pattern.'[44]

Social Efficiency and Adjustment to Industry

The rhetoric of social efficiency typically linked references to individual learners with the themes of industry or experimental psychology.[45] Children's individual abilities were depicted as measurable, definable, and classifiable. Individualized instruction involved providing each learner with a program of study that facilitated his or her progress toward a vocational and social niche with the greatest possible efficiency. A diversified system of schooling that included vocational training and specific classes for 'exceptional children' was depicted as both progressive and democratic.[46] Marion Goode Hodgins expressed the efficiency of progressivist aims succinctly: 'The ultimate end of education is the production of efficient citizens.'[47] Schools, like industry, were in the business of production and were compelled to pursue the most efficient means possible.

From the social efficiency perspective, it was essential to classify children according to their individual abilities and inclinations. Hodgins, a teacher at the Central High School of Commerce in Hamilton, believed that the most pressing objective for progressive education was training students for a future vocation.[48] Similarly, Donald Peat of Toronto's Church Street School for Boys explained that classifying children according to their abilities and intelligence was commensurate with providing them 'the right to an opportunity to develop their talents, no less than other children, to the greatest extent commensurate with the good society.'[49] A general education failed to provide exceptional learners with an opportunity to flourish; it also denied them equality of opportunity.[50] Conversely, a progressive education able to formulate a way of classifying children according to their abilities would liberate those children from an oppressive, general, and academic system of schooling.

Special programs designed for special children would provide exceptional children with particular instruction. They would focus attention where required. Such a progressive system would give Ontario's children the support they deserved; it would also help classes operate more efficiently in a democratic society. Identifying individual intelligence would thus make the entire system of schooling in Ontario more efficient and, indeed, more democratic.[51] If Ontario students were classified according to their abilities, all the students would better value their time in school. As Peat explained it, the value of classification and specialization of study in schools lay in its increased efficiency: 'Average classes will cease to be clogged with ill-adjusted troublemakers; children of average and higher intelligence will get fuller value for the time they spend in school; courts and reformatories will save expenses now incurred through preventable delinquency; and the lower I.Q. boys and girls will have the chance to claim their birthright of useful, happy citizenship.'[52]

Peat's arguments are saturated with the language of efficient management and administration. The focus on IQ as a means of understanding the individual would cure society's ills and usher in democratic opportunity for all.[53]

According to S.R. Laycock, Professor of Educational Psychology at the University of Saskatchewan, Canadians were entitled to equal educational opportunity, which meant that 'every child, dull, average, and bright, shall have the chance to develop in accordance with his own particular abilities and needs.'[54] But Laycock here was concerned mainly with a particular category of exceptional students – Ontario's highly gifted students, whom he estimated to be 5 per cent of the student body. He expressed concern that, because they were not receiving learning commensurate to their abilities, they were being denied their right to a fitting education: 'If the teacher is incompetent, these children may suffer somewhat more than the average child. If she [sic] is an alert and progressive teacher, they do not suffer unduly in their development.'[55] Only a system that identified and classified students on the basis of intelligence could fully realize learners' cognitive potential, with the support of teachers who provided classes with challenges appropriate to their abilities.[56]

A progressive education that directly addressed individual learners' cognitive abilities was often described in business terms, as entailing a 'return on investment.' C.W. Greer of Earlscourt Public School in Toronto offered Ontario's educationists the following anecdote:

> He said: 'Fertilize that hillside field? Heck, I've wasted enough good manure and seed on it to cover the country. Every rain there's a run-off that washes everything away except the fences. A man can't do a thing with that field. It ain't fit to plant pig-weed in, let alone wheat!' Then he added, thoughtfully: 'Son, put your effort where it'll net you some profit. Every hour spent on this field is money in my pocket. But the other one – last time I worked it, I seeded it four times, and never got a crop.'[57]

Greer's anecdote depicted a situation in which the capabilities of learners, like the fecundity of fields, had long been established. The farmer knew what would pay dividends and what would not. Educational attainments were intimately related to intelligence, which was a fixed entity.[58]

Progressive educationists with an efficiency orientation knew what traditional educationists did not: schools could find ways to maximize the returns on society's investment in education. Trying to take children identified as slow, or defective, and bring them to the intellectual ability of others who were deemed normal, or intelligent, was a waste of time and energy.[59] Instead, schools should administer intelligence tests and grade children according to their abilities rather than their school ages; efficient and progressive schools would be organized according to intelligence and ability rather than other concerns.[60]

The benefits of this sort of progressivist practice would trickle down to all levels of society. Each individual would benefit greatly from an education that maximized his or her potential learning. Thus, a gifted pupil would develop into a future leader of society or industry,[61] while a 'below-average' child would have many positive experiences in school that would contribute to the development of a healthy attitude as well as useful skills.[62] Returning to Greer's analogy between farming and educating, a progressivist system would maximize society's return on its investment: 'The farmer knew by experience what would, and what would not, pay dividends. Should formal education fail to recognize what is obvious to practical economists?'[63]

Maximizing educational returns was closely linked to eliminating educational waste.[64] These considerations, especially in articles in *The Canadian School Journal*, were depicted as consistent with the ideals of a democratic and Christian state. The diagnosis and treatment of 'sub-normal' children was represented as a noble service.[65] It was incongruous with democratic and Christian principles to eliminate children of low intelligence from society; it was perfectly acceptable to give such children fitter and happier lives.[66] 'Unless we adopt the Nazi plan of doing away with below-average individuals,' explained Laycock, 'we have no alternative but to guide them to the fullest life which they are capable of living and into channels of work and play where they can best serve their fellows.'[67] For each individual there were ideal channels based on ability. It followed that one of the principal aims of progressivists was to eliminate wasteful and inefficient courses of study. Diagnostic information about each learner would facilitate this efficient channelling;[68] the same information could guide remedial school programs, which were seen as a means to correct each individual's life course.[69]

David Russell of UBC's Department of Education told Ontario's educators that education required a reorientation in priorities: 'Teachers and administrators are content to have classes conducted in the same old way, thinking nothing of the human waste involved. With a few exceptions, Canadian schools generally have been slow to adopt the diagnostic and remedial point of view, which has done much for retarded children in other systems.'[70]

The diagnostic perspective, then, emphasized gathering information about students for needs assessments as well as tailoring instruction for efficient progress in society. This approach was predicated on the collection of reliable and objective data on individuals.[71] It was particularly relevant for individuals who would be assuming vocational careers and who thus required training in particular sets of skills or habits before entering the workforce. So explained W.H.H. Green, the principal of the Vocational School in Fort William, Ontario. Green was certain that 'intelligence tests, mechanical aptitude tests, art ability tests, stenographic ability tests, the school nurse reports, and personal interviews, play an important part in helping pupils to find their right places.'[72] A special type of education was needed for each student, and selecting the appropriate path meant eliminating the ones that would distract the student and that would not reflect his or her intelligence and ability.[73]

Standardizing assessments and collecting data on individual learners is a very contemporary concern in education, mainly in the United States. In the journals, these were depicted as educational means to the progressivist end of social efficiency. From the efficiency perspective, then, collecting diagnostic information on individual students' aptitudes and interests was the lynchpin of an efficient and progressive schooling system, because of the information it would provide to administrators, parents, and guidance counsellors. Every teacher needed to be familiar with the potential of each student and with his or her interests and potential vocational opportunities.[74] Marion E. Goode, who emerged in 1940 as a consistent advocate of vocational guidance and testing in Ontario's journals, believed that it was the responsibility of every teacher to lead students toward their vocational goals. To maximize efficiency and comprehensiveness, teachers' instructional decisions would be based on data gathered from seven sources: personnel records, research, tests, interviews, try-out experiences with work, more lengthy placements, and follow-up interviews.[75] Also, general intelligence tests were to be administered several times in each pupil's school career so that any necessary adjustments to the program and curriculum could be made.

John A. Long of the Ontario College of Education advocated objective examinations that could facilitate a teacher's involvement with an individual learner's progress along vocational channels. The strength of 'objective' testing was that it could quantify students' mental abilities reliably and consistently.[76] The assumption was that a person's intelligence operated within certain parameters. All students could be trained to learn more about particular subjects, but their ability to think about matters intelligently was fixed and relatively rigid.[77] Traditional examinations were both unreliable and too closely linked to particular content. Intelligence tests, by contrast, eliminated unreliability as well as the subjectivity of an individual teacher's grading system and thus produced information regarding native ability that was independent of subject matter.[78] In short, they promoted efficiency among both students and administrators.[79]

It was all fine and well to attempt to organize the system of schooling to promote equality of opportunity, explained some progressivist articles, but the maintenance of an efficient social order also required that particular skills and habits be produced.[80] The explicit teaching of proper conduct, including character traits that would not disrupt society, was necessary if individuals were to adjust efficiently to an established social, industrial, and economic order.[81] Individuals who could not find appropriate work and who were potentially disruptive of the status quo were described as deviants and future criminals. Efficient schools could also, then, prevent crime and disorder by sufficiently preparing students to adjust to their places in the world.[82] This involved, above all, training future citizens 'in habits of work in such a way that they will be self-supporting in later life, and to develop in them such desirable social qualities as honesty, self-control, reliability, truthfulness, and the ability to live and work contentedly.'[83]

That character education should have as its aims conformity and the inculcation of specific habits or attitudes desired of citizens in life was an idea consistent with the efficiency orientation in progressivist articles.[84] A progressive school board was envisaged as one that considered the psychological aptitude of individual students and that made provision for special attention that could enable future social adjustment.[85] In language startlingly inconsistent with the typically democratic or scientific rhetoric of efficiency progressivists, educator C.L. Burton argued that if schools were to prepare students for lives in business and industry, they needed to be organized like corporations.[86]

For the good of all students, Burton argued, those who could not be placed efficiently in a modern and progressive workplace should not be in school along with their peers: 'Mental defectives should be separated … Not only should the mentally unfit be weeded out, but the mentally alert and those showing special promise along various lines should be encouraged to proceed further than the average along the lines of special abilities.'[87] Each child had a vocational niche in life, and schools should prepare him or her to fill that niche.[88] Harold Hill of Harbord Collegiate Institute in Toronto interpreted the intellectual abilities of students in equally undemocratic terms. He discerned among students social classes that need not mingle.[89] While the gifted and the delayed received much attention, Hill explained, the middle class of children of average intelligence made up the majority of school populations and of society.[90]

In spite of these seemingly elitist conceptions, it was also a common complaint that there was too much emphasis on identifying and placing exceptional children at the expense of the 'gifted' learners: 'So often the so-called "brilliant" students have turned out in later life to be utter failures or to achieve only mediocre success, while the steady plodders with only average ability have scaled the heights to fame and fortune.'[91] The public school system, from this perspective 'has left the gifted children in the regular grades, with a great deal of spare time on their hands, and with very little outlet for their abundant energies and creative abilities.'[92]

This trend was very commonly described in terms of socio-economic classes. Fully integrated classrooms were the educational equivalent of forcing the rich to stay with the poor and middle classes, rather than maximizing their economic advantage. As a result, such special students ended up squandering their potential and living average or mediocre lives. In a progressive environment, where their assets could be put to full and efficient use, vaster fortunes could be made; the benefits of this would then trickle down to all others in society. Modelled on the principles of social efficiency, a progressive educational system in Ontario would provide a specialized channel of study for students commensurate with their abilities and their interests. This would enable them, later in life, to assume responsible places in the social order.[93]

Social Meliorism and Engagement with Social Ills

The New Education Fellowship (NEF), an international organization established in Europe to explore and promote progressivist educational ideas, held its annual conference at the King Edward Hotel in Toronto on 23 and 24 April 1937. Professor Harold Rugg, a noted American progressivist from Columbia University's Teachers College, who represented the PEA at NEF gatherings, spoke to Ontario's educators about the themes and meanings of progressive education.[94] The new education, he argued, 'demands that pupils should be given a chance to learn self-government in social co-operation, and that pupils should be introduced to a knowledge of our [sic] changing culture.'[95] Dr Boyd H. Bode of Ohio State University spoke about the relationship of education to the social order. *The School* summarized Bode's thesis as follows:

> He believes, as others do, that education should be adapted to our changing social order, that our pupils should learn to co-operate in school as they must co-operate later in adult life; but he urges that they must be brought to a just evaluation of our present social order and to a sane judgement of what changes should be made, not by indoctrination but by training in reading, in observation, in discussion, and in thinking for themselves.[96]

According to *The School*, the conference's entire proceedings were notably charged, not only because of the presence of internationally renowned educationists, but also because Ontario was in the midst of a progressivist revolution in its own curriculum.[97] The editorial was notable because it isolated the term *progressive education* by placing it within quotation marks and argued that Ontario's educationists had participated in the conference out of a keen 'desire to learn what the "new education" really is.'[98]

The meanings of progressive education were not fixed, and their implications for the province's educationists were still being explored. The general theme of the conference was 'Tradition and Freedom in Education.' Delegates discussed how progressive education interacted with individual freedom and how it broke from traditional models of schooling.[99] Rugg presented two speeches; in both, he emphasized meliorist progressive concerns: for correlating school studies with social settings, for fostering social cooperation, and for paying heed to the changing nature of culture.[100] From this orientation to the progressivist concern for individual education, Ontario's schools were being asked to develop training in observation, discussion, and critical thinking free from any indoctrination.[101] Chapter 6 of this book will discuss how by 1940, with the advent of the Second World War, meliorist calls had grown loud for a new education that would promote democracy by engaging students in free discussion, cooperative organization, and democratic debate.[102]

For social meliorists, individualized education had a social and cooperative aim: the individual student had to learn to be responsible for the welfare of his or her peers. 'Individualism,' Dalhousie University Professor B.A. Fletcher told Ontario's teachers, 'is the quality that more than any other sharply distinguishes the democratic from the totalitarian idea ... It is the concept that is finding expression in all the recent efforts to provide equality of opportunity.'[103] But, he continued, 'individualism does not imply licence. The growing child needs to be surrounded by a ring of prohibition, both to save society from his [sic] disturbing egoism, and also to foster the shapely growth of his later personality.'[104] A progressive school should not think of the individual student either as some functional element within an imposed social structure or as an unfeeling egotist. The former view would lead to suppression of individuality and self-right, the latter to narrow and selfish ends.

The only way for a democratic society to proceed, particularly in times of toil and trouble, was on the basis of individual self-sacrifice for communal welfare and service.[105] Almost immediately on assuming the position of Deputy Minister of Education for Ontario, Duncan McArthur started using *The School* as his pulpit to announce a bold vision of sustainable democratic citizenship.[106] He declared that education in Ontario needed to break with the spirit of competition and the ethos of individualism in order to cultivate cooperation, community, and interdependence.[107] For him, among the foremost principles of progressive school reform was the relating of individual interests to the concerns of society so that students would learn to show concern for the entire community in which they lived.[108] His rhetoric was vivid and eminently quotable:

> The old wine of unrestrained individualism, of laissez faire, the 'God's in His Heaven, all's well with the world' complacency of the Victorians will not be contained within the new bottles of respect for human rights of a planned economy, and of subordination of individual freedom to the well-being of the community. If the school of to-day is to discharge adequately its responsibilities, it must recognize that the old order has changed and prepare the new generation to adjust itself harmoniously in an independent and integrated society.[109]

In this meliorist vision, the good of one learner was inextricably bound to the good of the whole community.[110] By contrast, the traditional school's concern for teaching and testing academic content fostered a spirit of competition.[111] Similarly, the more efficiency-minded trend of streaming children into classes destroyed any possible sense of community and mutual support by aggravating the differences among individuals.[112] Meliorist progressives also condemned examinations and report cards that placed greater emphasis on where Ontario's children stood in relation to one another than on their attitudes to work and on their abilities to work cooperatively.[113]

The individual learner had to learn to be adaptable, for the modern world was being overwhelmed with change. In 1937, Joseph McCulley of Pickering College published a bold article in *The Canadian School Journal* in which he urged progressive schools to teach individual children ways of coping with change by helping them develop the skills to think critically and independently.[114] The world was ripe with change, he argued, and as a consequence, the future could never be predicted and laid down in blueprints. To usher in a new social order students would need to be able to question the world around them and reshape it accordingly.[115] After reminding his audience that self-discipline and cooperation were the foundations of democratic living, he continued:

> Children must be freed from any authoritative concepts or any blind wor-

ship of tradition or the status quo. In their school days they must have some opportunity to learn how to choose, – to choose between opposed alternatives that path which will ultimately be good for the maximum good of all. Biological structures and civilizations themselves which have shown an inability to adapt to new conditions have perished; the school of tomorrow must, above all things, turn out citizens who are capable of facing their very different problems intelligently, courageously and with sympathy for all living beings.[116]

McCulley was expressing here a sentiment repeated time and again in articles by meliorist progressives interested in promoting, through the schools, habits of mind in students that would enable them to think critically about social problems.[117]

Modernity appeared to mark all phases of life with what John Long of the Ontario College of Education referred to as 'a climate of mystifying change.'[118] An education that would be in any way useful or relevant in a modern world was one that prepared minds to respond to conditions that were rapidly becoming increasingly complex.[119] Critical thought and adaptability of ideas were antidotes to narrow, specialized, skills-based education, which would only promote conformity and subjugation to the dominant industrial and social orders.[120] In a 'progressive, industrial world, nothing is taken for granted,' stated a 1933 editorial article in *The Canadian School Journal*, which defended the individual's right to think critically and to doubt.[121] From this perspective, initiative and self-reliance – particularly in the tumultuous context of the Depression – depended on critical doubt: 'the student who approaches life's problems with a mind unfitted to think things out is greatly handicapped.'[122]

The Depression was often referred to as proof that Ontarians needed to adapt and to expect change, that no space of employment was safe, and that any job or trade might be deemed expendable.[123] For progressive schools to prepare individual students for all this dramatic change and instability, they would have to concentrate on developing individuals who were adaptable to modern life. The idea that school should train students based on their abilities to perform particular tasks was, from the meliorist perspective, unreasonable.[124] The most practical knowledge that any individual student could gain in a progressive school was the ability to live adaptively and critically in social contexts that were constantly evolving.[125]

That was the message repeatedly propagated by meliorist progressives, and as the Depression dismantled many educationists' faith in a predictable world for which one might prepare students to live, even the Premier of Ontario, George S. Henry, admitted that all children should know the truth of their situation: 'We live in a world of change ... nothing is perfect. What satisfies us to-day will not satisfy us to-morrow.'[126] In other words, the course of studies in progressive schools needed to prepare students for a world of change. Again, this was related to the belief than every individual's learning and education extended beyond the parameters of schools.[127]

The home, the church, and agencies such as the Girl Guides and Boy Scouts, the Junior Red Cross, and the YMCA and YWCA, as well as adult education initiatives, all contributed to the progressivist vision of social justice and welfare outside the schoolhouse. Participation in social extracurricular agencies was a way for students to learn that their responsibilities to community were to be taken seriously.[128] A 1933 editorial in *The School* praised community organizations for their communitarian concern for the development and welfare of all Ontarians, whatever their ability, intelligence, and socio-economic status.[129] Cooperation among schools, families, and community groups could help develop a progressive vision for a socially just and regenerated world.

Extracts from two notable addresses, 'Some Problems of Government' and 'The Endless War,' by Nicholas Murray Butler, President of Columbia University, commemorating the 183rd year of his school, were reprinted for Ontario's educationists in October 1936.[130] Butler argued that, if it was to be useful and robust, education needed to foster cooperation and build a greater sense of community.[131] A self-reliant critical intelligence was necessary to a healthy democracy if individuals were to promote social justice and respect for democratic institutions.[132] In 1933, before the black cloud of the Depression lifted, it was particularly important for meliorist progressives to advocate justice and democracy as the bedrock of hope for all students.[133] No one who as a child had developed a critical orientation to life would submit to demands that he or she become a cog in some industrial machinery. In the words of Henry Conn, an Ontario teacher, 'we cannot make the pupil fit the school. But it should be quite possible to make the school fit the pupil.'[134] In a progressive society, the child need not fit into an extant order; that order was changing and could be reformed in accordance with its citizens' will.

Watson Kirkconnell wrote that progressive education should never 'think of the state as a machine in which the citizen is a mere cog.'[135]

Likewise, Joseph McCulley described education that did not address actual social problems and cultivate critical intelligence as displaying an ostrich-like avoidance of necessary controversy.[136] The world might very well be changing, explained a 1935 editorial in *The School*, but humanity had shown a remarkable ability to adapt to change.[137] Progressive schools could challenge students to think critically about their world and prepare them for that change; schools need not suppress conflict and instability, thereby putting socially minded criticality at risk.[138] In the words of John Cook, an Ontario teacher, 'the developing in the pupil of the spirit of co-operation is one of the teacher's most vital responsibilities.'[139]

In this chapter, themes for thinking about the meanings of individualized instruction expressed by progressive educators in *The School* and *The Canadian School Journal* have been explored from three progressivist orientations. First, from the child study orientation, individualized instruction entailed the holistic study of each learner's normal development; concern for individuals' freedom, happiness, and well-being; and future citizens' adjustment to social contexts. Second, from the social efficiency orientation, individualized instruction entailed maximizing the returns on educational investments, eliminating educational waste, standardizing assessment and data collection of mental aptitude, and maintaining social order. Third, from the social meliorist orientation, individualized instruction entailed teaching individuals responsibility for their peers, preparing children to be adaptable in contexts of social change, and developing habits of mind related to critical intelligence and social cooperation. In the following chapter, the same three orientations toward progressive education will be used to shed light on the final domain of analysis, the progressivist concern for closer bonds between schools and society.

5 Progressive as Contemporary: Critiques of Learning Correlating Schools and Society

Relate the school to life, and all studies are of necessity correlated.*

This chapter examines how the concern for relating schools more close-ly to society was depicted from the perspective of the three orienta-tions framing the progressive rhetoric: child study, social efficiency, and social meliorism. Considered from the first orientation, the pro-gressivist concern that schools and society be interrelated focused on child health, human security, and parent involvement through home and school associations. From the second orientation, social efficiency, schools could relate better to social realities by providing students with the appropriate skills, knowledge, and guidance for their adjustment to vocational life. From the third orientation, meliorism, progressive schools could be model democratic communities that fostered critical thinking, promoted civic responsibility, and helped society become more equitable and just.

Child Study and Developmental Psychology

The Institute of Child Study came to symbolize the linking of schools to society and of studies within schools.[1] The trend in education was toward specialization of training; in counter to that trend, child study progressivists believed that specialization led to the isolation of subjects from one another and from actual life.[2] They emphasized the develop-

---

* John Dewey, *The School and Society* (Chicago, IL: University of Chicago Press, 1907), 107.

ment of projects and enterprises that related various subjects of study to one another.[3]

Two other themes – health, and home and school groups – are also rooted in the progressivist educational practices of the Institute of Child Study and its founding director, William Blatz.[4] Improving the physical and mental health of children was seen as vital for the province. Parent education and parental involvement in school activities were another means of strengthening synchronicity between students' domestic and educational spheres.

With regard to school and society, health and human security were core themes in child study progressivist rhetoric. The source journals contained many frank discussions about how health matters provided the strongest justification for relating schools to society. Indeed, entire issues of *The Canadian School Journal* had health as their central theme.[5] Each individual child's physical health was a concern. Besides that, however, a healthy society was founded on habits learned both at home and in school.[6] The first duty of all parents, then, was to protect and develop their children's health; schools, as places where all children were brought together, needed to care for the health of all students in order to promote their happiness and enjoyment of life.[7]

In Ontario's revised 1937 curriculum, health was made a separate 'division' of study. This was seen as a formal recognition of health's importance as just described. The province's Chief Inspector of Public and Separate Schools, V.K. Greer, informed teachers that 'the division of health is given first place in the new course. Nevertheless it is not intended that health teaching shall appear too prominently on the teacher's time table.'[8] Health, he informed teachers, was a subject that related to the entirety of children's lives and to all the school subjects. Consequently, it should not be scheduled as a subject separate from others in daily study.[9]

Throughout the interwar years, medical inspections grew increasingly common in Ontario's school system. These inspections came to signify that health promotion was a responsibility to be shared by home and school.[10] Dr John T. Phair, Chief Medical Officer of Health for Ontario, explicitly addressed the overlapping concerns between the provincial Departments of Education and Health.[11] He noted that despite decades of increased cooperation between schools and social medical agencies, many people still regarded health as the sole responsibility of parents.[12] School health service in Ontario actually began in 1909 with an amendment to the School Act of 1907, reported Edna

Moore in *The School*. That act had permitted medical and dental inspection in schools.[13] But it was not until 1924 that services were amalgamated and extended across the province.[14]

This concern for health, both physical and psychological, prompted discussion in the journals about reforming and modernizing Ontario's spaces of schooling. The beautification of school grounds was seen by some as an important element of school progress. The periodicals reported scholarships and awards presented to beautified schools.[15] In 1940 the Department of Education sponsored a survey of school grounds in the province. Various horticultural societies in the province became interested in working with Ontario's students to build sustainable planting programs in and out of school.[16] The province had come to believe that the state shared with parents a responsibility for health promotion.[17] Ideally, the two ought to cooperate closely on the matter. School gardening clubs, extracurricular groups that worked on beautification projects on school grounds and in the community, were presented as examples of this cooperation.[18]

Upgrades to school buildings – for example, the modernization of heating systems and improvements to lighting – typically were discussed in terms of their central importance to children's health.[19] Such upgrades were portrayed as closely linked to progress in school.[20] According to O.T. Walker, Chairman of the Property Committee in Brampton's Public School Board, improved school buildings made for better and happier educational experiences.[21] Walker's particular concern was the provision of adequate lighting, which would amount to 'a decidedly forward step' for Ontario's schools.[22] Improvements to the school plants would improve the entire life of the school. 'Better light gives brighter, more cheerful surroundings,' he explained, 'These are naturally reflected in brighter, happier children. The advantage to those children who are actually backward or slow because of inability to see well, will be inestimable. Better lighting certainly makes for more thorough assimilation of knowledge, better education, and more school co-operation.'[23] These benefits would then extend beyond the child's school life into all social life.

Suitable playgrounds and safe spaces for exercise on school property were portrayed as necessary for the development of children's bodies and minds; they would also serve the entire community.[24] Growth and development were important factors to consider in education, declared an editorial in *The Canadian School Journal*, and schools had to facilitate 'not only growth of mind, but of body and soul.'[25] Jessie Beattie, former

Director of Recreation with the Community Welfare Council, saw the development of sanitary, well-heated, and attractive school buildings as indicative of all that was best in 'new education.'[26] In very similar terms, he argued that beautified school grounds reinforced the progressivist idea that schools should be concerned with more than the training of healthy minds. Places to play developed healthy bodies, but the aesthetic and spiritual dimensions of life also needed cultivation: 'Our world is not only a world of the material but of the spiritual, using the term in its broader sense. It was planned to satisfy more than the hunger of the body. To know this, we have only to look at the colour of the sunset on a spring night, to smell the fragrance of a rose.'[27] Better school buildings enabled happier learning experiences, and these would remain more memorable throughout life.

Proper nutrition, medical care, dental maintenance, and education were important to all Ontarians, but particularly to school-aged children, who needed to be treated holistically in the home and at school.[28] Social progress and prosperity were inseparable from physical health and healthy habits.[29] School records could go beyond the purely academic to log a child's physical development, health particulars, weight, and measurements; this would require doctors, nurses, and parents to work closely together.[30] The progressive school, explained a 1937 editorial in *The Canadian School Journal*, was one that joined with the home and the church to promote the healthy and harmonious development of physical and intellectual abilities.[31]

The individual child's mental health was seen as persisting though life, necessarily implicating all social institutions. Corbin Brown, Inspector of Public Schools in St Catharines, expressed this recurring sentiment most cogently: 'One of the most important features of present practice in our elementary schools is the increased interest shown by teachers in the mental health of their pupils. If each child is to achieve the maximum of happiness and usefulness in his [sic] life, he should have, not only good physical health, but in addition, a wholesome mental outlook.'[32]

The need for increased cooperation between home and school, Brown went on to say, had been emphasized by many speakers and writers and was implicated in the growth of home and school associations.[33] The most important reason for this cooperation, he added, was the promotion of children's affective security in the world.[34]

The concept of security, as it related to a child's ability to face the world with self-reliance and confidence, was one of William Blatz's favourite topics.[35] If home and school were correlated effectively, both helping produce healthy habits, the student's world would be more secure. The child would then become independently secure; that is, he or she would be able to take responsibility for his or her own behaviour and actions.[36] This in turn, Blatz argued, would liberate the child from depending on parent and teacher for guidance.[37] A fit life, in affective terms, required a secure outlook, which was predicated on self-direction as well as on healthy habits of mind and action.[38]

Medical doctor Charles Alexander, assessing the role of health in schooling, came to a similar conclusion. Educational and medical institutions needed to work together to help children develop the skills necessary for a healthy, happy life: 'Education should be a training in not only how to make a living but a training in how to live.'[39] R.H. Roberts, an educator, echoed Alexander when he described the school as a community in which the child dwells. Relating this community to real life entailed more than knowledge. It included healthy habits with respect to relaxation, food, and cleanliness.[40] He argued strongly for 'the importance of integrating the entire life of the school child in a programme of physical, mental, emotional, and moral health.'[41]

The health of students in Ontario's schools was a dominant theme in child study progressivist articles; children's health in the home was a corollary concern. From the beginning, parent education in the province focused sharply on the promotion of healthy homes.[42] Throughout the interwar years, educationists urged that schools offer lectures to parents about the value of good health and how proper exercise and a balanced diet would increase weight and growth.[43] A 1936 editorial in *The Canadian School Journal* maintained that with regard to health, parent education was as important as children's education:

> Lectures could be sponsored and paid for by the school board for the benefit of the whole community. A public health nurse or a speaker from one of the many health organizations ... could be secured giving the parents useful information on the care and supervision of the child. Parent education is as essential as the education of the child. The parents prepare the child's lunch, clothe the child, and should understand the necessity of proper care and the results of neglect of some of the minor defects which in time may prove to be incurable.[44]

Such lectures were coordinated by interested parents, who founded the Home and School Movement in 1916. That movement had grown to become a provincial organization by 1919.[45] Various home and school associations were established in local districts, and boards emerged as principal advocates for the belief that a child's domestic and educational experiences required greater complementarity.[46] The movement's advocates were particularly interested in the early, formative years of human life, when, according to one account, 'the twig is bent, the sight is taken and the race of life has begun.'[47] The movement proclaimed itself an 'essentially fundamental and progressive educational one.' Within it, teachers in schools and parents at home, representing 'two great forces,' could 'work together harmoniously and in a spirit of intelligent co-operation.'[48]

The Home and School Movement's lobbyists changed how parents and teachers interacted throughout the province.[49] The extracurricular activities and social services offered in schools and the expanding popularity of 'parents' days' and community meetings increased the influence of schools in family life.[50] At the local level, home and school groups mediated between parents and educational administrators, discussing everything from homework to celebrations.[51]

These home and school groups – the forerunners of today's Parent–Teacher Associations (PTAs) – also communicated with educational authorities on behalf of parents and expressed the concerns of families to the school boards. Sometimes they incurred the wrath of educationists;[52] other times, they were depicted as attempting to interfere with the school board's management of teachers. Attendees at OEA conferences reported that school trustees were discussing the role of these groups as mediators between parents' interests and the school boards' authority.[53] In rural regions, the home and school associations also supplied books to schools and selected texts for libraries that local parents considered important for their children to read.[54] Generally speaking, increased communication between the home and the school was deemed vital to the holistic development of children. Parents and teachers needed to keep in close contact so that each child's two spheres of life could complement each other.[55] As *The Canadian School Journal* put it in December 1939, this cooperation helped 'influence and train children to become healthy in body, mind and soul in this present world of great activity.'[56]

Social Efficiency and Adjustment to Industry

As has been reinforced throughout this book, progressivist texts stressed that Ontario's schools should no longer devote themselves strictly to the inculcation of academic content. Reinforcing the idea that schools needed to relate more explicitly to the social realities of life, a 1934 editorial in *The School*, aptly titled 'School and Society,' celebrated that educational activities had become increasingly relevant to vocational training: 'the "three R's" has now been extended to embrace the specialized training of boys and girls for every sphere of commercial, industrial, and professional activity.'[57] The schools were represented as laying the foundations for a socially efficient and progressive society, particularly in industrial and economic terms. The cultivation of skills, habits, and character traits conducive to such gains was the responsibility of a progressive educational system.[58]

Relating schools to society meant, in many respects, assessing the needs of industry and the business community. These needs would then be translated into educational objectives. In the words of G. Fred McNally, Alberta's Supervisor of Schools, schools preparing students to take up gainful work in industry needed to be organized as if they were industries, meaning that 'education should be required to justify itself by the return of definitely recognizable dividends.'[59] The needs of any society were akin to those of business and industry. For that reason, progressivist schools would necessarily base their curriculum on principles that provided communities most efficiently with essentials such as food, clothing, and shelter.[60] The relationship between schools and society, from the social efficiency orientation, will be explored further in this section, building on sections in chapters 3 and 4 of this book.

Progressive schools were depicted as playing an important role in society's commercial, technical, and industrial progress.[61] With this in mind, students needed to learn many of the basic principles of industry, including business ethics, retail practice, contracts, taxation, and banking.[62] The more specific instruction could be in these areas, the better; as one of Ontario's secondary school teachers, J. Ferris David, put it, 'every large business institution demands highly trained and educated men [*sic*], each an expert or specialist in his own particular field.'[63] According to another teacher, students required training in business if they were to find their vocational niches in the community.[64] Progressive education was thus depicted as the adjustment of educational facilities to give students training in the skills they would need in their vocations.[65] Having been reconstructed to prepare Ontario's youth for successful careers in business or industry, schools would be more inclined to 'train' the mind to complete particular tasks efficiently rather than 'stuff' it with facts and figures.[66]

If school learning was to be more closely related to life in business or industry, the business model was an apt one for school organization.[67] C.L. Burton, President of the Robert Simpson Company, contended that 'educational objectives, so far as business is concerned, should be set with a view of preparing those who will enter the ranks of industry and business enterprise for their future work.'[68] Burton depicted children as a natural resource that could be used to stimulate society's progress. Education, it followed, had to include much more than academic study.[69] It needed to adapt business models not only as means but also as ends.

As noted in the previous chapter, eliminating waste in educational practice was one way to promote efficiency. This would entail a review of the management and control of schools, as well as the course of study.[70] In terms of the curriculum, subjects that did not facilitate adjustment to the economic realities of life were deemed wasteful, removed as they were from what Dalhousie University Professor of Education B.A. Fletcher called 'the *fundamental principles*' of life.[71] J. Ferris David made this point clearly when he argued that all 'frills of education must be done away with at once and the curriculum adjusted so that the education received in our secondary schools will be such that a boy or girl will be properly fitted.'[72] Frills were those subjects that did not direct a child toward some useful vocational niche.

Vocational guidance and support programs can best be understood as progressivist projects relating to the aims of social efficiency. In a paper presented by the Deputy Minister of Public Welfare, Milton A. Sorsoleil, before the Supervising and Training Department of the OEA, the promotion of vocational guidance was depicted as essential to the shift toward increased efficiency in schools.[73] Students' vocational paths were largely dictated by intelligence tests, which were seen as reliable predictors of mental ability.[74] Guiding students toward their vocational niches in life, explained Florence Dunlop, psychologist for Ottawa's public schools, involved collecting a range of information beginning with that related to intelligence, but also including 'pertinent data on health, developmental history, physical condition, personality, mental age, rate of mental maturation, school progress, special abilities and disabilities, interests, desires, home and community conditions.'[75]

Vocational guidance was predicated on the belief that each person had a niche in the established order. Informed guidance from the schools could facilitate future citizens' transitions to fitting careers. As W.G. Martin, Minister of Public Welfare, explained in a speech at an OEA conference, 'education is training in the principles of citizenship, enabling the boy or girl to find his or her proper groove in order that they may make a worth-while contribution to the day and generation in which they are privileged to live.'[76] Discovering students' aptitudes and abilities went hand in hand with their training in an efficiently managed and progressive system of schools.[77]

Efficient schools, then, would require students to think about their vocational opportunities and their potential fit within the larger structure. 'Modern industrial and progressive conditions have made vocational guidance imperative,' declared an editorial in *The Canadian School Journal.* 'Without proper guidance both the individual and the state may suffer loss.'[78] In the first four years of the 1930s, as the Depression brought concerns about employment to the forefront of educational talk, *The School* and *The Canadian School Journal* together carried more than twenty articles on vocational preparation in the province's schools. It was in this climate that the Ontario Vocational Guidance Association was organized, in 1934, to study the principles, problems, and techniques of guidance.[79]

The emphasis on vocational guidance gained strength into the mid-1930s. Then, as the Depression lifted, that emphasis shifted from finding students work to finding them work that would promote the greatest happiness for them. Marion Goode, a counsellor as well as a frequent contributor to the source journals on the subject of guidance, believed that the greatest concern of vocational guidance programs needed to be the negotiation of students' abilities and interests. Looking forward to a new decade, the 1940s, Ontario's schools needed to accept that helping an individual find a niche where he or she could perform 'successfully and happily' was a proposition that should receive 'the very ready assent of persons of sane mind.'[80]

Interesting and meaningful work was depicted as an elixir for good health and personal happiness.[81] Vocational guidance was the most efficient way that a school could use data collected on individual students to facilitate their transition to useful, suitable, and happy lives.[82] The task of helping Ontario's future citizens find their future niches in society was far too important to be left to chance.[83]

In an age of increasing specialization, Goode argued, educationists with expertise in vocational guidance were carrying out a vital social task more efficiently than parents could: 'As for the great mass of working-class parents, it is obvious that limitations of knowledge, experience and ability must often make it impossible for them to offer wise counsel. In many cases they accept chance opportunities without regard to their suitability; and in many cases they allow children who deserve a better fate to drift into blind-alley occupations, more heedful of immediate gain than of future advancement.'[84]

The economic and industrial order in Ontario was increasing in complexity, and traditional models of apprenticeship for training were vanishing. For those reasons, the educational machinery required greater expertise and specialization.[85] Electa Bissell, an elementary school teacher, expressed her faith that guidance was the very core of modern education. She summarized the efficiency progressivist view succinctly: 'From his [sic] baby ways, teach him to walk by himself, and make him realize that he is an important cog in the machinery of a smoothly-running world.'[86]

Social Meliorism and Engagement with Social Ills

While the efficiency progressivist articles sought to pursue a business model to reform Ontario's schools, the meliorist texts often presented business interests as a scourge in schools.[87] An education that promoted competition among students or that valued conformity was presented as anti-democratic. It was more important for schools to develop in students the ability to think critically and promote social justice than it was to adjust them to an extant order. According to an editorial article in *The School*, the aims of education involved 'a wider distribution of material benefits, fundamentally by a wider distribution of three related abilities: the ability to recognize the universal good, the ability to recognize the good in others, and the ability to assume responsibility in co-operation with others to achieve the common good.'[88]

As seen earlier, meliorist articles readily admitted that the circumstances of life had changed. According to Joseph McCulley, Ontario was in the midst of its greatest period of change, and if schools were to relate to social life, they also required reforms.[89] The most important of these was infusing schools with the spirit of democracy and cooperation.[90]

The social meliorist lens in Ontario's progressivist concerns for relating schools to society reveals an interest in reforming society to better the lot of all humanity. In the words of W.G. Martin, Minister of Public

Welfare, 'if there was ever a time in history when there was a need for a great crusade of youth and older men for the betterment of the lot of humanity that hour is to-day.'[91] A truly progressive society was one built on the principle of cooperation.[92] During the years when the Depression affected school funding most significantly, 1932 and 1933,[93] John A. Cook, a member of the Rural Section of the OEA, made the case that 'co-operation of individuals has aided them to build up our great civilization faster and more satisfactorily, and so to live more success-fully than individuals could possibly do by living alone and individu-alistically.'[94] Ontario's schools, consequently, needed to build links to the community; they also needed opportunities to work cooperatively in order to improve society.[95] One editorial in *The School* called on edu-cationists to see schooling as a way of reforming society along more equitable lines: 'A new world is in the making, or so they tell us. Civili-zation has struck its tents, and is on the march.'[96]

Meliorist progressivists often questioned the aims of education in articles that explored the meaning of schooling and the purposes of reform in a democratic state.[97] One persistent theme throughout the interwar years was the teacher's role as a figure of authority in the classroom. How could debate and freedom of discussion be fostered in a system with mandated curricula and examinations? Were educa-tors facilitators, guides, or indoctrinators? Questions like these, exam-ined in earlier chapters, persisted and indeed dominated the journals between 1940 and 1942.[98] Typically, arguments in favour of democratic schooling contrasted Ontario with fascist or Nazi states, which were characterized as overly concerned with indoctrination. But besides the war, this discussion of indoctrination had another driver. In 1939, George Counts of Columbia University spoke about indoctrination at a meeting of the Toronto Branch of the NEF. In characteristically dramatic fashion, he told his audience that indoctrination represent-ed the greatest threat to democracy.[99] 'Is indoctrination just another name for education?' asked W.C. Keirstead, Professor of Education at the University of New Brunswick, 'or may indoctrination be used in education?'[100]

Keirstead's article in *The School* likened individuals in a democratic community to active cells in a living body, which have independent and yet cooperative functions. Each part of the body depended on the health of other parts, and no society could be healthy unless it tended to the well-being of all its elements. When the whole of a community worked in harmony, everyone prospered and there could be 'increased richness for all.'[101] What, then, was the teacher's role in the protection of individual freedoms within a centralized, structured system of schooling? The editors of *The School* answered that question in 1939 in strongly meliorist tones: 'What can teachers do? They must not attempt to merely indoctrinate their pupils, first, because such education is futile, and secondly, because a certain section of the public will not allow us to indoctrinate their children or their young people. Teachers can, however, do much. In general they must educate their pupils to gather information, to weigh evidence, to analyze propaganda, and to come to their own conclusions.'[102]

Democracy, not business, was depicted as the ideal model for progressivist school reforms, because it enabled educationists and students alike to explore, debate, and express opinions.[103] Ideally, democracy permitted and indeed *required* rational debate and dissent. Furthermore, it led to decisions and aims that were pragmatic and mutable in a complex and evolving world.[104]

Occasionally, articles advocating democratic schooling as a means of furthering social reforms reported on progressivist occurrences in the United States. An editorial in *The School*, for example, cited at length a front-page article in the *Times Educational Supplement* the day after a meeting of the National Education Association, on 6 July 1935.[105] Having discussed the American context, the editorial equated a democratic approach to debating educational reforms with freedom of speech. To develop a democratically minded and critical citizenry, Ontario's schools needed to promote academic freedom; 'administrators and schools should have full opportunity to present differing points of view on all controversial questions, in order to aid students.'[106]

Promoting democratic communities in the schools that would lead to social justice and cooperation was made difficult by what John Cook called 'our so-called capitalistic system.'[107] The ethos of civic cooperation and the spirit of laissez-faire capitalism were at odds with each other, Cook argued; the former could lead to equity, while the latter had led to economic depression and dramatic inequities.[108] Progressive education should be about building community and reforming society through democratic citizenship.[109] This message seemed to be emphatically reinforced throughout the Depression, which devastated Ontarians and thrust concerns for children's health, stability, and welfare into the limelight:

In all industrial sections of Canada the problem of looking after children whose mothers are working in industry is becoming more acute. Many school-age children are subsisting on a very ill-balanced diet – some leaving home in the morning after a breakfast of bread, returning at noon to an empty and cheerless house for an inadequate or injudicious lunch, and ending the day with a dinner prepared by one already tired from other employment.[110]

Inequality of opportunity, in both educational and economic terms, was seen as rooted in laissez-faire competition, leading to gross injustices.[111]

In 1935, at the High School Boards' Annual Convention, Joseph McCulley proclaimed the death of laissez-faire and asked educationists to strive for a more just and cooperative world for which 'a wider socialized viewpoint on the part of teachers and trustees is necessary.'[112] As Frederick Minkler explained, progressive education aimed 'to develop the emergent generation that it will formulate a better and better democratic society.'[113] Minkler's definition of progressive education reveals how very different the progressivist orientations were with respect to relations between school and society. He essentially critiqued other progressivists' 'attempts to fit the child into a pre-determined mould, to train to fit into the social order to which he belongs.'[114]

In the context of the journal articles, perhaps because debate itself was not possible given the medium, these varying definitions of progressive education sometimes resembled a spirited marketing campaign. The development of Education Weeks by teachers' federations was a clear example of the perceived need for teachers' federations in Ontario, as one editorial put it, 'to put up a persistent sales campaign for education.'[115] But the article failed to qualify what type or vision of education was being sold.[116] A progressivist vision, explained E.A. Corbett, 'like any other commodity, has to be sold to the people, and ... a certain amount of showmanship is always necessary in promoting a program ... In other words, the pill has to be sugar-coated.'[117]

McCulley, a prominent advocate of the meliorist progressivist orientation, knew this well; advertisements for Pickering College, the private school founded in 1842 as a Quaker institution, which McCulley operated, were published regularly in *The Canadian School Journal* with the banner 'Education in a changing world.'[118] McCulley was so successful at selling the meliorist vision of progressive education that he was elected chairman of publicity and promotion for the conference of the western New York branch of the PEA in the United States.[119] While it might appear curious that progressivists arguing for cooperation and community advertised their beliefs, the espousals and editorials were consistent with the vision of democracy for which meliorists advocated.

Freedom of speech, diversity of opinion, and freedom of choice were still the foundations of democratic schooling and were vital to debate.[120] C.C. Goldring, speaking at the 1937 Urban Trustees Association meeting in London, Ontario, stressed that training for life involved learning how to live in a functioning democracy. In his opinion, which he expressed in uncharacteristically convoluted terms, 'democracy consisted of making choices, consequently our schools should aim in preparing students to prepare themselves for the time when they will have to make their own choices in life.'[121]

Marketing was not indoctrination; so it was with great horror that an editorial in *The School* reported on some of the Nazi policies that were shaping German schools.[122] Such policies were antithetical to democratic principles because they forced students to conform rather than to doubt. A.S.H. Hill, a teacher at Oakwood Collegiate Institute, referred to this divide as the 'struggle between two ways of life, "Hitlerism" and "Democracy."'[123] Progressive democracies aimed to cultivate critical thinking, democratic debate, intellectual curiosity, and equality of opportunity.

'Democratic education,' explained a 1941 editorial in *The School*, consisted of 'challenging the rigid procedures of tradition, [and] showed disdain for any emphasis on efficiency – at least in theory.'[124] Two months later, Professor David H. Russell of UBC expanded on this definition by explaining that any citizen actively participating in democratic life necessarily had a critical and inquiring view of the world. 'Democracy,' he argued, 'would wither if citizens' critical faculties atrophied.'[125] It was primarily in schools that this critical perspective should be nurtured; this would require education itself to operate democratically. Angela A. Hannan, citing James G. Gardiner, former Minister of National War Services, said that this would entail 'freedom to live, freedom to think, freedom to learn, freedom to agree or disagree, freedom to choose one's calling, freedom to change one's mind, leavened by a healthy community spirit, which permits us to bear one another's burdens.'[126] No quotation in the sources encapsulates the meliorist progressivist concern for the schools and society more comprehensively.

This chapter has examined various progressivist depictions of the relations between schools and society. From the child study orientation, proposals were made for relating schools to society by promoting health and establishing home and school associations. From the social efficiency orientation arose visions that would relate the course of study more closely to society's industrial progress by establishing vocational guidance programs in schools. From within the social meliorist orientation, progressive schools were seen as vital to the creation of a more cooperative, democratic, and socially just society.

The following chapter will examine journal articles that were critical of progressive education and school reforms. Humanistic studies will be presented as foils to progressivist rhetoric.

6 Humanists as the Foil to Progressivists: Resistance to Progressivist Reforms in Ontario

> I wonder how far we must go before we begin to realize that modern education is gradually turning its back on all that is cultural and thereby betraying its most fundamental purpose.*

Humanists, like their progressivist counterparts, were not contesting that the world around them, whether contemplated in industrial, economic, social, or intellectual terms, was changing.[1] It would have been impossible for any educationist of the times to be oblivious to the dramatic changes sweeping through Ontario's culture and society.[2] 'It is generally accepted that society is going through a period of radical changes,' explained Reverend L.J. Bondy of St Michael's College in Toronto.[3] 'Some of these changes are inevitable, many are unquestionably good, a few are alarming.'[4] The times were changing, admitted the humanists, but they always had been evolving, and would never cease to do so.[5]

All aspects of life, explained Sir Arthur Currie, President of McGill University, 'grow and change indeed. But the more they change, the more they remain, in essence, the same things.'[6] Nothing, not even education, could keep up with the mutable nature of life. What was essential in the presence of turmoil and change was the steadying influence of tradition.[7] Maurice Hutton, University of Toronto classicist, expressed this sentiment most clearly upon his retirement in 1928 following nearly half a century of leadership in the field: 'We had learned from

---

* L.J. Bondy, 'The Present Situation in Modern Languages in Our Schools,' *The School* (October 1938): 121.

the Greek philosophers and from the New Testament, to find reason and purpose, and mind and God in the world and then Darwin interposed and brought back chance and luck and accident and the doctrine of casual survival of the lucky ... the world has again become all chaos and confusion.'[8]

For Hutton, the modern pursuit of science and progress had ushered in one world war as well as untold atrocities. In the words of W.H. Fyfe, Principal of Queen's University, the '"grand, old fortifying" classical curriculum ... provided for the young mind problems that had permanent interest disentangled from contemporary passion.'[9] Facing the onslaught of progressivist arguments, humanist articles in the periodicals fought for the survival of the classics, albeit from a position referred to by A.B. McKillop as 'dethroned and generally diminished.'[10] Until the curriculum reforms of the late 1930s, Latin had remained a prerequisite for entry into the four-year Bachelor of Arts degree in university.[11] The reforms would diminish Latin's prestige as a qualification for university.

Humanists saw progressive education as the ascent of fads and frills in Ontario's schools; this, they warned, would lead to scattered and confused ends. Quite correctly, they anticipated that in the pursuit of what was new and contemporary, the aims of schooling would become utterly confused and entangled. Humanists such as Fyfe depicted progressivist ideas as entangled in a passionate but ultimately futile struggle to relate schools to contemporary life. If social conditions were, indeed, always evolving, education could not keep up with these changes. Henry Bowers, a teacher from Fergus, Ontario, characterized progressive education as a 'millipeducation.' The title of his article, 'Guesswork,' highlighted what he called the fundamentally 'contradictory tendencies' embedded in progressivist modern thought. Progressive education was, for him, 'a great millipede, the legs of which reserve to themselves the right to independent action. Some move forward; others, with delightful contrariety, insist that backward is forward.'[12]

In the same issue of *The School*, Evangeline Lewis from the Mount Allison School for Girls blamed progressivist ideas for the modern concern for specialization of study.[13] The traditional humanistic curriculum was, by contrast, broad and encyclopedic. It enabled exploration of the relationships among personal, contextual, and eternal phenomena. The classics remained classic because of their eternal value, whereas the future was contingent, mutable, and unpredictable. Predicated on that same argument, Bowers presented his most derisive characterization of progressivist millipeducation: '"Gressives" they are, no doubt;

but which is "pro-" and which "retro-"? Certain legs agree that lateral movement is desirable, but half of these maintain that the true path is on the right, while the others are equally positive that it lies to the left. Indeed, there are wistful legs that find on solid earth no rest for the soles of their feet and sigh for the wings of a dove."[14] Bowers's depiction of progressivist ideas stands out for its sarcasm and originality; more commonly, though, progressive education was slandered as being overly concerned with 'fads and frills.'[15]

These humanist critics maintained that the concerns of progressivists would change and sway ephemerally and subjectively, whereas more academic subjects were lasting and substantial.[16] Citing a forty-five-year-old article that had appeared in the *New York Evening Post*, a 1934 editorial in *The School* equated the progressivists' concerns for school reform with the passing of crazes, one always supplanting some other:

> The history of education in this country for the past fifty years has been a history of crazes – the method craze, the object-lesson craze, the illustration craze, the 'memory-gem' craze, the civics craze – calling upon children of eight to ten for information as to custom-houses, post-offices, city councils, governors, and legislators – the story-telling craze, the phonics craze, the word-method craze, the drawing and music craze, beside the craze for letters and business forms, picture study and physics. Now arrives manual training.[17]

The 1937 and 1938 revisions to Ontario's *Programme of Studies* were viewed by many humanists as another example of what the above editorial called mere 'fluctuations, shiftings, and tinkerings.'[18] Speaking two years after the first curriculum revisions were published, the Principal of the Normal School in London, C.E. Mark, felt that he spoke for a great many educationists when he expressed doubt about the revisions' value and substance.[19] Critics of the progressivist craze for reform were fearful, he explained, of being labelled ultra-conservatives; the swing toward progressive education in the province, however, was too extreme and dramatic to be sustainable:

> Progress is best achieved, not by repudiation of the past, but by a reconstruction of the past. Some of the best thought of the ages has been built into our educational theory, and practices worthy of that theory have been based in the main on principles that are eternal. And so, young teacher, give ear to the first note of warning, to view that past with a full sense of

indebtedness and gratitude, and to beware of turning too far to an extreme just because it is new and different.[20]

Progressivists, for Mark, were akin to petulant and overly excitable youth.

Professor L.J. Bondy lamented that 'one of the first results of the *progress* has been the passing of the classical languages; Greek already buried and Latin with one foot in the grave.'[21] Bondy poked fun at the lofty claims of progressivists who believed that the schools should address all of society's ills; noting different possible destinations for progress, he challenged those who advocated progressive education to define its aims with greater accuracy.[22] If the humanists' voices in the educational literature were losing their prominence, they refused to go silently. Fyfe blamed certain progressivists for the Depression, accusing them of being inspired by the ignoble motive of producing fodder to work in factories. In his view, they cared not for 'slow mental growth but training for trade or industry. It is a short-cut which has landed us in the Slough of Despond.'[23]

R.B. Liddy, Professor of Psychology at the University of Western Ontario, made a similar argument to Fyfe's, insisting that 'the chief emphasis, although not the only emphasis, of the school should be upon intellectual development.'[24] The so-called traditional schools criticized so heavily by progressivists, he acquiesced, might have 'spent relatively too much time worshipping at the shrine of the purely intellectual' at the expense of the emotional and the practical.[25] But he felt that the pendulum of progressivist reform in Ontario's schools had swung too far and had overly relegated academic content: 'We must not lose perspective when we recognize the need for a richer curriculum; and we must continue to emphasize the fact that the primary scholastic function is intellectual education. The chief emphasis of the school must be upon what the title of this paper designates, rather loosely perhaps, the making of the mind.'[26] Intellectual progress, he concluded, founded on knowledge of the heritage of past human achievements and developed by the language and number arts, was the most valuable basis for curriculum construction.[27]

The humanists were on the retreat, as was evident in the faltering of faculty psychology as a framework for thinking about curriculum and learning. Faculty psychology entailed the belief that individuals had different mental abilities, or faculties, such as the faculties of reason and of memory, which were like muscles in the body; each required conditioning, testing, and stretching in order to develop.[28] It was held that for each faculty, there was a subject that could best facilitate that training.[29] This view of mental development was predicated on the belief that learning in one context was generally transferable to another. In other words, if educators developed a child's faculty of reason via the discipline of mathematics, the child would be more reasonable generally.[30]

Just as it is today, the idea that education was in some way related to the training of the mind was a potent one that educationists found difficult to relinquish.[31] A.J. Husband, Principal of Brockville Collegiate Institute, addressing the English and History Section of the OEA, argued that the value of history lay in the subject's ability to cultivate the faculties of memory and imagination.[32] A year later, J.H. Smith, Public School Inspector for South Perth, offered Ontario's educationists a very similar message. He began: 'Most of us think, that we are going to school to prepare us for the earning of a living, but I would say we are sent to school to learn to live a life, there's a big difference.'[33] This, Smith explained, could not happen if schools prepared students only for work in factories by teaching them a narrow range of skills. Education needed to be more holistically concerned with the cultivation of *all* the mental and emotional faculties.[34]

As late as 1935, Samuel Ramsey's mental disciplinarian introduction to *The English Language and English Grammar* was being cited in *The School*:

> That great body of knowledge known as learning is valuable indirectly rather than directly. By it are formed habits of calm, thoughtful observation and discrimination that modify the whole character of men. If a savage could be induced to give his [*sic*] attention for half an hour to the drawing of a circle, to the equality of its radii, its relation to the hexagon – he would be a little less of a savage all his life after. All honest pursuit of knowledge has a humanizing effect.[35]

This citation expressed the most endearing and hopeful aspect of the humanists' educational vision – an undying faith in the transformative power of education to touch all people, regardless of their backgrounds or abilities. But at the same time, there was within it an alienating elitism that represented the uneducated person as uncivilized.[36]

Experimental psychology would, ultimately, deal the most striking blows to the established faith in the potential for certain subjects to develop mental faculties. 'With the dawn of experimental psychology,' explained E.D. MacPhee, 'the concept of faculties was called into question, and with the development of that science, the theory disappeared.'[37] Peter Sandiford, Professor and Psychologist at the Ontario College of Education, reported to Ontario's educationists that the research of Edward Thorndike and William James in the United States had debunked any possible correlation between the training of faculties and general mental ability.[38] James, Sandiford explained, in a modest experiment with his graduate students at Harvard University, had found that memorizing all of *Paradise Lost* had not helped any of them learn Victor Hugo's *Satyr* any more quickly.[39] Thorndike's research at Columbia University supposedly confirmed James's hypothesis that skills learned in one context could not be transferred to another:

> When Thorndike and Woodworth planned more elaborate researches and used a number of subjects, the paucity of transfer effects began to be realized. Practice in estimating areas of one shape did not always improve the ability to estimate areas of other shapes. There could be negative and zero transfer as well as positive. This study is also historically important in that it first suggested how transfer takes place.[40]

The implications of this research for progressivists were evident: if learning was to be relevant and practical to life, it had to be specific and contextual. The reasoning underpinning the preservation of classical subjects – namely, that these disciplined faculties of the mind – was therefore faulty.[41]

Humanists were compelled to demonstrate the utility of their subjects for contemporary life – a game they were destined to lose. Ancient Greek could never meet the utilitarian criteria that, for example, Social Studies or Health could. With the demise of faculty psychology as a defensible justification for including classics in a modern course of studies, humanists turned their arguments in the source journals to more utilitarian themes: preservation of the cultural heritage of Western civilization and its importance for understanding the present world.[42] Fyfe, lamenting the declining knowledge of Greek, worried that Ontario's students were being deprived of 'the language which unlocks the only door that leads into their full intellectual inheritance.'[43] Humanists, in similar terms, swung to the defence of classical subjects, particularly Latin, explaining that these accompanied richer and deeper understanding of present life, language, and meanings. Oshawa Collegiate and Vocational Institute teacher Charles Ewing described Latin as a beacon that illuminated the derivations of terms in language, science, and mathematics.[44] He argued: 'Etymology is no highly specialized science to be pursued only by the erudite. It is actually the "Open Sesame" to that mastery of words without which thought can never be fully and accurately conveyed from one mind to another.'[45]

Some humanists argued that if classical studies seemed useless or merely abstract, this was due only to poor instruction that had not sufficiently emphasized the enormous debt that modern languages and sciences owed to the past. As J.M. Paton explained, the key to better English was increased study of Latin and Greek.[46] Citing a 1936 editorial published in the magazine *Saturday Night* titled 'An Illiterate Nation,' Paton associated the declining study of classical languages with 'the prevalent inability of otherwise educated Canadians to use the English language with accuracy, to say nothing of literary effect.'[47] The decreased skill in the use of modern languages was depicted as a consequence of the demise of ancient ones, confirming what E.D. MacPhee had termed the 'direct utility values of classics.'[48] MacPhee's argument for the contemporary value of classics sought to establish a utilitarian argument for Latin while denying the plausibility of faculty psychology.[49]

An editorial in *The School* implored teachers of Latin to make more explicit the connections that the language had to modern life and contemporary subjects.[50] Classicists could make their courses more appealing by using lively activities and by celebrating student successes as opposed to stressing precision in grammar and penalizing errors.[51] Latin clubs and Latin societies, for example, were envisaged as part of the solution to poor teaching and dull subject matter.[52] The introduction of such programs in schools, explained B.C. Taylor, a teacher at the University of Toronto Schools, required 'skilful manipulation. A flat statement to the effect that a Latin Society is about to be founded may result in demonstrative nose holding in some quarters. A good teacher is three parts salesman, so that the idea must be sold as worthwhile.'[53]

A brief introduction to the article by the editors of the journal makes very clear that, by the early 1940s, the focus of humanists had shifted from arguments for mental development to ones of direct utility.[54] A decade earlier, R.H. King, the first principal of Scarborough High School, had argued that educators needed to reinforce the many relationships between classical languages and subjects and contemporary life in a modern democracy.[55] Time and again, humanists claimed that classics could be saved if teachers could make evident their eminent practicality to life.[56] What was at stake with regard to these progressivist reforms, argued an editorial piece published in 1941, was the destruction of all that was best in education, namely, 'the foundations of that higher life which alone preserves the good and which is the only basis of true progress.'[57]

What was perhaps most interesting with regard to the humanist retreat was the elevation of school libraries in the anti-progressivist rhetoric; libraries were depicted as the last bastion for the humanities, where the classics could survive and, perchance, thrive in the school context. Even as the articles published in the source journals from Ontario sketched a picture of the humanists' retreat in face of progressivist advances, they also portrayed an intriguing humanist concern and advocacy for school libraries. It appears that as proponents of liberal education and the study of classics found themselves marginalized in discussions of curriculum reforms to Ontario's schools, they increasingly threw their support behind public and school libraries, which would be storehouses of great literary works and historical texts.

These libraries were represented as capable of cultivating intelligence and appreciation of various aspects of the human spirit by enlarging the scope of education to include interaction with masterpieces of literature, art, and history.[58] According to L. Irene Cole, who instructed at the Ontario College of Education's Library School, libraries were not only supplements to school, but also essential institutions for broadening the entire population's knowledge base.[59] Cole explained: 'It has been said the public library is the "university of the people," if this statement is true, then the elementary school library is the key that unlocks its door.'[60]

Particularly during the Depression, when the burden on Ontario's 'communities to fill in the leisure time of the unemployed and preserve morale' was of grave concern to educationists, libraries were seen as spaces where adult education could flourish.[61] Study groups were organized in various public libraries in the early 1930s, inviting Ontarians to enlighten their minds and contemplate great literary works and human accomplishments.[62] In April 1934, J.D. Campbell, Assistant Chief Inspector of Public and Separate Schools, published a lengthy article in *The Canadian School Journal* outlining the history of Ontario's elementary school libraries. 'The library is an ancient and mediaeval institution as well as a modern one,' Campbell explained.[63] His concern, in tones reminiscent of other humanist articles, was that past human achievements be seen as relevant in a contemporary context.[64]

The libraries were thus represented as safe, enlightening spaces where all Ontarians could develop their minds and pursue learning.[65]

Arthur Slyfield, a librarian at Oshawa Collegiate and Vocational Institute, explained to educationists that libraries were pleasant and instructive places where the public and all students could pass their time amid 'pictures, trophies, museum specimens, and growing plants, not to mention books.'[66] The reading resources, unlike the increasingly utilitarian resources required for subject study, were for both business and pleasure, as instructive as they were interesting.[67] The best kind of education was guided by intelligent reading of great books, those capable of developing a vivid and robust intelligence. Lillian Morley, a librarian from Milverton, Ontario, expressed the belief, for example, that it was quite possible for quality reading alone to help a child become well educated; this faith, she explained, had been marginalized by the 'comparatively recent swing towards the inclusion of manual arts in the school curriculum.'[68]

Libraries, guardians of academic knowledge, were also described in terms revealing a faith in mental discipline. Different books were able to develop different aspects of the mind and spirit.[69] Such development, explained a 1933 editorial in *The Canadian School Journal*, was 'a necessary part of an intelligent man's [sic] life. He reads as naturally as he eats. His mind is fed as regularly as his body. As with physical food, so with the mental – it has to have a balanced ration.'[70] The classical curriculum might no longer have been available to Ontario's students, but the essence of the humanists' faith in a liberal curriculum could be retained within the province's libraries. The institution seemed to respond to Harvard University President James B. Conant's call for a 'modern equivalent' to the classical curriculum.[71] Conant's plea, repeated by George Rogers, the Chief Inspector for Public Schools in Ottawa, held that the study of classics provided a common framework to ground the thinking of an educated society.[72]

Articles in the source journals maintained that Ontario's libraries, public and educational, seemed to fulfil this role. In 1935, *The Canadian School Journal* published the opinion that libraries, like the academic curriculum, could help develop and discipline the mind: 'A circulation of books through a community is of vital importance to the mental fitness of the people. Books are great levellers. They give to all who will faithfully use them, the society, the spiritual presence of the Greatest of our race.'[73] If the progressivists were the prevailing influences on life at school and work, the humanists seem to have become more interested in life at times of leisure.[74] To develop a fuller and richer life of liberal study in times of leisure – even if school led directly into industry – remained an admirable and achievable aim.[75] 'Learning for learning's sake was no longer the slogan of schools,' lamented George Rogers, who felt that the modern age in education had become a strictly utilitarian one.[76]

The educational aim of cultivating a love for and interest in great books and classical themes was an important one for humanists.[77] Refining children's literary tastes was just as important as developing their minds.[78] Mae Locklin, a school librarian, stressed that the librarian's task was ultimately to help children 'cultivate a taste for good fiction, for poetry and biography, and to discourage the reading of cheap and useless stories.'[79] If libraries could develop in children the habit of selecting and reading books that developed their faculties broadly, these would be taken home, shared with the family, and spread to the community.[80] Ideally, each home could establish its own library with its own classic texts.[81] In the words of Isabel Wilson of Ryerson Public School in Toronto, reading and education were largely about appreciating 'beauty of expression' and cultivating 'harmony of thought.'[82]

The humanists also argued that literature, history, and the classics had the power to inspire students to carry out great acts and to achieve their potentials. History teaching through stories of great lives, which involved presenting heroic figures accomplishing noble feats, was related to the study of Western society's classic texts.[83] The publication of an annual list of 'essential books' in *The Canadian School Journal* was largely about establishing a canon.[84] One teacher noted in 1932 that 'children are great hero worshippers and will find many ideal characters in books by which to pattern their own lives.'[85] Classical history and languages might not appear immediately and directly useful, but the inspirational and motivational aspects of such studies were beyond measure.[86] Libraries, then, had limitless potential to house and disseminate the knowledge to support broad and liberal learning.[87] A 1939 editorial in *The Canadian School Journal* posited that even if public schools existed for the purpose of starting education, libraries were able to continue and broaden the public's studies.[88] At a time when the humanist influence on the school program was receding, school libraries were a potential bastion of classical, academic knowledge that could develop children's minds and spirits.[89]

Humanists were grasping at utilitarian straws, which evaded them. When one reads through articles in the source journals, it is impossible not to notice that an increase in progressivist rhetoric and reform language was intertwined with the decline of the classical, academic model of schooling. The study of Latin, in particular, suffered a severe decline. By 1934, it was clear to teachers of the subject that they could make no 'claim that Latin be made compulsory for all students in the academic department of our secondary schools.'[90] A progressivist curriculum, concerned more with the specialized study of contemporary life than with past achievements and general training of the mind, was in its ascendency; what mattered most to progressive educators was a subject's utility in the modern world.[91]

By 1935, a year after the election of a Liberal government in Ontario and following years of brutal economic depression, progressivists' calls to seriously interrogate the aims and organization of schools had been heeded. An editorial in *The School* that year maintained that schools had been thrust to the forefront of the public's mind and that they were now seen as a powerful tool for reforming all of society: 'In its search for the causes of our present social and industrial muddle, the public has not been slow to question whether faults in our educational system may account, in part at least, for our present troubles.'[92] For schools to relate better to a modern world, their primary concern would have to be the utility of the subjects they taught. The same editorial pointed out that across the province, 'teachers and administrators alike feel that the curriculum must be examined critically in order to ensure that the courses offered are really useful for the youth of the present day.'[93] No subject or discipline could be retained if it did not fit perceived wants or needs:

> For instance, the teachers of Classics in Ontario felt that they must justify afresh the place given to Latin in the provincial schools. The result has been the presentation to the Classical Section of the Ontario Educational Association of a formal report, not only on the value of the study of Latin, but on the best way of teaching the subject. Latin must justify itself or go, and so must the other subjects.[94]

In the latter years of the interwar period, humanists were wrestling with ways to demonstrate the utility of the classics to Ontario's educationists.

By the end of the 1935 school year, the frontal attack on the humanities and the classics seemed hardly justified when one considers the already marginalized position of those fields of study in Ontario's educational framework. In 1936 it was reported in *The School* that many humanists had resolved to cut their losses; 'the so-called Latin question' could be resolved if the subject was retained in the curriculum as a matriculation subject only for those students for whom it was necessary.[95] Other humanists, such as the Classical Section of the OEA, were more hopeful

that Latin could stand firmly in spite of incoming tides of reform. At
their annual convention in 1935, they reported the findings of a committee that had investigated the state of Latin in Ontario's schools.[96] The
report argued that classical subjects had been too marginalized in the
province; it then recommended that the situation be ameliorated via the
promotion of Greek and Latin, improved teacher preparation, and revisions to examinations and the curriculum.[97]

Latin, the report outlined, was not a compulsory study either in the
secondary schools or in any one of the five universities in the province,
nor was it being offered as a subject of study in the technical and commercial schools. It was not required by the Department of Education for
a high school graduation diploma or for admission to a normal school.
Also, students could enter any of Ontario's universities without Latin
and could enrol in the Faculties of Applied Science, Household Science, and Forestry. In the Faculty of Arts, the Commerce program did
not have Latin as a prerequisite. Middle-school Latin was required in all
other areas of the Faculty of Arts, as well as in the Faculties of Medicine
and Dentistry. Upper-school Latin remained a requirement for Honours
programs.

After the report was released, the Council of the Faculty of Arts at
the University of Toronto, whose members included professors from
the sciences, mathematics, history, economics, and ancient and modern
languages, tried to unite behind the committee's recommendations.[98]
By a vote of sixty to eleven, the council 'decided that at least Middle
School Latin should continue to be a prerequisite for those who wished
to proceed to the degree of Bachelor of Arts.'[99] But the pendulum had
swung by then, and progressivist reform visions had all the momentum.
By 1938, Greek and Latin were being denied to first-year high school
students in lieu of a common, general program of courses.[100] Furthermore, language requirements for university study were being loosened,
so that students were now permitted to elect French or mathematics in
lieu of Latin.[101] In fact, Duncan McArthur, the Minister of Education,
believed that the 'greatest service the teaching profession could render
to humanity would be to make French and Latin optional instead of
compulsory subjects.'[102] McArthur saw no value in students memorizing passages of Latin text.[103] Such practices – elevating content over
individual interest, promoting rote memorization and recall, and teaching that which bore no relation to contemporary life – were at odds with
the core sensibilities of Ontario's progressivists.

7 Continuities and Change: Reforming the Curriculum and the War's Impact on Progressivist Rhetoric, 1937–1942

Social virtues are not things merely to learn about. They are to be achieved only by practising them. They are to be accepted willingly as desirable forms of conduct; they cannot be developed by coercion. The school, therefore, must be organized to permit their exercise and growth in situations that require their practice. Hence, opportunities should be provided for children to work together in groups, each child sharing in the planning, execution, and completion of worth-while tasks.*

This final chapter considers the years between 1937 and 1942, during which broad and thorough revisions were made to Ontario's curriculum. Canada's participation in the Second World War and the very significant threat that global conflict posed to democracy brought about shifts in progressivist rhetoric. The source journals, which had heretofore been almost stubbornly adverse to discussing political matters, rallied behind the cause of a democratic education for a progressive world. Still, the progressivist articles did not engage in any rhetorical disputes regarding different visions for school reform.

The source journals were willing to engage with democratic pedagogical themes on a large and international scale, but they also remained diffident with regard to oppositional progressivist discourses in Ontario. Thus, there was a stark absence of editorial critiques about the curriculum reforms or of commentary on the government's stance on matters such as labour disputes. The journals were, in general,

---

* *Programme of Studies for Grades VII and VIII of the Public and Separate Schools, 1942* (Toronto, ON: Department of Education, 1942), 6.

supportive of the Ontario government.[1] Many voices were absent in these sources. Those that were included weighed in on pedagogical matters with cautious optimism, leaning toward the consensus view that democracy was a beacon of hope in times of darkness. Duncan McArthur, a major figure in the curriculum revisions and a strong voice in the periodicals, attempted to weave progressivist currents of opinion into a broad and cohesive vision for Ontario's school reforms.

In 1934, with the worst of the Depression beginning to ease, a new government led by Mitchell Hepburn was elected to lead Ontario to better days. Among his many campaign promises, Hepburn had vowed to overhaul the education system. That had particular appeal to Ontario's educationists, who for fifteen years following the end of the First World War had presented progressivist visions in the periodicals. Ever since 1923, Ontario's premiers had retained the education portfolio for themselves; consequently, Hepburn argued that the Department of Education had been led by men lacking 'particular training' in educational matters.[2] Dr Leo J. Simpson, the new Minister of Education, had been a school board trustee in Barrie and was considered a good party organizer with grassroots support among trustees and educators.[3] The new Deputy Minister of Education and Chief Director of Education, Duncan McArthur, would become the driving force behind the department's reforms to Ontario's schools. According to Robert Stamp,

> actual leadership was assumed by the new deputy minister, Duncan McArthur. This was the outstanding educator Hepburn had been seeking for over a year – a Queen's University history professor, member of the Kingston Board of Education, and a man who had the respect of the province's teachers. Hepburn had failed to lure McArthur into the political arena as a Liberal candidate in the 1934 election, but the subsequent offer of the senior civil service position in the department had its appeal. Eventually, McArthur would have a taste of both worlds, for he moved from deputy minister to minister following Simpson's death six years later.[4]

Among the first announcements by the newly formed Department of Education was a promise to review and revise Ontario's course of study.[5]

The curriculum of Ontario's schools did undergo considerable change, most notably in 1937 and 1938. The reforms to the program of study in those years represented a culmination of the progressivists' reform energies and an attempt to institutionalize progressivist practice in schools. The revised curriculum embodied all three of the core progressivist principles, making provisions for individual learners, active learning, and studies of relevance to contemporary society. E.J. Transom from the Central Public School in Timmins, trying to be objective in his assessment of Ontario's curriculum revisions, explained the primary difference between the 'old' and 'new' courses of study as follows: 'The old course stressed, almost exclusively, subject matter to be learned. The new course introduces other factors, like personality development, and socialization or citizenship.'[6] It also brought together many of the concerns raised in progressivist journal articles since 1919, including the study of extant social problems, the fostering of community, enterprise learning, health studies, and opportunities for students to have options regarding their courses of study.[7]

As far back as 1911, reference had been made to the need for Ontario's educational system to broaden the course of study so that it related better to the modern world's various needs.[8] There was a strong focus on the need to differentiate between a program that would provide general learning leading to university matriculation and a program that would prepare students more narrowly for particular domains in society.[9] But not until 1937 did the shift toward a progressivist paradigm fully transform Ontario's program of study.

A strong theme in the revised program was the need to balance a common curriculum with individual choice. Thus, all Ontario students as they entered high school were introduced to a grade nine program featuring certain compulsory subjects: 'English, social studies, health and physical education, business practice and writing, mathematics, general or agricultural science, French, general shop for boys and home economics for girls, and music and art.'[10] English, social studies, and health remained compulsory subjects in grade ten; then in grades eleven and twelve, history replaced social studies as the third compulsory subject. Furthermore, students had to select four of the following optional subjects to supplement their core curriculum: 'mathematics, science or agriculture, shop or home economics, and music and art or music or art.'[11] There were slight variations in the optional courses available to students in the industrial, home economics, commercial, and art courses.

W.G. Fleming argues that with respect to program revisions for elementary schools, the *Programme of Studies for Grades I to VI of the Public and Separate Schools, 1937* 'was an event of considerable importance of the evolution of curriculum in elementary schools in Ontario because of the progressive outlook defined in the introduction and embodied in the recommendations.'[12] The Ontario program had been developed by a committee of educators led by Thornton Mustard and S.A. Watson and had been heavily influenced by the Deputy Minister of Education, Duncan McArthur.

In 1936, McArthur had selected Mustard, of Toronto Normal School, and Watson, from Keele Street Public School, to lead the committee charged with reforming the province's curriculum. These two educationists 'were pragmatists, convinced by the realities of the depression that a different approach to class-room learning was necessary to prepare students for an uncertain future.'[13] In light of the dramatic effects wrought by modernity, faith in a stable, predictable future had been shaken.[14] Their report and the ensuing revised program drew many ideas and phrasings from reports of the Consultative Committee of the Board of Education in Great Britain, which dealt with the topics of adolescence, primary schooling, and nursery schools.[15]

The Ontario program dealt with many similar interests, but not exclusively so. Health, a relatively new domain for education stressed in the revised curriculum, involved the maintenance of healthy environments in schools and the provision of experiences that could produce lifelong healthy habits. The instructional aspects of health education were framed in terms consistent with this book's definition of progressive rhetoric as described most consistently by child study progressivist articles. In other words, the instructional aspects should relate to social life and activity as experienced outside the school.

So important was health promotion that the Department of Education issued a handbook for teachers in 1938 to facilitate its implementation in the schools.[16] The teaching aid, titled *Health: A Handbook of Suggestions for Teachers in Public and Separate Schools*, was prepared by members of a Joint Committee on the Teaching of Health, appointed from the province's Departments of Education and Health.[17] Its chapters addressed a variety of topics, including the 'Need and Meaning of Health Education,' 'Health Instruction in the Grades,' 'The Human Body: Scientific and Technical Information for the Teacher,' and 'Communicable Diseases.'[18] This handbook also included a glossary that related the daily school program to health instruction.[19] The definition of *homework* offered in the handbook is notable, for it struck all the chords of progressivist rhetoric:

The child needs to play out-of-doors. For his [sic] growth he requires an adequate amount of sleep. Homework which curtails the child's time for recreation and sleep is open to serious question. There are types of homework which have important values in linking up the activities of the school with the child's home and community life. These types give the child an opportunity for outdoor and creative activities and may lead him to explore his own latent abilities. Such homework becomes a contribution to his physical, mental, and social health.[20]

Here, the three domains of progressivist thinking (see chapters 3 to 5 of this book) were clearly interrelated and demonstrated as applicable to educational studies. The individual child's interests and development, his or her active participation in learning tasks, and the linking of school to society were being brought together under the canopy of health.

This handbook did not veil its progressivist rhetoric: 'More and more does the progressive teacher appreciate the importance of the physical, mental, emotional, and social capabilities and limitations of the individual pupils under his [sic] care.'[21] The progressivist themes were projected as offering a viable pedagogical alternative to the traditional curriculum, which was depicted as inflexible, narrow, and overly academic.[22] This alternative sought to actively engage Ontario's teachers in ongoing experimentation with and definition of progressivist schooling, while building a community of educators who would be stakeholders in the province's educational future.[23]

McArthur described health education as a powerful way to approach education holistically. He took into account various aspects of students' development, and he linked children's school lives to their home lives.[24] He described the revised curriculum initiated during his tenure at the Department of Education as

essentially an educational program involving the training of both body and mind. It will endeavour to improve the health of our youth by providing greater facilities for games and out-of-doors recreation. We will endeavour to bridge the gap between school and home even should that involve a drastic revision of our traditional views regarding the function of the school. Whatever affects the physical and mental well-being of the children is properly the concern of the educator. The interest of the school in the boy [sic] must not be confined to what happens in the classroom between 9 a.m. and 4 p.m.[25]

With the introduction of health study into the *Programme of Stud-*

ies, McArthur found a means of knitting together all three domains of progressivist concern. Health involved activity and active learning; it concerned the individual development of students; and it related studies to life outside school. Healthy habits, for instance, were described as the results of *doing,* not 'reading and talking. Instruction in Health, therefore, should be active rather than formal in its nature, and should be linked as closely as possible to the child's daily experience.'[26] Health, the document argued, 'should not be regarded simply as a "subject" of the curriculum but as a programme pervading the whole life of the school and the whole life of each pupil.'[27]

With respect to individual subjects, English represented the core of the curriculum. It was seen as occupying 'first place among the intellectual exercises of the elementary school. It is of prime importance that children learn to speak and write their mother tongue clearly, accurately, and gracefully.'[28] Emphasis was placed on clarity of expression and mastery of reading and writing, both oral and written. Supplemental reading was described as 'the most important phase of the English course ... [because] the child who has learned to love reading is not only likely to continue his [sic] education all through life, but is prepared profitably to enjoy his leisure.'[29] A child who developed a love for reading and who mastered the required skill set was capable of self-directed, lifelong learning. Libraries were positioned as important sources of this supplementary reading. A list of suggested topics and resources for each grade was provided in the program; it included domains of English instruction such as conversation, reading, verse speaking, verse making, storytelling, dramatization, letter writing, word study, sentence study, and writing.

Social studies was the most meliorist progressivist element of the 1937 curriculum revisions in Ontario. This new subject was specifically designed to link school learning more closely to provincial society.[30] It strove to engage students in active examinations of the world as it presently was and could be, not with its past or its heritage. McArthur himself noted that as soon as he entered the Department of Education, it was apparent to him that 'both elementary and secondary school courses were out of harmony with the times, and accordingly [he] sought a remedy.'[31] The expressed aim of the social studies course was 'to help the child to understand the nature and workings of the social world in which he [sic] lives ... The course aims, also, to develop in the pupils desirable social attitudes.'[32] The subject matter would be drawn from contemporary problems and issues in the world, which would then be contextualized in light of geographical and historical study. The progressive concern for active learning was not neglected; it was 'expected that much of the course will be carried out through co-operative activities of various kinds.'[33] Active learning – a means of developing the right attitudes of mind – should be encouraged. Teachers should 'guard against *merely talking* about the duties of boys and girls, but must provide, instead, daily co-operative activities through which the practice of mutual helpfulness will grow.'[34]

The revised description for the natural science course reinforced this theme that the new style of education should emphasize the cultivation of habits of mind more than the absorption of facts or figures. The sciences were important because they could foster in students 'a genuinely scientific spirit,' wherein a community of scholarship would thrive.[35] To engage students, as a community of learners, in active scientific inquiry would be to cultivate an orientation to learning that future citizens would require in a progressive, evolving world. The purpose of the course would be to provide experiences for children so that they might learn 'to observe carefully and dispassionately, to formulate one's observations in words or in other ways, and to make proper inferences from what has been observed.'[36] Experiential interactions 'with real things' in the scientific realm, such as field excursions and experiments, were more preferable means of achieving these aims than 'lessons at set periods' in a day.[37]

An emphatic concern for relating school studies to actual life beyond the confines of classrooms permeated the program. There was a persistent emphasis on active learning that would be somehow self-directed or that would factor in the individual child's interests. Mathematics education, for example, would involve helping the child see the 'value of numbers in the ordinary affairs of life, to provide him [*sic*] with training in the use of numbers for his own practical purposes, and to form the foundation upon which his subsequent mathematical knowledge will be built.'[38] Art and music, while portrayed as useful media for the active and creative expression of instinctive urges in children, were also means of correlating all other subjects and of permitting individuals to construct and 'express more and more successfully *their own ideas*.'[39]

Uniting the revised curriculum document with McArthur's broad vision for progressivist reform of schools was a desire to transform a course of studies that up until then had seemed overly concerned with inculcating academic knowledge. Such knowledge was viewed as bearing little or no relevance to contemporary life, social activity, or democratic citizenship. This is why the revised course of study refused to authorize a standardized textbook or reader for each subject and discouraged the use of examinations as the sole measures of progress.[40] McArthur, shortly after his appointment within the department, had advised Ontario's educationists in 1934 that 'the relaxation of the examination system may prove to be of definite encouragement to teachers to promote reading beyond the limits of prescribed texts.'[41] Indeed, by 1940 only the departmental examinations for high school entrance remained.[42] Textbook learning, he continued, was narrow, and furthermore, its mandate compelled teachers to push through textbooks at the peril of ignoring broader student interests, activities, and explorations:

> The system of authorizing special text-books for courses of study has likewise led to the encouragement of the formation of habits of mind which cannot be regarded as otherwise than undesirable. The authorizing of a particular book as a text gives to the printed word within the book a literal inspiration. It becomes easy for the student to assume that all of the truth relating to a subject is contained within the covers of the book.[43]

In addition to that, the facts and figures contained in textbooks, once 'committed to memory are soon forgotten. The information temporarily acquired is seldom related to the structure of knowledge or experience possessed by the pupil.'[44] Standardized departmental examinations were as ill-suited to progressivist thinking as was the authorization of any single textbook for a subject, because both reinforced a passive, acquisitive model of learning.[45] Consequently, McArthur explained, 'the relaxation of the examination system may prove to be of definite encouragement to teachers to promote reading beyond the limits of prescribed texts.'[46]

Besides liberating students from prescribed texts and rote learning, the new model aimed at liberating the teacher. In seeking to dethrone an academic curriculum taught through authorized textbooks and tested via provincial examinations, McArthur was staking his progressivist vision on the teachers of Ontario who would necessarily be enacting his principles. As reported in a 1941 supplement in *The School*, reporting on the new curriculum in Ontario, 'the successful operation of any plan of education depends upon the teacher. The full benefits of the new curriculum can be realized only if the teacher understands the objectives and is able to secure results.'[47] If the traditional academic curriculum depended on standardized texts and assessments, the progressivist program of study would succeed only if teachers and principals were permitted freedom to make activities relevant, interesting, and interactive.[48] There is a cliché regarding a French inspector of schools who boasted that on any given day he could know what page of the textbook every child in the country was reading. It was against such highly standardized visions of schooling that the 1937 and 1938 programs were positioned.[49]

It is because the notion of standardization, at its very core, conflicted with the progressivists' emphasis on individualized instruction and the freedom to choose a personally meaningful course of study that the curriculum revisions provided ample opportunity for electives. McArthur contended that beyond the common grade nine program, there should be 'a wide range of studies available for the various qualities of minds in the boys and girls.'[50] It is in this context that the Department of Education's loosening of language requirements and the demise of Latin and Greek as compulsory subjects can best be understood.[51] McArthur told J.F. McDonald, in response to the University College professor's argument that the loss of Latin would make Ontario a weak and effeminate culture, that 'the psychology that it doesn't matter what you teach a boy [sic] so long as it's unpleasant is antiquated.'[52] McArthur, with his progressivist sensibilities, held that compulsion in learning was neither useful nor desirable.[53]

Beyond its implications for Ontario's curriculum reforms, this exchange between McDonald and McArthur indicated clearly the extent to which the periodicals were willing to go to isolate pedagogical statements from political controversy and rhetorical debates. First, neither *The School* nor *The Canadian School Journal* published articles directly critical of McArthur's progressivist reforms. Second, McArthur's debate with McDonald was not reported at all in the journals – only in the newspapers that covered the OEA conference that year, the *Globe* and the *Toronto Daily Star*. *The School* provided no account of the conference. *The Canadian School Journal*, the official organ of the association, offered a terse but positive summary of McArthur's thesis that 'the greatest service the teaching profession could render to humanity would be to make French and Latin optional instead of compulsory subjects.'[54] There is no mention of McDonald or of any critical response to McArthur's address. The summary does remind the reader that 'Dr. McArthur said that the universities in this province are more rigid in their requirements than Oxford, Cambridge or Aberdeen.'[55]

In general, Patrice Milewski's assessment that 'the *Programme* can be understood as signifying a fundamental transformation that broke with previously existing pedagogies' is generally correct.[56] Milewski identifies the 1937 curriculum as 'a rupture in educational *discourse*.'[57] In his view, 'it conditioned or defined what could be said about teaching, learning, children and schooling for the greater part of the twentieth century.'[58] In Robert Stamp's assessment, both 'culturally and politically, the revised program of 1937 implied a partial rejection of absolute values passed on to former generations of pupils.'[59] The new *Programme* emphasized preparation for the present and the future more than it did transmission of past triumphs, heritage, and tales.

The extent to which progressive discourse and rhetoric actually affected classroom practice is debatable; so are, even, educationists' conceptions of which direction progress should pursue. But a rupture in official discourse, however dramatic or bold, did not necessarily correlate with a rupture in the modes and methods of instruction. W.G. Fleming touches on this point directly:

> The *Programme of Studies for Grades I to VI of the Public and Separate Schools, 1937* demonstrates a highly progressive orientation and might have set the schools of Ontario on an entirely new path had certain circumstances been more propitious. The main reason why the point of view expressed in the document was 'ahead of its time' was that the short period of preparation for elementary teachers ... made it impossible to induce them to abandon the patterns by which they themselves had been taught.[60]

Fleming is right: progressive rhetoric takes on a very different character within the confines of a school or a particular classroom. If, however, as is the case here, the language of progressive schooling is of primary interest, the 1937 and 1938 curriculum documents represented significant ruptures in the discourse of systematized and departmentally sanctioned visions of progress.

Throughout this book, progressivist concerns have been described from the perspectives of different orientations. At this juncture, it is fitting to ask how Ontario's curriculum revisions in the late 1930s and early 1940s can be assessed in light of the different progressivist orientations described throughout this study. In other words, to what extent did the revised *Programmes of Study* reflect the distinct concerns about educational reform that were evident in the source journals?

First, to review, progressivist articles concerned with child study revealed a concern for developmental psychology. From this orientation, progressive educational reforms posited the individual learner as the focal point of pedagogy. Throughout life, human beings passed through stages of development, each of which was qualitatively distinct. Educational activity was described as providing learning experiences appropriate to a particular stage of development. Such experiences would lead the student gradually to the next stage of development and growth.

The developmental model resembled the common vision of evolution, wherein a species adjusts to its environment and becomes increasingly complex. As such, child study as an orientation was steeped in the biological sciences and concerned with the promotion of health. In fact, many of its most vocal advocates, including William Blatz of the Institute of Child Study, had begun their careers as medical doctors. The application of medical principles, such as resiliency, security, and hygiene, was common. The child, a natural organism like a flower, passed through particular phases and needed a healthy environment and nurturing in order to adjust to each stage and thereby flourish.

By contrast, progressivist texts revealing concern for social efficiency promoted educational reforms that approached individual students as cogs in an industrial and social machine. Education was more akin to management of industry than to nurturing or cultivating a garden. The aim of pedagogy was to assess, as precisely as possible, the abilities and inclinations of students in order to prepare them for vocational paths. Educational aims were not to be left to chance. The more specifically they could be identified, the more efficiently they could be realized.

Advocacy for standardized testing and intelligence measures, as well as for vocational guidance programs, the surveying of professions, and auxiliary education programs, was very closely associated with social efficiency progressivists. Education needed to be specific in order to train future citizens for their future careers. A progressive education was one that would prepare students as efficiently as possible for life in the complex modern world.

Progressivist texts revealing the social meliorist position depicted the preparation of students for the modern world in a very different way. The social meliorist position hinged on the unpredictability and mutability of social life. Wars, financial crises, and industrialization had wrought tremendous and widespread changes to Ontario and to the entire world. Furthermore, unrestrained individualism, in education as in economics, led to social injustices as well as to a prevailing ethos of competition.

From the meliorist orientation, for Ontario's schools to be progressive they would need to combat the spirit of competitiveness by promoting active citizenship and social cooperation. Schools could play a vital role by inculcating in the province's future citizens the skills and habits of mind necessary for them to join together and deal with society's problems. Individual citizens were depicted as inextricably tied to their communities. Educational activity needed to promote a critical spirit and mind; this in turn would enable students to face a world consumed by change.

The differences among these three progressivist orientations have been discussed throughout this book; so have the domains of common concern. The various progressivist texts differed in their handling of the three dominant and overarching themes: activity, individuality, and the relationship between education and society. In other words, each offered a different perspective on what progressive education meant, but all were progressivist in that their reform rhetoric addressed the same themes. As an example, let us consider the individual's relationship to Ontario's social order.

As mentioned in previous chapters, efficiency progressivists concerned themselves mainly with the maintenance and management of the existing economic and social order. Progressivist reforms would help that order run more smoothly and efficiently. Schools could be managed and operated as industries were run. Ultimately, they would need to follow industrial models so that school studies could be related as closely as possible to the province's vocational realities. Students' aptitudes and interests could be gauged, businesses could be surveyed, training programs could be implemented, and guidance programs could help individuals find their vocational niches.

The meliorist position was most frequently (at the very least implicitly) critical of business, rampant individualism, and laissez-faire capitalism. The social order was, from this progressivist orientation, not only changeable but also in need of change. Greater social cooperation was necessary so that future citizens, the students in Ontario's schools, would be able to deal adequately with social problems. A healthy democracy required active citizens who would challenge the established social order and think critically about it. The good of any one person was indivisible from the good of all.

Similarly, child study progressivists depicted cooperation and social activity as vital in education, but for different reasons. Development and adjustment to different stages throughout life was characterized as a necessarily social process. Individuals had freedoms, and they needed to exercise those freedoms in order to retain a distinct sense of self throughout life; but at the same time, all actions had social consequences. Social adjustment was not the same as social conformity, and the latter was unacceptable because it imposed a pattern of living and thinking that limited the individual's activity and creativity.

A review of the various progressivist positions described in this book reveals how difficult a task the Department of Education faced in terms of bringing those positions together with any coherency. As mentioned earlier, the introduction of health studies was one way of emphasizing the common concerns of Ontario's progressivists. V.K. Greer's appraisal of the new *Programme of Studies* made it clear that the department was casting its net broadly in order to appeal to *all* progressivists:

> Those successful teachers who had found the former courses somewhat rigid now enjoy the freedom which they may use in the choice of subject matter ... The parents are also keenly interested, and very largely because they have noted the increased interest on the part of the children. A prominent University professor states that the psychology of the course is thoroughly sound and quite abreast of the present-day opinions of leading psychologists. The man on the street comments that his child is reading more and enjoying the activities and projects of the classroom. On the whole, there can be no doubt that a child-centred programme is a better programme than a subject-centred one.[61]

The Department of Education believed that centring the new course of studies on individual students as opposed to academic content would give Ontario's educational stakeholders an agreeable foundation for reform. At the conclusion of his long appraisal, Greer stated confidently: 'There need be no turning back. All are agreed that we are now making progress under this new programme.'[62] If Greer's assessment of the situation was accurate, what did the curriculum revisions offer in order to attract the support of progressivists of fundamentally different orientations?

Health, which reached out to all progressivists, would have had particular appeal to child study concerns. Indeed, the core themes in the revised *Programme of Studies* appear to have been influenced largely by developmentalist concerns. In the program's discussion of 'The Child's Need for Success,' for instance, Blatz seems to have written the following statement on the topic of security:

The development of the individual takes place largely through social participation. Indeed, many capacities of the individual are brought out only under the stimulus of associating with others. But in order that development may be continuous, the efforts of the individual must be attended by success. It is true that 'we learn from our mistakes,' but it is equally true that continued and prolonged failure stops growth altogether.[63]

An introductory section titled 'Fostering Individual Talent' was similarly imbued with child study rhetoric: 'This Programme of Studies accordingly attempts to provide for differences in the abilities, tastes, and interests of individual pupils; and requires that the teacher be alert to detect and foster the growth of individual talent.'[64]

Health studies were intended to be woven through all aspects of the school; similarly, the ethos of developmental psychology permeated the entire document. It suggested, for example, that mathematics be taught in a way that respected the learner's stages of development and understanding.[65] Furthermore, promotion from one grade to another would be based on the student's age and not solely on annual external examinations.[66] The notion that school activities needed to be centred on the learner's interests in order to engage him or her in studies that were meaningful and motivating was woven throughout the same document.[67]

The social efficiency progressivist rhetoric also wove in and out of the document at various points. Sometimes it was wedded to a child study theme in a way that seemed to show the two orientations as perfectly compatible: 'Learning takes place most efficiently when the interest of the learner is aroused.'[68] Such instances begged the question as to whether a teacher should aim to arouse the learner's interest in order to make education more meaningful for the student or more efficient for the teacher. Clearly, the *Programme of Studies* was seeking to establish common progressivist ground; in this case, the engaged student was less likely to provoke disturbance and more inclined to work fastidiously on a task. Similarly, the provision of greater options and elective courses following the common grade nine program seemed favourable to both child study and efficiency progressivists. For the former, elective subjects would allow for greater experimentation and individual choice in school; for the latter, freedom to select courses would permit the tailoring of educational programs suitable for particular abilities or vocational channels.

In other sections of the *Programme of Studies* the school's role was depicted as 'assist[ing] the pupil to master those skills that are essential to human intercourse in a modern society.'[69] These skills included those involving 'the conversion of materials to serve human purposes,' such as agriculture, home economics, manual training, and crafts.[70] The descriptions of these subjects in the *Programme of Studies*, however, did not go nearly as far in their espousal of efficiency rhetoric as the mildest of such articles in the source journals. The value of the course in crafts, for example, is stated in very Deweyan language:

> The value for older children of some training in the traditional crafts is now generally recognized. In doing and making, students not only develop manual skill, but the ability to think their way through the difficulties presented by materials and processes. Handwork has value also in helping children to realize the importance of accuracy, for mistakes in the concrete are easily recognized and can seldom be erased or wholly corrected. Moreover, it cannot be too strongly emphasized that the brighter children require manual activity of this type as much as those of lower mental capacity.[71]

Manual and craft work was thus presented as helping students develop useful skills and habits independently of any vocational pursuit. Furthermore, manual training was not to be treated as a subject toward which students would be streamed if their academic work was insufficient. The message promoted greater inclusivity, not classification.

Home economics was a very notable exception. The program stated clearly that the subject

> possesses a definite educational value, not unlike that of craftwork for boys, but more important in its practical bearing. Chief among these educational values is the development of a girl's natural interest in her home, together with the cultivation of desirable attitudes towards the privileges, duties, and responsibilities of life in the home. Scarcely less important, educationally, is the opportunity afforded by the work in Home Economics to train the girls in proper habits relative to their personal appearance, the care of their belongings, and the conservation of their health.[72]

In terms of the efficient management, maintenance, and preservation of social order, nothing in the *Programme of Studies* made a statement as transparently social efficiency progressivist as this: 'The practical value of skill in the various activities of the home must be apparent to all. Regardless of their station in life, practically all girls will share, sooner or later, in the management of a home.'[73] Judging from the descriptions of courses offered in the curriculum alone, one might surmise that only Ontario's girls required particularized training for their predestined domestic role in society.[74] On the whole, however, the *Programme of Studies* did not go as far in its espousal of efficiency rhetoric as it did with the language of child study and meliorism.

The social meliorist emphasis was emphatically clear in a number of instances, most notably in relation to social studies. 'The aim of the whole course in Social Studies is to help the student to understand the social world in which he [*sic*] lives,' declared the provincial curriculum document.[75] The meliorist concern for studying current events in the contemporary context was encapsulated in this new subject, which offered an opportunity to relate historical, geographical, and social studies to problems in students' lives outside of school.[76] Discussion was identified as a useful tool for the teaching of social studies, a tool by which students could develop critical habits of mind: 'Children will acquire in a very meaningful way a great deal of geographical and historical material, and what is more important, learn to think geographically and historically and to watch for further items of information confirming or refuting the views expressed in class.'[77] While espousing such meliorist ideas, the *Programme of Studies* weighed in far more cautiously than many of the discussions in the source journals did.

Teachers were advised to confine the discussion of current events to matters of fact rather than opinion: 'Little good and much harm can come from airing *opinions* upon international, political, or religious problems – opinions probably founded on inadequate information.'[78] The note of caution can be interpreted as suggesting that teachers lead their students to make claims based on warrants and evidence, which would stimulate research. It can also be seen as a way of limiting potential controversy associated with this new subject arising from overly provocative discussions or critical attitudes expressed in school. Ultimately, the *Programme of Studies* was firm in its assertion that the principle of cooperation and the ideal of democratic citizenship were foundations for future social growth and activity. The 1942 edition of the document, published in the midst of the Second World War, asserted that 'the world has become an interdependent social and economic unit, and the future advancement of civilization, following the settlement of our present troubles, will be dependent upon the establishment of ideals of co-operation rather than those of rivalry.'[79]

Social studies, of course, came at the expense of history and geography, which were no longer treated as separate subjects in Ontario's elementary schools. The province's humanists would have, at the very least, found the centrality of English in the *Programme of Studies* valuable. The first aim for English study identified in the document was the cultivation of 'a genuine and abiding love of good reading,' which implied that literature would persist in schools.[80] In fact, every classroom was seen as requiring 'a small, well-chosen, attractive library [that would help] to cultivate properly the love of reading and to form the habit of finding in books information and enjoyment.'[81] The second aim, 'to develop in the students the power to express themselves correctly and effectively in oral and written language,' suggested that the formal study of grammar and usage should remain in the school program.[82]

V.K. Greer's assessment of the new curriculum stated clearly that a progressive program did not imply unfettered activity catering entirely to children's 'whimsical desires' and 'changing interests.'[83] In fact, Greer seemed to acquiesce to humanists' critiques of progressivist reforms, stating that Ontario's schools would maintain their academic rigour:

> It will be wrong to interpret the new course as inviting the teacher to do away with all distasteful tasks. It will also be wrong if the acquiring of factual knowledge is belittled. It will be dangerous also if too much emphasis is placed upon play and upon activities which have very little or no worth-while purpose. The inexperienced teacher may easily mistake physical bustle for mental activity, with the result that much energy may be spent and little progress made. Drill, review, and examinations will still be needed, and it will continue to be very important that the child's factual knowledge at the end of any period will be at least equal to, if not greater than formerly.[84]

Citing Charles W. Eliot, President of Harvard University, Greer stated that the pupil should 'use his own language with exactness, freedom, and charm.'[85] For the time being, English, a broad term 'made to include English literature, English grammar, English composition, supplementary reading, spelling, and writing,' remained useful in Ontario's *Programme of Study*.[86]

As the 1940s and the Second World War neared, certain minor revisions to the 1937 and 1938 curriculum documents were undertaken. In W.G. Fleming's assessment, the 'general nature of the recommended approach remained essentially the same. The introduction was rewritten in 1941 with much greater stress on the objective of preparing children to live in a democratic society.'[87] Indeed, 'Education for Social Living' was the first theme treated in the 1942 publication by the Department of Education.[88] 'Co-operation in a democratic group' was depicted as the highest social value, and this required that students practice 'self-control, intelligent self-direction, and the ability to accept responsibility.'[89] Ontario's schools, the introduction argued, needed to facilitate opportunities for students to work together in order to plan, execute, and complete worthwhile and common learning tasks.

So vital were these cooperative activities to the vitality of democratic education that a lengthy, nine-page description of 'Enterprises' was included in the document immediately following the introduction.[90] The 1937 curriculum had stressed individualized learning and self-direction; in the 1941 version, in light of the war experience, the individual learner was depicted as having to learn and practise cooperative and democratic habits of mind.[91] Fleming has argued that in the late 1930s and early 1940s, the emphasis on democratic citizenship also affected themes and topics in Ontario's textbooks and educational resources.[92]

Modifications made to the province's curriculum documents when they were reprinted in the early 1940s reflected the dominant theme running through *The School* and *The Canadian School Journal* between 1940 and 1942. During those years, the editorial articles in the two journals repeatedly emphasized the need to foster democratic habits of living in Ontario's schools in order to counter the forces of Nazism and fascism.[93] Duncan McArthur, as befit the Minister of Education, demonstrated his commitment to the idea of democratic education in a flurry of speeches and publications between 1941 and 1942.[94]

On 7 December 1941, for example, McArthur published an article in *Saturday Night* titled 'Education for Democracy' that *The Canadian School Journal* found compelling enough to discuss at length for trustees and ratepayers throughout Ontario.[95] In that article, McArthur stated that the purpose of education was to create good citizens. There were no self-contained individuals, he argued; all individuals were social beings with responsibilities to the school, town, municipality, province, Dominion, and Empire. Ontario's schools had to prepare the province's youth to 'undertake the responsibilities of citizenship, fortified by habits of mind which accustomed them to the recognition of the rights of others and to their obligations to the community.'[96] The war would eventually end, McArthur stated, and when it did, society would require citizens who had courage, endurance, and understanding and who were capable of building a new and forward-looking world.

In his Christmas message to Ontario's trustees and ratepayers, the Minister of Education reminded readers of *The Canadian School Journal* that the strains generated by world war had imposed extra responsibilities on the province's schools.[97] Because many fathers were engaged in military service and many mothers were occupied in war industries, 'the home has too frequently become one of the first of our war casualties.'[98] Teachers, in particular, were bearing a greater burden in providing anchorage for boys and girls in the province, through curricular and extracurricular supervision. Education had come to represent for McArthur a great model of public service and citizenship committed to the preservation of democracy.

'In no other war or national crisis,' read an editorial in *The Canadian School Journal*, 'has the school occupied such an important place as at the present time.'[99] Ivan Schultz, Minister of Education for Manitoba, echoed this sentiment when classifying 'teaching as a war profession.'[100] The first duty of teachers, he argued, was to the schools and the children. Schultz implored educators across the country to remain in the classrooms, where they could be of best service to the community and to the youth of society.

The Canadian Broadcasting Corporation (CBC), whose radio broadcasts reached homes across the province, was increasingly regarded as having 'direct responsibilities, educational and cultural' with regard to the fostering of democratic citizenship.[101] 'The citizen's task,' intoned the CBC's Gladstone Murray, 'might be described as learning how to play his or her individual part – through self-sacrifice, discipline and initiative – in adaptation to new conditions.'[102] Preserving democratic ways of life was the primary responsibility of schools; radio, like education, touched the lives of all Ontario citizens. In times of war, Murray argued, the responsibility of public institutions was to exert a unifying influence on the public's temper and thought, thereby stimulating national consciousness. In times of peace, which would follow, educational organizations would be required to impart information and opinions that enabled citizens to participate in democratic life, 'i.e., reconstructing and reshaping the Post War [*sic*] world.'[103]

It is, perhaps, these last two points that best describe the responsibilities that Ontario's periodicals appeared to assume in the context examined by this book. Because oppositional discourses were excluded from, for example, socialist and separate school sources, the range of definitions regarding progressive education was limited. It can even be argued that the progressivist editorials in the journals represented a consensus view of educational reform, in that the net they cast was not broad enough to capture actual debate, tension, or rhetorical cutting and thrusting. Both the journals considered here depended on subscriptions for their survival. Generally speaking, *The School* reached an audience of teachers, teacher educators, and teacher candidates, whereas *The Canadian School Journal* appealed directly to taxpayers and school trustees. The generating of political debates and controversy was not in the interests of either source journal, and – perhaps to a fault – the journals isolated pedagogical matters from any political entanglements.

There certainly were differences between the publications, but these were most evident outside of the editorial articles and reports that concern this study. *The School*, for instance, included sections on model lessons, assessments, and templates that could be of immediate practical use to educators. The journal reported on matters that were happening in schools and were of interest to those who worked in schools. *The Canadian School Journal* reported on meetings of trustees, school councils, and school boards. The journal brought to the attention of its readership events related to taxation, policy, jurisdiction, and funding. This journal, in particular, focused its editorial content during the early 1940s on themes related to democracy and citizenship. This emphasis reflected the journal's base in the OEA, which, in the early years of the Second World War, had emphasized the idea of education for citizenship, with the aim of bringing together Ontario's educationists for that purpose.[104]

This is not to say that *The School* neglected the war effort and its implications for Canadian students. The journal's angle on events was one that typically addressed classroom practice. In 1940, for example, under the editorial management of Charles Phillips, *The School* began publishing a monthly diary that teachers could use to help their pupils 'follow the course of momentous events in Europe.'[105] The diary recounted significant events happening in Europe during the war, and suggested that students mark these happenings on an outline map, follow the reports in local newspapers, and write a monthly essay recounting the 'Achievements of the Month.'[106]

Two months later, a lengthy article by H.E. Smith from the University of Alberta reminded Ontario's teachers that the basis of the educational philosophy 'caught up in the phrase "progressive education"' could be summed up in 'an abiding belief in the superiority of the democratic way of life over any other known way of life.'[107] Living democratically, he explained, entailed an emphasis on 'the desire to co-operate rather than to compete, tolerance of the rights of others rather than selfishness, critical-mindedness rather than suggestibility, and concern with present conditions of living rather than with the life of the past.'[108] For the most part, progressivist rhetoric in the early 1940s asserted democratic attitudes and dispositions in educational contexts. In this meliorist progressivist vision, active and critical citizens were the greatest hope for democracy.[109]

Both journals, though they edited out certain controversial or oppositional discourses, were forums where the moulding of Ontario's educational future could be explored. Particularly with regard to citizenship education and training, progressivists depicted this future as broadening the vision of education to include more than book learning and academic knowledge. Schools were means of bringing Ontario's youth into contact with the realities and problems of life outside the classroom. Faced with global conflict and world war, progressivist articles generally described the school's role as promoting national unity, greater interest in public affairs, and a readiness to subordinate individual welfare to the common good.[110]

The Co-operative Commonwealth Federation (CCF) was a socialist party that had emerged from the Depression years as a national political force. In Ontario, partly in response to 'Hepburn's anti-Labour policies during the 1930s and the substantial growth in labour organizations and collective bargaining during the war years,' many of Ontario's educationists rallied behind the CCF.[111] Robert Stamp writes that a 'mixture of status consciousness and utopian idealism … prompted some Ontario teachers to flirt with the C.C.F. and other left-wing political groups in the early 1940s.'[112] This perhaps explains why the Canadian Association for Adult Education put forward a 1943 document advocating greater social responsibility and social planning, and why the National Council for Canadian–Soviet Friendship gathered 15,000 people in Toronto's Maple Leaf Gardens that same year to call for teacher exchanges between Russian and Canadian institutions. In the 1943 election, Ontario's Liberal government was ousted by Colonel George Drew's Progressive Conservatives, who secured a minority government by gaining a mere four more provincial seats than the CCF.[113]

The Second World War shifted progressivist rhetoric toward meliorist espousals of democratic citizenship; however, that war would last longer than the almost singularly meliorist visions for progressive education. In Robert Stamp's assessment, 'while a few educational leaders would keep the progressivist spirit alive throughout the war years, its viability as an educational philosophy was now under consistent attack. Education for peace had been shelved in favour of military preparedness.'[114] The League of Nations, which had been held up as the model of educational cooperation and democratic citizenship, had proven toothless when confronted by Nazi and fascist threats.[115] In 1945, with the war in Europe clearly won, Drew lost a vote in the Ontario legislature and called a new provincial election.

Emphasizing the word *progressive* in his party's name, Drew equated the CCF with fascist Germany's National Socialism and represented the impending election as one between the warring forces of fascism and freedom.[116] This time, the Conservatives did secure a majority government, with the CCF slipping to eight seats. As W.G. Fleming suggests, the 1937 *Programme of Studies* would have borne very different fruit had certain events transpired differently; this is abundantly clear in light of the politics of postwar Ontario. Less than four months before the sudden death of Duncan McArthur, Drew made it clear that he had assessed progressivist ideas and found them wanting: 'Teaching democracy was important, but there's been a little too much carrying the ideas of democracy to the point that children have as much right to express opinions as the teachers.'[117]

The *Toronto Daily Star*, with an ominous tone, predicted the end of progressivist thinking in the Department of Education: 'What the Colonel has overlooked is the fact that the only way to learn democracy is to practise it. And the best way the teachers can put their lesson across is by fostering and encouraging self-confidence, initiative, and independent thinking among children. Col. Drew would have the youth strapped into obedience.'[118] Drew, like his Conservative predecessors George S. Henry and Howard Ferguson, would maintain the Education portfolio and would steer the department in a different direction than his Liberal predecessors, including the progressive-minded Duncan McArthur.

Robert Gidney, whose historical account of Ontario's school system *From Hope to Harris* begins where this study ends, at the Second World

War, described the province in 1945 as 'just beginning to emerge from fifteen years of wrenching dislocation and haunting insecurity.'[119] The war had stimulated the economy and instilled a sense of common purpose, thus solving some of the serious problems caused by the Depression; but it had also 'bred its own dislocations, of people and resources, and the dominant mood of the immediate post-war years was a deep yearning for normality, security, and stability.'[120] Gidney's general observations regarding Ontario's population in the latter part of the 1930s and the early 1940s have some relevance with regard to progressivist rhetoric in the province's journals.

Canada's active involvement in the Second World War began in 1939; and by 1940, the sense of common purpose just referenced had taken shape as a common interest in democratic education. Though they had different interpretations of what progress in schooling might entail, the discursive communities brought together by the journals agreed that democratic schools providing opportunities for active learning and citizenship training were vital to the nation. Stamp notes that 'teachers' magazines and teachers' meetings were preoccupied with the question of how best to teach citizenship and democracy.'[121]

Perhaps, beyond the war effort, this coalescence can be attributed to efforts by the province's Department of Education, which, under McArthur's influence, had brought together various progressivist themes in the revised *Programmes of Studies*. The curricula introduced in 1937 and 1938 were attempts to weave together distinct visions for progressive schools in the province and to derive some order and consistency from them. The revised course of studies rejected a strictly academic model of learning based on the memorization of textbook facts and figures. In so doing, it aligned itself with the domains of progressive education treated in this book: active learning, individualized instruction, and links to contemporary society.

Prominent in the revised curriculum, and woven into all other subjects, was the new domain of health study. Social studies, a new course at the time, was likewise intended to bring together various subject matters. Social studies, history, geography, and civics could be interrelated thematically for the purpose of addressing contemporary social questions. Enterprise tasks and project-based learning were depicted as useful ways to engage students in the active and cooperative study of issues that had actual relevance outside of academic texts.

Students in secondary schools were given a common foundation through a general grade nine program that would allow them to explore various subjects before deciding on a focus. From grade ten onward, they had increasing opportunities to select courses of study that were both useful and relevant to their interests and vocational or academic paths. The loss of Latin as a mandatory subject caused some concern, but it was, McArthur argued, the only way to ensure that the individual learner could 'try himself [*sic*] out along different lines under the guidance and direction of teachers, that he might reach conclusions regarding his particular capabilities and aptitudes.'[122] The varied program enabled Ontario's students to actively engage with 'different lines of approach to education' in order to free them from the bonds of a strictly academic and traditional course of study.[123]

Conclusion: Progressive in a Parallel Way

The most popular new ideas were associated with progressive education, which represented a revolt against existing formal and traditional
schooling. It also meant expansion of the school's purpose and curriculum
through emphasis upon the child's place in the larger society. New pedagogical ideas founded on research and growth in psychology were central
to the changes of the progressives. Within this broad framework, however,
there were many variations and differences in philosophy of practice.*

The principal aim of this study has been to weave consistency and
order out of the various meanings of progressive education articulated
by Ontario's educational communities, whose members encountered
progressivist ideas and used these as a means of revisioning public
education. This aim led me to the discovery of two journals, *The School*
and *The Canadian School Journal*, which were widely distributed and
largely accessible at the time. These monthly journals published editorial and opinion articles that sought to describe and understand what
an educated individual looked like in a seemingly modern, progressive
society. How could public education be reshaped to prepare the next
generation of citizens for the realities of contemporary life, which was
so dramatically different from that of Victorian society and was still
evolving?

In many respects, progressivist thinking was a manifestation of exis-

---

* Robert S. Patterson, 'Society and Education during the Wars and Their Interlude', in
  Canadian Education: A History, ed. J.D. Wilson, T. Stamp, and L.P. Audet (Toronto, ON:
  Prentice Hall of Canada, 1986), 373.

tential angst. Global warfare, mechanization, urbanization, immigration, the effects of the Depression, and a multitude of developments in technology, communication, and transportation had wrought great change on the world, rendering it almost unrecognizable. Contributors to the journals constantly remarked on this change, reflected on its accelerated pace, and wondered about the future. How did Greek and Latin, the classics, and matriculation exams help students cope with change? And how could schools be used as a medium for transforming this yet untold future, for rendering that future more socially just, more efficient, and more respectful of individual strengths and interests?

The three themes of progressivist rhetoric around which educational reformers would cluster reflected these questions. Schools had to free themselves from Victorian pedagogical norms and curricula in order to make way for pedagogical notions that would be of value to the modern age. At the core of progressivist thinking was the promotion of active learning, of individualized instruction, and of education relating to contemporary life. These notions were, of course, variously interpreted. Advocacy for child study and developmental study of learners, for increased social and administrative efficiency, and for social meliorism and reform led to different interpretations of, for instance, how to cater instruction to the individual child. In the name of individualization, notions as conceptually oppositional as the implementation of intelligence tests to understand the intellectual capacities of students and the conviction that human resiliency and need for freedom could permit all learners to pursue particular interests and loves in life were woven into the rhetoric of schooling.

Progressivist ideas were not engaged in warfare; rather, they overlapped and paralleled one another. Curiously, *The School* and *The Canadian School Journal* can be seen as metaphors for the parallel progressivist thinking that pervaded the times. Progressivist ideas were published, sometimes beside one another; but beyond the critiques of traditional schooling, they did not engage critically with one another within the framework of progressive education. The meanings of progressive schooling were thus laden. Consequently, we must consider not only the broad framework of progressive education but also the different orientations to and interpretations of its themes. Within the model defined and used in this study in order to confront the problem of progressive education – in brief, the conceptual confusion regarding what the movement was as well as how to describe the complexity within – the different orientations to progressivist schooling can be discussed under the canopy of broad domains. I hope this book has shed new light on familiar themes, including the potential relationship between the decline of classical studies in Ontario's schools and advocacy for school libraries as citadels of great literature and canonical texts.

The curriculum reforms introduced by Ontario's Department of Education in the late 1930s and early 1940s, which were heralded for their progressivist vision for the province's schools, can be seen as appealing to fundamentally different progressivist orientations for different reasons. This book has identified the progressivist rhetoric during Ontario's interwar years as a meaningful source for descriptions of pedagogical and programmatic responses to social change and modernization – one that reveals and brings together three sets of common concerns in the critique of provincial education. The rhetoric of progressive education – at least with respect to official state discourse on education, and despite internal divisions regarding the reasons for or the aims of educational reform – reveals that there was a common concern for relating schools more closely to contemporary society, for stimulating students' individual interests and abilities, and for encouraging inquiry as well as active learning skills.

This study opens exciting apertures for future historical research. An examination of the distinct progressivist orientations in the rhetoric of educational reform after the Second World War might reveal whether and how child study, social efficiency, and social meliorism persisted as orientations to school reform in the province. The *Living and Learning* report, crafted by the Provincial Committee on Aims and Objectives of Education in the Schools of Ontario and published by the province's Department of Education in 1967, thirty years after the revisions to the program of study, could be interpreted as an attempt to combine and give coherent expression to disparate progressivist tendencies. How did the humanists' critiques of progressive education evolve during the postwar years? Hilda Neatby's *So Little for the Mind* (1953) represented a significant marker in the postwar anti-progressivist (or, *later humanist*) rhetoric. One might examine whether her critiques of progressive education addressed any particular progressivist orientation, or whether they treated more general domains.

To describe what progressivists meant when they demanded an active curriculum, chapter 2 addressed the question from three different orientations. From the perspective of the first progressivist orientation, child study, active learning entailed learning tasks that were developmentally appropriate, that bundled different subjects around unifying themes, that facilitated socialization, and that allowed some degree of self-direction or nonconformity. From the perspective of the second progressivist orientation, social efficiency, active learning involved applying skills and knowledge in particular contexts that would facilitate adjustment to industry or a vocation. From the perspective of the third progressivist orientation, social meliorism, active learning was an educational process that developed a critical attitude toward an unpredictable world with the ultimate aim of fostering active citizenship and engagement with civic problems.

With regard to the second progressivist domain, individualized instruction, chapter 3 first explored the child study orientation. The orientation described a process of holistic child study the intent of which was to understand each learner's needs with regard to freedom, happiness, and well-being, as well as future citizens' adjustments to social contexts. Second, the social efficiency orientation described individualized instruction as a process beginning with the scientific measurement of each learner's mental aptitude with the aim of tailoring the course of study to individual ability. Third, from the social meliorist orientation, individualized instruction entailed preparing children to be self-directed citizens who were responsible to their peers in a democracy.

Chapter 5 considered different orientations toward the role of schools in contemporary society. From the child study orientation, relating schools to society entailed improving child health, in part through medical inspections and improvements to school buildings, and in part through including parent education and participation within the definition of schooling. From the social efficiency orientation, bringing schools and society closer together was depicted largely as a process of relating the courses of school study more closely to industry's demands, as well as helping students make wise vocational choices through guidance programs. From the social meliorist orientation, schools and society were positively related to each other when students learned to take an active role in the creation of a more just, democratic, and cooperative world.

Chapter 5 also discussed how the common ground among progressive educators in Ontario was their disavowal of a humanistic curriculum that trained the mind and developed the spirit. The humanists first defended the belief that a classical curriculum could strengthen students' mental faculties. They then attempted to demonstrate the utility of subjects such as Latin for the study of modern contexts. Humanists also threw their weight behind the development and maintenance of school libraries that would house classic works of literature and that would make these available to children who no longer studied them in school. For the humanists, the interwar years in Ontario were years of decline. In terms of the rhetoric of schooling, those years witnessed, conversely, an efflorescence of progressivist ideas in all their contradictory diversity.

These various currents of progressivist discourse ran parallel courses in the source journals without engaging in an epic struggle for influence over the domain of schooling, as they might have in other media. Representations of progressivist practices entrenched at the Institute of Child Study by child study advocates such as William Blatz could thus be juxtaposed with depictions of intelligence testing and vocational adjustment or social reconstructionist arguments without advocates of these positions necessarily crossing swords. Thus, someone like Duncan McArthur could weave consistency and order out of the various strands of progressivist rhetoric, planning educational reforms that brought together distinct visions for schooling into a unified program of study.

The two primary sources used for this study, *The School* and *The Canadian School Journal*, proved useful resources for mining progressivist rhetoric in the province. In terms of editorial content, both journals explored and published visions for progressive education. Each cast a net wide enough to access and address a broad discursive community, but one might never gather that other oppositional discourses – including those from socialists, secondary school advocates, and many private school representatives – were posing critiques of traditional modes and models of schooling in the province. The journals obscured fundamental conflicts in the province, particularly those that appeared overtly political or controversial. In terms of the non-editorial content, it is evident that the two journals were primarily intended for distinct, albeit parallel, communities of Ontario's educationists. *The School* addressed teachers, teacher candidates, and school administrators. *The Canadian School Journal* addressed trustees, taxpayers, and administrators at the school board level.

Each journal represented the model of an educational journal that no longer exists in Ontario.[1] They focused sharply on pedagogical matters in isolation from political ones, and they avoided overly controversial subjects and sources; that said, both journals published, side by side, a rather disparate group of educationists. In any given issue, progressivist visions written by professors of education ran side by side with those of school inspectors, classroom teachers, administrators, community group representatives, and representatives from the Department of Education.

In Ontario's environment, which had been shaped by two world wars and the severities of the Depression, the forces of modernity altered the culture in dramatic ways. Ontarians saw their world as shifting, progressing, and evolving. Educationists (and others) saw schools variously as instruments for enabling social adaptation, for managing or controlling relationships to the changing order, and for making the world a more just and equitable place. The journals were forums that many educationists read in order to interpret the aims and effects of progress in relation to education.

The notion of public intellectuals might appear foreign today, including among educationists; but it was quite a powerful one in the journals being studied here. Instead of discussing progressivist visions in separate spheres, educationists in schools, school boards, and the Department of Education shared these journals as forums for their ideas. These journals eschewed debate and controversy, perhaps because they were deemed inimical to these forums. As this study has shown, *The School* and *The Canadian School Journal* apparently existed not to foment controversy but rather to explore distinct visions, meanings, and interpretations of progressive education in Ontario.

It is important to consider the enduring quality of progressivist thinking in public education. The accelerated rate of change in technology, communication, and travel, the potential for economic and industrial collapse, and the unfortunate consequences, as well as the inevitability, of war together compelled progressivists to seek means of reforming schools in order to prepare students to cope with contemporary realities. Those same forces confront us today. We are children of the progressives, pedagogically. We strive to incorporate the latest technologies in classrooms and to administer schools and school districts more efficiently; we saddle public education with increasingly burdensome responsibilities; we increasingly seek to make educational studies a science, the beacon of progress and careful study. Schools can remedy all social ills, and students can develop their individual personalities, even as they conform to social norms and find worthwhile jobs that can contribute to the economy and to society.

Perhaps the humanists, who implored educationists to seek the solutions to the present in the past, had a valuable insight that we have yet to recognize in public education. If we try to bring schools into alignment with contemporary society – and this modern age is evolving more and more quickly – we will find that we are chasing our tails. We are, to use a metaphor cited earlier, millipedes, with legs pulling in different directions, ever moving and never arriving. It may be – and I suspect it is so – that the progressives had it, in many ways, wrong in seeking to outright dismantle the traditional curriculum. Humanist critics of progressivist thinking in education – most notably Allan Bloom and Hilda Neatby – were equally wrong to blame the likes of John Dewey for destroying the fabric of schooling in society. Dewey had warned us against pursuing either extreme: 'The fundamental issue is not of new versus old education nor of progressive against traditional education but a question of what anything whatever must be to be worthy of the name *education*.'[2] Perhaps we need to slow down our reformist agendas and define the qualities of an educated individual for our own time.

Appendices

Appendix A. Public School Enrolments in Ontario

Year	Number of students		Number of schools	
	Elementary	Secondary	Elementary	Secondary
1912	429,030	32,608	5,939	148
1917	458,436	33,024	6,103	162
1919	471,729	33,036	6,179	167
1923	519,271	48,263	6,334	183
1927	535,691	59,692	6,426	197
1931	476,892	65,029	6,411	207
1935	565,777	67,395	7,049	212
1940	543,323	73,102	7,120	228
1942	525,441	62,671	7,048	233

Sources: Reports of the Minister of Education to the Government of Ontario.

Appendix B. Composition of the Department of Education

Premier of Ontario	Minister of Education	Deputy Minister of Education	Chief Director of Education
James P. Whitney 1905–14 (Conservative)	Robert A. Pyne 1905–18	Arthur H. Colquhoun 1906–34	John Seath* 1906–19
William H. Hearst 1914–19 (Conservative)	Henry J. Cody 1918–19		
Ernest C. Drury 1919–23 (United Farmers of Ontario)	Robert H. Grant 1919–23		**
G. Howard Ferguson 1923–30 (Conservative)	G. Howard Ferguson 1923–30		Francis W. Merchant 1923–30
George S. Henry 1930–34 (Conservative)	George S. Henry 1930–34		George F. Rogers 1930–34
Mitchell F. Hepburn 1934–42 (Liberal)	Leonard J. Simpson 1934–40	Duncan McArthur 1934–40	Duncan McArthur 1934–43
	Duncan McArthur 1940–43	George F. Rogers 1940–45	
George A. Drew 1943–48 (Progressive Conservative)	George A. Drew 1943–48	John P. Cowles 1945–46	John G. Althouse 1944–56
		Frank S. Rutherford 1946–51	

Sources: Reports of the Minister of Education to the Government of Ontario.

*Until the passing of John Seath, the Chief Director of Education position was titled Superintendent of Education.

**The position of Superintendent/Chief Director did not exist between 1919 and 1923. Other empty spaces in the figure denote vacant positions.

Appendix C. Circulation Statistics for Source Journals

Year	The School	The Canadian School Journal
1919	5,250+	
1920	5,500+	
1921	6,000+	
1922	6,000+	—a
1923	6,750+	—
1924	6,682*	—
1925	7,072*	—b
1926	7,470*	—
1927	7,062*	—
1928	7,631*	6,500+
1929	7,460*	6,500+
1930	7,388*	6,500+
1931	6,970*	6,500+
1932	7,251*	6,500+
1933	6,859*	10,000+
1934	6,554*	10,000+
1935	5,129*	10,000+
1936	5,229*	10,000+
1937	5,510*	5,000+
1938	6,074*	6,000+
1939	5,745*	6,000+
1940	7,713*	5,250+
1941	7,882*	4,500+
1942	8,000+	4,500+

Sources: McKim's Directories of Canadian Publications.

+ Where a number is followed by the (+) symbol, an affidavit of circulation was not furnished, and the circulation rating listed by *McKim's* was provided as accurately as possible. The figure represents a minimum number of readers.

* Where a number is followed by the (*) symbol, the publisher of the journal furnished an affidavit of circulation confirmed by the Audit Bureau of Circulations in order to confirm circulation ratings for advertisers.

a. Before 1922, *McKim's* has no record of the source journal. In 1923, it appears under the title *Ontario School Board Journal*. No circulation rating is available. The record shows that the journal is published in Port Perry, Ontario, at the press of the *Port Perry Star*.

b. In 1925, the journal description in *McKim's* is modified to reflect a new title, *The Canadian School Journal*. The journal's publisher is listed as the OSTRA, based at 1104 Bay Street in Toronto. The printer remained in Port Perry, Ontario.

Notes

Introduction

1 'Editorial Notes: Progress in Education,' *The School* (November 1930): 213.
2 The interwar context is extended into 1942, the year of the death of Duncan McArthur, Minister of Education in Ontario. McArthur featured prominently in the province's progressivist reform rhetoric.
3 John Dewey, *Experience and Education* (New York, NY: Touchstone, 1938), 17.
4 George S. Tomkins, *A Common Countenance: Stability and Change in the Canadian Curriculum* (Vancouver, BC: Pacific Educational Press, 2008), 144.

1. Ontario's Educational Context in the Interwar Period

1 There would be a later, neo-progressive iteration of reform discourse and policy in the 1960s and 1970s, but the interwar period is one where Ontario's educationists initially adopted and interpreted the rhetoric of progressive education. *Living and Learning,* published by The Provincial Committee on Aims and Objectives of Education in the Schools of Ontario, appearing in 1968 and commonly referred to as the Hall–Dennis Report, is perhaps the best example of this neo-progressive discourse in the province.
2 John Herd Thompson and Allen Seager, *Canada, 1922–1939: Decades of Discord* (Toronto, ON: McClelland and Stewart, 1985), 155.
3 Rosa Bruno-Jofré, 'Citizenship and Schooling in Manitoba, 1918–1945,' *Manitoba History* 36 (1998–9): 26–36; Robert Patterson, 'The Implementation of Progressive Education in Canada, 1930–1945,' in *Essays on Canadian Education*, ed. N. Kach, K. Mazurek, R.S. Patterson, and I. DeFavery (Calgary, AB: Detselig, 1987), 79–93; Amy von Heyking, *Creating Citizens: History and Identity in Alberta's Schools, 1905 to 1980* (Calgary, AB: University of Calgary Press, 2006).

4 Robert Patterson, 'Society and Education during the Wars and Their Interlude: 1914–1945,' in *Canadian Education: A History*, ed. J. Donald Wilson,
   Robert M. Stamp, and Louis-Philippe Audet (Toronto, ON: Prentice-Hall of
   Canada, 1970), 360.
5 Tom Mitchell, 'The Manufacture of Souls of Good Quality: Winnipeg's 1919
   National Conference on Canadian Citizenship, English-Canadian Nationalism, and the New Order after the Great War,' *Journal of Canadian Studies*
   31, no. 4 (Winter 1996–7): 21, cited in Rosa Bruno-Jofré, 'Citizenship and
   Schooling in Manitoba,' 103.
6 Paul Axelrod, 'Beyond the Progressive Education Debate: A Profile of
   Toronto Schooling in the 1950s,' *Historical Studies in Education* 17, no. 2
   (2005): 227–41; Ken Osborne, 'Teaching History in Schools: A Canadian
   Debate,' *Journal of Curriculum Studies* 35, no. 5 (2003): 585–626.
7 Lynn S. Lemisko and Kurt W. Clausen, 'Connections, Contrarieties, and
   Convulsions: Curriculum and Pedagogical Reform in Alberta and Ontario,
   1930–1955,' *Canadian Journal of Education* 29, no. 4 (2006): 1097–126.
8 Ian Drummond, *Progress without Planning: The Economic History of Ontario
   from Confederation to the Second World War* (Toronto, ON: University of
   Toronto Press, 1987).
9 Ibid.
10 Henry V. Nelles, *The Politics of Development: Forests, Mines, and Hydro-Electric Power in Ontario, 1849–1941* (Hamden, CT: Archon, 1974).
11 Kieran Egan, *Getting It Wrong from the Beginning: Our Progressivist Inheritance from Herbert Spencer, John Dewey, and Jean Piaget* (New Haven, CT: Yale
   University Press, 2002), 2. Herbert Spencer, Egan notes, acutely assessed the
   context of modernity when he argued that it permeated all things and was
   evident in 'the progress of civilization as a whole, as well as in the progress
   of every nation.'
12 Egan, *Getting It Wrong from the Beginning*, 2.
13 Ibid.
14 Robert Stamp, *The Schools of Ontario, 1876–1976* (Toronto, ON: University of
   Toronto Press, 1982).
15 The Act to Confer the Electoral Franchise Upon Women took effect 1 January 1919.
16 James Naylor, *The New Democracy: Challenging the Social Order in Industrial
   Ontario* (Toronto, ON: University of Toronto Press), 42–4.
17 Ibid., 42–3. According to Naylor, 'unprecedented working-class militancy
   greeted the end of the war.' He backs up this statement with staggering
   statistics: 'Strike activity, which tended to level off in 1917, albeit at a rather
   high level, climbed to new heights as the war drew to an end. In the region

as a whole, the number of worker-days lost in strikes climbed from 25,000 in 1915 to more than 120,000 in 1918 and to an astounding 850,000 in 1919.'

18 James Spelt, *The Urban Development in South-Central Ontario* (Assen, Netherlands: Koninklijke Van Gorcum, 1955).
19 Peter A. Baskerville, *Ontario: Image, Identity, and Power* (Toronto, ON: Oxford University Press, 2002), 157–9.
20 Ibid.
21 Naylor, *The New Democracy*, 114–16.
22 Thompson and Seager, *Decades of Discord*, 224–30.
23 Patterson, 'Society and Education during the Wars,' 360.
24 Ibid., 360.
25 Baskerville, *Ontario*, 180–4.
26 Doug Owram, *The Government Generation: Canadian Intellectuals and the State, 1900–1945* (Toronto, ON: University of Toronto Press, 1986).
27 Patterson, 'Society and Education during the Wars,' 360.
28 Ibid., 361.
29 Ibid., 361.
30 Craig Heron, *The Workers' Revolt in Canada, 1917–1925* (Toronto, ON: University of Toronto Press, 1998).
31 Ibid.
32 Patterson, 'Society and Education during the Wars,' 360.
33 Ibid., 360.
34 Robert Bothwell, *The Penguin History of Canada* (Toronto, ON: Penguin Canada, 2006); Thompson and Seager, *Decades of Discord*.
35 David Tyack, *The One Best System: A History of American Urban Education* (Cambridge, MA: Harvard University Press, 1974).
36 Stamp, *The Schools of Ontario*.
37 E. Brian Titley, 'Editor's Introduction,' in *Canadian Education: Historical Themes and Contemporary Issues*, ed. E. Brian Titley (Calgary, AB: Detselig, 1990), 81. 'This century' refers to the twentieth century.
38 Ibid., 81–2. Titley believes that the basic tenets of these movements were based on 'reformist, not revolutionary, sentiments. Progressive education … became one of the instruments of these movements.'
39 Robert S. Patterson, 'The Canadian Experience with Progressive Education,' in *Canadian Education: Historical Themes and Contemporary Issues*, ed. E. Brian Titley (Calgary, AB: Detselig, 1990), 95–110. In fact, Patterson believed it 'virtually impossible to provide a simple, capsule statement about how the nation was influenced by and dealt with this phenomenon,' 95.
40 Ibid., 95.
41 'The Challenge of Childhood,' *Canadian School Board Journal* (June 1928): 2.

42 Ibid., 2.

43 'The Aims of Education,' *Canadian School Board Journal* (June 1928): 4. The speaker cited was President of the Trades and Labor Congress of Canada. The article summarized events occurring at the 1928 Convention. Moore also, the article related, spoke of the League of Nations and introduced its publication, *A New World*. His speech is notable because of the expression he gave to the changes that modernity wrought on Ontario, but also because he saw these changes as ongoing: 'No one can possibly forecast what the educational needs of the next decade will be because of the rapid development in industry, agriculture, and science.'

44 See, for example, F.P. Gavin, 'Recent Social Changes and the Schools,' *Canadian School Journal* (May 1935): 134–5, 157.

45 R.J. McCracken, 'Facing the New Order,' *Canadian School Journal* (May 1942): 144.

46 Ibid., 144–5, 166.

47 Bruno-Jofré, 'Citizenship and Schooling in Manitoba,' 102.

48 R.H. Grant, *Report of the Minister of Education for the Year 1919* (Toronto, ON: Legislative Assembly of Ontario, 1920), vi.

49 'Need Craft Training,' *Canadian School Board Journal* (January 1928): 13.

50 Stamp, *The Schools of Ontario*, 137–8.

51 G. Howard Ferguson, *Report of the Minister of Education for the Year 1926* (Toronto, ON: Legislative Assembly of Ontario, 1927), xiii.

52 Ibid., xiii.

53 Ibid. In Ferguson's words: 'The foreign-born, both parents and children, trained in an atmosphere inimical to Canadian ideas of citizenship are quickly developing into loyal and law-abiding Canadians,' xiii.

54 G. Howard Ferguson, *Report of the Minister of Education for the Year 1927* (Toronto, ON: Legislative Assembly of Ontario, 1928). The majority of immigrants were identified as having mid-European origins. The school car was 'adding its quota to the loyal and intelligent citizenship of Ontario,' 6.

55 See, for example, George S. Henry, *Report of the Minister of Education for the Year 1931*, vi.

56 Rosa Bruno-Jofré, 'Manitoba Schooling in the Canadian Context and the Building of a Polity: 1919–1971,' *Canadian and International Education* 28, no. 2 (1999): 1–22.

57 Howard Palmer, 'Reluctant Hosts: Anglo-Canadian Views of Multiculturalism in the Twentieth Century,' in *Cultural Diversity and Canadian Education: Issues and Innovations*, ed. J.R. Mallea and J. Young (Ottawa, ON: Carleton University Press, 1984), 21–40.

58 Ibid.

59 Baskerville, *Ontario*, 159–60.
60 V.K. Greer, 'Report of the Chief Inspector of Public and Separate Schools,' *Report of the Minister of Education for the Year 1933* (Toronto, ON: Legislative Assembly of Ontario, 1934), 14.
61 Stamp, *The Schools of Ontario*, 137–8.
62 Patterson, 'Society and Education during the Wars,' 365.
63 W.L. Grant, 'The Education of the Workingman,' *Queen's Quarterly* 27, no. 2 (1919): 163.
64 Patterson, 'Society and Education during the Wars,' 364.
65 Stamp, *The Schools of Ontario*, 138.
66 Ibid.
67 See, for example, G. Howard Ferguson, *Report of the Minister of Education for the Year 1929* (Toronto, ON: Legislative Assembly of Ontario, 1930), x. Ferguson notes: 'The lessons returned are examined by well-qualified teachers in the employ of the Department, who find that the majority of those taking these lessons make just as good progress as they would in a well-conducted school … In fact, the general results have been successful beyond all expectations, and too much cannot be said in praise of the co-operation of the parents, and the perseverance of the children in carrying out this work, no doubt, in many cases, under very unfavourable circumstances,' x.
68 Robin S. Harris, *Quiet Evolution: A Study of the Educational System of Ontario* (Toronto, ON: University of Toronto Press, 1967), 47.
69 Patterson, 'Society and Education during the Wars,' 372.
70 Robert A. Levin, 'Debate over Schooling: Influences of Dewey and Thorndike,' *Childhood Education* 68, no. 2 (1991): 71–5.
71 'Peter Sandiford,' *The School* (November 1941): 186.
72 W.G. Fleming, *Ontario's Educative Society*, vol. 5, *Supporting Institutions and Services* (Toronto, ON: University of Toronto Press, 1972), 166.
73 Ibid., 166–7. Fleming comments on the expanding role of the Research Department during the Second World War, including the application of intelligence testing to military assignments: 'Test development, of course, remained an area of primary emphasis. During the war a contribution was made toward the practical problem of selecting suitable armed forces personnel for special tasks. Investigations into measurement theory began at the same time to add a new dimension to the work.' The use of standardized intelligence tests for the streaming of military personnel is consistent with the way these instruments were described as being useful tools for diagnosing students' individual abilities in schools. See, for example, the discussion of this topic in ch. 4, 'Standardizing Assessments and the Collection of Data on Individuals.'

74 Levin, 'Debate over Schooling,' 71–5.
75 H.E. Amoss, 'Report of the Inspector of Auxiliary Classes,' *Report of the Minister of Education for the Year 1929* (Toronto, ON: Legislative Assembly of Ontario, 1930), 33.
76 Stamp, *The Schools of Ontario*, 69.
77 Ibid.
78 Patterson, 'Society and Education during the Wars,' 362.
79 Ibid., 362.
80 Frank T. Sharpe, 'What Would I Do If I Left School under Present Conditions?' *Canadian School Journal* (October 1933): 355.
81 William E. Blatz and Helen MacMurchy Bott, *Parents and the Pre-school Child* (Toronto, ON: J.M. Dent and Sons, 1928), v.
82 The institute's idea was consistent with the progressivist advocacy for interrelation and integration of subject areas and topics. As an interdisciplinary centre for study, it was designed to bring different academic areas, including medicine, psychology, education, and sociology, together for research on problems of mutual interest – in this case, children and human development.
83 Jocelyn Motyer Raymond, *The Nursery World of Dr Blatz* (Toronto, ON: University of Toronto Press, 1991), ix.
84 Fleming, *Supporting Institutions and Services*, 187. Fleming acknowledges the influence of the institute on Ontario's child study research in relation to education, but situates its inception in a broader context beginning in the United States before the First World War: 'The beginning of the movement that led to the founding of the Institute of Child Study may be traced to the establishment of the Child Study Laboratory at the State University of Iowa in 1911 through the efforts of Carl E. Seashore and associates. The experiment was sufficiently successful that similar steps were taken at other leading universities such as California, Minnesota, Harvard, Yale, and Columbia.'
85 See, for example, E.A. Bott, 'Founding of the Institute of Child Study,' in *Twenty-five Years of Child Study: The Development of the Programme and Review of the Research at the Institute of Child Study, University of Toronto, 1926–1951*, ed. Karl S. Bernhardt, Margaret I. Fletcher, Frances L. Johnson, Dorothy A. Millichamp, and Mary L. Northway (Toronto, ON: University of Toronto Press, 1951), 15–17.
86 J.T. Phair, 'School Medical Inspection,' *Canadian School Journal* (September 1932): 295. Mental hygiene was an important theme in the child study movement. Key sources for the history of mental hygiene include the following: Neil Sutherland, *Children in English-Canadian Society: Framing the*

Twentieth-Century Consensus (Toronto, ON: University of Toronto Press, 1976); Norman Dain, *Clifford W. Beers: Advocate for the Insane* (Pittsburgh, PA: University of Pittsburgh Press, 1980); Wilbur Cross, *Twenty-Five Years After: Sidelights on the Mental Hygiene Movement and Its Founder* (New York, NY: Doubleday, 1934); Nina Ridenour, *Mental Health in the United States: A Fifty-Year History* (Cambridge, MA: Harvard University Press, 1961).

87 Viola Henderson, 'The School Child's Lunch,' *Canadian School Journal* (September 1932): 296.

88 D.R. McClenahan, 'Observations on Rural Public Health Work in Ontario,' *Canadian School Journal* (December 1932): 314.

89 Ibid., 313–14.

90 Frederick Minkler, 'The Progressive Education Conferences in Hamilton and Windsor,' *The School* (January 1939): 379.

91 Ibid., 379.

92 W. Line and J.D.M. Griffin, 'Education and Mental Hygiene,' *The School* (April 1937): 647–8. Surveys concerned classroom organization, punishment, and rewards. In terms of discipline, it was commonly acknowledged that intrinsic interest in the school work itself could be regarded as the key to preventative discipline.

93 Ibid., 647.

94 Margaret S. Gould, 'Education at the Expense of Health,' *Canadian School Journal* (October 1934): 343.

95 Ferguson, *Report … 1929*, vii.

96 'Health Education: Editorial Notes,' *The School* (March 1936): 550–1.

97 Cynthia Commachio, *The Infinite Bonds of Family: Domesticity in Canada, 1850–1940* (Toronto, ON: University of Toronto Press, 1999).

98 George S. Henry, *Report of the Minister of Education for the Year 1932* (Toronto, ON: Legislative Assembly of Ontario, 1933), vii. See also 'The Depression and Its Impact on Education' in this chapter, as well as Appendix B for reference to Ontario's premiers and education ministers throughout the context of study.

99 R.W. Anglin, A.G. Hooper, A.G. Husband, W.A. Jennings, and I.M. Levan, 'Report of the High School Inspectors,' in ibid., 16.

100 John T. Phair, Mary Power, and Robert H. Roberts, 'An Experiment in Health Teaching in the Schools of Ontario,' *The School* (September 1936): 6.

101 Ibid. Bad health habits in children were seen as emerging from inadequate knowledge of hygiene; left unchecked, they would be repeated in the adult population.

102 Ibid., 6–12.

103 This can be attributed to growing concern over the effects of moderniza-

tion and the need to exercise careful management and control in times of change and unrest. Its influence can also be attributed to the growing interest in correlating business and industry with schools. The ideas of Frederick Winslow Taylor, who promoted the scientific management of factories for the promotion of increased production at decreased cost, as well as for better regulation and order, were particularly influential. For Taylor's seminal text, see Frederick W. Taylor, *The Principles of Scientific Management* (New York, NY: Harper and Brothers, 1911).

104 Baskerville, *Ontario*, 35.

105 For an elaborate description of how social efficiency modelled on F.W. Taylor's ideas affected educational aims and reforms, see Raymond E. Callahan, *Education and the Cult of Efficiency: A Study of the Social Forces That Have Shaped the Administration of Public Schools* (Chicago, IL: University of Chicago Press, 1962.

106 H.M. Cooke, 'Secondary Education,' *Canadian School Journal* (November 1932): 381.

107 G.F. Rogers, 'Present Day Problems in Education,' *Canadian School Journal* (May 1933): 173.

108 Ibid. Rogers, while recognizing the changing needs of schools and school organization in Ontario, maintained that the study of classics and history provided a common foundation for the province's students.

109 'Secondary School Costs,' *Canadian School Journal* (January 1933): 15. It is worth noting that this editorial was presented at the very height of the Great Depression. The effect of the Depression on schools will be considered in 'The Depression and Its Impact on Education' in this chapter.

110 'Educational Experiments, Research, and Progress in Canada,' *The School* (December 1940): 278.

111 'Supplement: Reports on Educational Progress in Canada and Newfoundland, 1940–1941,' 907.

112 Ibid., 907. Certainly, the war effort accounted for much of the concern for practicality and industrial need, but the trends noted in 1940 were, generally, those that dominated conceptions of social efficiency.

113 Patterson, 'Society and Education during the Wars,' 362.

114 Canadian Teachers' Federation, 'CTF History,' http://www.ctf-fce.ca/e/organization/about/ctf_history.asp (accessed 15 June 2010). The 1920 mandate established by the Canadian Teachers' Federation remains in place today.

115 W.G. Fleming, *Ontario's Educative Society*, vol. 7, *Educational Contributions of Associations* (Toronto, ON: University of Toronto Press, 1972), 38.

116 Ibid., 38.

117 Patterson, 'Society and Education during the Wars,' 362.
118 Ibid.
119 Fleming, vol. 7, 124.
120 'Association for Childhood Education,' *Canadian School Journal* (January 1932): 39.
121 Ibid., 39.
122 Baskerville, *Ontario*, 186. See Appendix B for a list of premiers, education ministers, deputy ministers, and chief directors of education throughout the context.
123 Ibid., 186–90.
124 George S. Henry, *Report of the Minister of Education for the Year 1930* (Toronto, ON: Legislative Assembly of Ontario, 1931), v.
125 George S. Henry, *Report of the Minister of Education for the Year 1931* (Toronto, ON: Legislative Assembly of Ontario, 1932), v.
126 Baskerville, *Ontario*, 180.
127 Stamp, *The Schools of Ontario*. See esp. his ch. 7, 'The Ontario Taxpayer and the Depression,' 143–63, for a particularly rich source of information on the impact of the financial crisis on the province's schools.
128 Ibid.
129 Ibid.
130 W.G. Fleming, *Ontario's Educative Society*, vol. 1, *The Expansion of the Educational System* (Toronto, ON: University of Toronto Press, 1971), 93. Fleming notes that the Adolescent School Attendance Act actually went into effect in 1921, contributing to 'a rapid subsequent increase' in the school population.
131 *Report of the Minister of Education of Ontario* (1917, 1927, 1934, and 1942). For a statistical table, see Appendix A.
132 Robert Stamp, *Ontario Secondary School Program Innovations and Student Retention Rates, 1920s–1970s: A Report to the Ontario Study of the Relevance of Education and the Issue of Dropouts* (Toronto, ON: Queen's Printer for Ontario, 1988), iv–v.
133 Ibid.
134 Charles E. Phillips, *Development of Education in Canada* (Toronto, ON: W.J. Gage, 1957), 225.
135 Ibid.
136 Stamp, *The Schools of Ontario*, 143–51.
137 Ibid., 143–4.
138 R.W. Anglin, A.J. Husband, W.A. Jennings, and A.G. Hooper, 'Report of the High School Inspectors,' *Report of the Minister of Education for the Year 1933* (Toronto, ON: Legislative Assembly of Ontario, 1934), 19.

139 Henry, *Report … 1933*, 5.
140 V.K. Greer, 'Report of the Chief Inspector of Public and Separate Schools,' *Report of the Minister of Education for the Year 1934* (Toronto, ON: Legislative Assembly of Ontario, 1935), 10. Similarly drastic cutbacks were undertaken across the country by Departments of Education in response to the Depression.
141 Stamp, *The Schools of Ontario*, 146–7.
142 Greer, 'Report of the Chief Inspector,' 10.
143 Ibid., 10.
144 Stamp, *The Schools of Ontario*, 146–7.
145 Ibid. Stamp explains: 'Although salaries slipped, they decreased much more slowly than for wage earners and salaried employees in the private sector, with the result that the average Ontario teachers' income possessed more equivalent real purchasing power in 1933 than in 1929 – $1050 to $797.' See also Canadian Teachers' Federation, *Trends in the Economic Status of Teachers, 1910–1955* (Ottawa, ON: Canadian Teachers Federation, 1957), 58.
146 Ferguson, *Report … 1929*, x–xi; Leo J. Sampson, *Report of the Minister of Education for the Year 1934* (Toronto, ON: Legislative Assembly of Ontario, 1935), 3–4. A permanent certificate, First or Second Class, depending on educational background, required completion of normal school and practice teaching in a model school, leading to a teaching position in either a high school or an elementary school.
147 The Ontario Secondary School Teachers Federation publication, *Teachers' Bulletin*, for instance, ran an article throughout the Depression that was written by the federation's publicity representative, A.D.R. Fraser. See, for example, Fraser, 'Our Publicity Man,' *Teachers' Bulletin* (June 1931): 16–18. In this article, Fraser reviews media coverage relative to teacher salaries in a section titled 'News Notes.'
148 'Editorial: Education Week,' *The School* (November 1941): 181.
149 S.R. Laycock, 'Extra-curricular Activities in the Modern School,' *The School* (October 1941): 93–7.
150 Neil McKenty, *Mitch Hepburn* (Toronto, ON: McClelland and Stewart, 1967).
151 Ibid.
152 Stamp, *The Schools of Ontario*, 151.
153 Ibid.
154 Baskerville, *Ontario*, 185.
155 Drummond, *Progress without Planning*, 343.
156 Stamp, *The Schools of Ontario*, 151.
157 Robert M. Stamp, *The Historical Background to Separate Schools in Ontario*

(Toronto, ON: Queen's Printer for Ontario, 1985), 12. Emphasis in original text.

158 Ibid., 13.

159 Ibid., 13.

160 McKenty, *Mitch Hepburn*.

161 Stamp, *The Historical Background*, 29. Stamp notes, as mentioned earlier, that this represents an increase of 10 to 17 per cent in the proportion of the total elementary population since the turn of the century.

162 Stamp, *The Schools of Ontario*, 153.

163 Ibid., 30.

164 Stamp, *The Historical Background*, 26.

165 Ibid., 29.

166 Stamp, *The Schools of Ontario*, 152.

167 Ibid., 146.

168 McCulley was a fervent meliorist progressivist. His opinions will be discussed at greater length in chs. 4 to 6. William Blatz, Director of the Institute of Child Study, also features in chs. 4 to 6. The institute, while later affiliated with the University of Toronto, can also be considered part of the separate school network. The discourse community enabled by the sources, by definition, was one concerned with the improvement of education. One hypothesis is that the private school stakeholders, most notably from Upper Canada College, were more concerned with the preservation of a humanist emphasis on schooling and a traditional curriculum than they were with progressivist reformism.

169 W.G. Fleming, *Ontario's Educative Society*, vol. 3, *Schools, Pupils, and Teachers* (Toronto, ON: University of Toronto Press, 1971), 59.

170 Ibid., 59.

171 Harris, *Quiet Evolution*. Particularly relevant are the two chapters on 'Organization and Control, 1867–1966,' 104–25.

172 Ibid., 110.

173 R.A. Pyne, *Report of the Minister of Education for the Year 1906* (Toronto, ON: Legislative Assembly of Ontario, 1907), iii.

174 Harris, *Quiet Evolution*, 110.

175 For a table of premiers, ministers, deputy ministers, and chief directors of education, see Appendix B.

176 Ibid.

177 Fleming, vol. 3, 87.

2. Approaching Progressive Education

1 *Western School Journal* was published by the Manitoba Department of

Education. In 1963 it changed its name to *Manitoba School Journal.*

2 John Dewey, 'My Pedagogic Creed,' *The School Journal* 54, no. 3 (16 January 1897): 77–80.

3 For more precise statistics, see Appendix C. See also *McKim's Directory of Canadian Publications* (Montreal, QC: A. McKim), Editions 12 to 35. *McKim's,* published annually, listed all newspapers and periodicals published in Canada and Newfoundland, including circulation ratings and listings of advertisers. The source lists no circulation figures for *Canadian School Journal* until 1928.

4 C. Pelham Mulvany, *Toronto: Past and Present, A Handbook of the City* (Toronto, ON: W.E. Caiger, 1884), 206. Mulvany uses the term *liberal* to denote a position unfettered to any particular political party or platform. The journal, in his view, was educational, not political. It ran from 1879 to 1883.

5 W.G. Fleming, *Educational Contributions of Associations*, vol. 7 of *Ontario's Educative Society* (Toronto, ON: University of Toronto Press, 1972), 1. In recognition of its 'preeminent status in the field of voluntary educational effort,' the Ontario Educational Association is the first organization that Fleming discusses in his text.

6 Ibid., 5. Further, Fleming noted: 'The federations, however, continued their separate existence, remaining independent both of one another and of the Association. The result was that the latter paid less attention to protective concerns than would otherwise have been the case.' It is not surprising under the circumstances that the federations maintained their own publications and that federation representatives were not among the contributors to *Canadian School Journal.* The postwar formation of educational associations was discussed in 'Forging Educational Organizations' in ch. 1.

7 Fleming, *Educational Contributions of Associations,* 7.

8 See, for example, Ontario Educational Association, *Proceedings of the Fifty-Ninth Annual Convention of the Ontario Educational Association* (Toronto, ON: King's Printer, 1920). The 1920 OEA convention conference proceedings list the participating sections by department. The Elementary Department sections included the following: Public School, Kindergarten, Household Science, Technical and Manual Arts, Spelling Reform, Hygiene and Public Health, Home and School, and League of the Empire. The College and Secondary School Department sections included these: Modern Language, Natural Science, Classical, Mathematical and Physical, English and History, Commercial, Continuation School, and High School Principals. The Supervising and Training Department sections included

Inspectors, Training, and Music. The Trustees Department listed no sections.

9 Fleming, *Educational Contributions of Associations,* 7.

10 Edwin C. Guillet, *In the Cause of Education: Centennial History of the Ontario Educational Association, 1861–1960* (Toronto, ON: University of Toronto Press, 1960).

11 Fleming, *Educational Contributions of Associations,* 6.

12 Guillet, *In the Cause of Education,* 377.

13 Fleming, *Educational Contributions of Associations,* 172.

14 'Introductory,' *Ontario School Board Journal* 1, no. 1 (12 December 1921).

15 'Report of the School Trustees' and Ratepayers' Association,' *Ontario School Board Journal* (April 1922): 21.

16 See, for example, *McKim's Directory of Canadian Publications* (Montreal, QC: A. McKim, 1929), 266.

17 Fleming, *Educational Contributions of Associations,* 175.

18 'The Challenge of Childhood,' *Canadian School Journal* (June 1928): 2.

19 Ibid.

20 The October 1934 issue, for example, included editorials (one page); extracts from addresses at local trustees' meetings (two pages); general articles on university extension, music, high schools in British Columbia and New Brunswick, homework, and the course of study in Ontario (sixteen pages); book reviews (three pages); reports from district association meetings (five pages); gleanings from a local educational conference (two pages); and advertisements (eight pages).

21 In October 1933 an editorial in *Canadian School Journal* commented on the actual relationship between the Department of Education and the periodical. The two were closely allied, the article explained, in part because the journal received financial assistance from the department: 'The Ontario School Trustees' & Ratepayers' Association is linked up with the Department of Education only through the closest co-operation. At no time has the Department of Education dictated or hinted at dictation, or even advised how or what our Association should do. Had it not been for the assistance the Department has given us financially we could not have functioned as we have.' 'Educational News,' *Canadian School Journal* (October 1933): 370. According to the editors, both the OSTRA and the OEA were 'thoroughly democratic' and not subservient to the government.

22 Articles by contributors outside the state were common, but their positions were never overtly controversial or oppositional to the department. See, for example, Arthur Herbert Richardson, 'Trees for Town and Rural Schools,' *Canadian School Journal* (May 1932): 188–92; 'Kindly Reference,' *Canadian*

School Journal (March 1933): 86; and W.J. Cairns, 'What To-Day's Business Man Asks of To-Day's Young Man,' *Canadian School Journal* (October 1936): 285–6.

23 See Charles E. Phillips, *College of Education, Toronto: Memories of OCE* (Toronto, ON: University of Toronto Press, 1977). Incidentally, Phillips's study of the Ontario College of Education, considering the period between 1920 and 1972, is an insightful study of an educational institution's role in the context of the emerging development and expansion of both the City of Toronto and the University of Toronto. Phillips also assumed the editorship of the journal in 1940. Phillips recalls that apart from regular features, the editor 'had to obtain, without payment to contributors, something like 300 articles per year,' 100. He later notes: 'To ensure a steady supply of articles for readers, with every type of interest, I kept getting the names of possible contributors from public school inspectors for the elementary edition and from the colleges staff and other sources for the secondary edition ... A large amount of correspondence was necessary, but we never had a shortage,' 102.

24 Ibid., 100.

25 Ibid., 98. Phillips offers an analysis of the contents of one issue – that of December of 1920 – which held consistently throughout the period. An exception of note was the publication in January 1941 of a fifty-page supplement on educational progress, research, and experiment in Canada. Phillips's analysis was as follows: 'short editorials (two pages), accounts of recent appointments (two pages), items of interest chiefly from books (three pages), book notices (five pages), current events (five pages), news items from other provinces (nine pages), full-page half-tones (two pages), Red Cross (three pages), general articles on measuring intelligence (seven pages), other articles on the Hudson's Bay Company, war poetry, teaching reading, seat work in the primary grades, teaching proportion and perspective (twenty-two pages), hints and helps used as fillers (two pages). Four of the articles were from Alberta,' 98.

26 The ratio of articles expressing progressivist:humanist rhetoric was approximately 15:1.

27 Phillips, *College of Education, Toronto*, 99–100.

28 Ibid., 101.

29 'History and Function of OISE,' *Graduate Studies in Education Bulletin, 2008–2009* (Toronto, ON: University of Toronto): 6.

30 Phillips, *College of Education, Toronto*, 100–1.

31 The masthead of the journal, presumably to reinforce this pedagogical emphasis, noted: 'Editorial Board: The Staff of the Ontario College of Education, University of Toronto.'

32 What Phillips did not recall when recounting this story in his text, *College of Education*, is that his editorial had actually anticipated a negative response from certain readers. In his conclusion, he asked readers to 'please delay an unfavourable verdict' of his thesis until they had read other editorials explaining how the new education applied to contemporary educational problems. See 'Editorial: Declaration of Faith,' *The School* (September 1940): 2.

33 Phillips, *College of Education, Toronto*, 101. Phillips refused to acknowledge the names of his accusers, and he did not summarize the accusations or defence. At the following staff meeting, six weeks later, he noted: 'The dean simply closed the meeting by saying that the editor had full responsibility for what went into the magazine, provided only that he sold enough subscriptions to keep it going.'

34 Phillips suggests that the readership of the journal increased throughout the interwar period. Subscription income neared $6,000 by the mid-1940s, but the figure is deceiving because the journal was sent free to all schools and to all teachers in larger schools who applied for it. Maintaining a steady authorship of educators entailed balancing the articles related to theory, psychology, and general concern with devices and techniques for teaching particular subjects or topics.

35 Ibid., 104.

36 Theresa Richardson has given the topic's ambiguous shape an apt description: 'Progressive education was pluralistic and often contradictory in its missions, motives, and degrees of success as was progressivism in general.' Richardson, 'Rethinking Progressive High School Reform in the 1930s: Youth, Mental Hygiene, and General Education,' *American Educational History Journal* 33, no. 1 (2006): 77.

37 See, for example, Gert J.J. Biesta and Siebren Miedema, 'Dewey in Europe: A Case Study on the International Dimensions of the Turn-of-the-Century Educational Reform,' *American Journal of Education* 105 (November, 1996): 1–26. See also the international journal of the history of education, *Paedagogica Historica*, which devoted both its first and second issues of 2006 to the reception and metamorphosis of New Education in various contexts.

38 Herbert Kliebard, *The Struggle for the American Curriculum, 1893–1958* (New York, NY: RoutledgeFalmer, 2004).

39 See, for example, Filene, 'An Obituary for "The Progressive Movement,"' 34. Note the epigraph to this chapter as well as the following, which concludes his essay: 'The "progressive" frame of reference, carrying with it so many confusing and erroneous connotations, must be put aside. It is time to tear off the familiar label and, thus liberated from its prejudice, see the

history ... for what it was – ambiguous, inconsistent, moved by agents and forces more complex than a progressive movement.'

40 Joseph J. Schwab, 'The "Impossible" Role of the Teacher in Progressive Education,' *School Review* 67, no. 2 (1959): 139.

41 Alfred L. Hall-Quest, *Editorial Foreword: Experience and Education*, (New York, NY: Collier, 1938), 10.

42 John Dewey, *Experience and Education* (New York, NY: Collier, 1938), 17.

43 Ibid., 17.

44 Ibid., 20.

45 Ibid., 20.

46 Kliebard, *The Struggle for the American Curriculum*, 271. In his afterword, 'The Search for Meaning in Progressive Education,' to the third edition of this text, Kliebard considers the history of texts dealing with progressive education. His historiography was a beginning point for my reflections on the field. He comments that 'the effort to depict a melange of reforms we have come to lump together as progressive education has itself developed something of a history; that is, apart from the history of the reforms themselves, the way historians have defined progressive education has acquired a kind of story of its own.'

47 Kliebard, 'Afterword,' *The Struggle for the American Curriculum*.

48 This has also been described as 'house history.' David Tyack, *The One Best System: A History of American Urban Education* (Cambridge, MA: Harvard University Press), 8–9.

49 Ellwood Cubberley, *Public Education in the United States* (Cambridge, MA: Riverside Press, 1919).

50 Ellen C. Lagemann, 'Does History Matter in Educational Research? A Brief for the Humanities in the Age of Science,' *Harvard Educational Review* 75, no. 1 (2005): 9–24.

51 Ibid.

52 Ibid. The anachronism is particularly apparent from the present perspective.

53 Ibid.

54 Lawrence Cremin, *The Transformation of the School: Progressivism in American Education, 1876–1957* (New York, NY: Alfred A. Knopf, 1961).

55 Ibid.

56 For further reading, see Bruce Curtis, *The Politics of Population: State Formation, Statistics, and the Census of Canada, 1840–1875* (Toronto, ON: University of Toronto Press, 2000); Ruby Heap and Alison Prentice, eds., *Gender and Education in Ontario: An Historical Reader* (Toronto, ON: Canadian Scholars'

Press, 1991); Martin Lawn, *Modern Times? Work, Professionalism, and Citizenship in Teaching* (London, UK: Falmer Press, 1996).

57 Arthur Zilversmit, *Changing Schools: Progressive Education Theory and Practice, 1930–1960* (Chicago, IL: University of Chicago Press, 1993).

58 Ellen Lagemann, *The Politics of Knowledge: The Carnegie Corporation, Philanthropy, and Public Policy* (Middleton, CT: Wesleyan University Press, 1989), 185.

59 In this case, as already noted, Thorndike's progressivist concerns used experimental psychology and administrative concerns as referents for change, whereas Dewey was more concerned with developing a comprehensive and pedagogically oriented theory of experience.

60 Tyack, *The One Best System.*

61 Thorndike can be included in the administrative camp and Dewey in the pedagogical one.

62 Herbert Kliebard, 'Vocational Education as Symbolic Action: Connecting Schooling with the Workplace,' in *Forging the American Curriculum: Essays in Curriculum History and Theory*, ed. Herbert Kliebard (New York and London: Routledge, 1992), 183.

63 David Labaree, like David Tyack, conceptualizes progressive reformers as either administrative or pedagogical. The former group affected schools and administrators, while the latter influenced teacher educators in universities. For further reading, refer to David Labaree, 'Progressivism, Schools, and Schools of Education: An American Romance,' *Paedagogica Historica* 41, nos. 1 and 2 (2005): 275–88.

64 Furthermore, it neglects the social meliorist domain, which was identified by Kliebard and which is a concern of mine.

65 Labaree, 'Progressivism, Schools, and Schools of Education,' 276.

66 Ibid., 279.

67 For examples of Canadian studies concerned with ascertaining the degree to which progressive education affected education in this country, see Paul Axelrod, 'Beyond the Progressive Education Debate: A Profile of Toronto Schooling in the 1950s,' *Historical Studies in Education* 17, no. 2 (2005): 227–41; and Robert Stamp, 'Growing up Progressive,' *Historical Studies in Education* 17, no. 1 (2005): 187–98.

68 See, for example, William Hayes, *The Progressive Education Movement: Is It Still a Factor in Today's Schools?* (Lanham, MD: Rowman & Littlefield Education, 2007).

69 David Levine, *Varieties of Reform Thought* (Madison, WI: State Historical Society of Wisconsin, 1964).

70 Filene, 'An Obituary for the "Progressive Movement,"' 20.
71 Ibid.
72 Ibid.
73 James W. Fraser, 'Who Were the Progressive Educators Anyway? A Case Study of the Progressive Education Movement in Boston, 1905–1925,' *Educational Foundations* 2, no. 1 (1988): 4–30; Julia Wrigley, *Class Politics and the Public Schools: Chicago, 1900–1950* (New Brunswick, NJ: Rutgers University Press, 1982); William J. Reese, *Power and the Promise of School Reform: Grass-Roots Movement during the Progressive Era* (Boston, MA: Routledge and Kegan Paul, 1982).
74 For a more descriptive summary, see Kliebard, *The Struggle for the American Curriculum.*
75 Raymond Williams, *The Long Revolution* (Harmondsworth, UK: Penguin, 1975).
76 Egan's approach is, perhaps, more conceptual and philosophical than strictly historical. Still, he describes three educational aims that coexist in modern education – academic idealization, individual development, and socialization – and he associates these with the progressivist concern for modern schools that relate more closely to individual learners.
77 Edward A. Krug, *The Shaping of the American High School, 1880–1920* (New York, NY: Harper & Row, 1964); *The Shaping of the American High School, 1920–1941* (Madison, WI: University of Wisconsin Press, 1972); Michael B. Katz, *The Irony of Early School Reform: Educational Innovation in Mid-Nineteenth Century Massachusetts* (Boston, MA: Beacon, 1968); Samuel Bowles and Harry Gintis, *Schooling in Capitalist America* (New York, NY: Basic, 1976); Joel Spring, *Education and the Rise of the Corporate State* (Boston, MA: Beacon, 1972).
78 Lagemann, 'Does History Matter in Educational Research?'; Diane Ravitch, *The Revisionists Revised: A Critique of the Radical Attack on the Schools* (New York, NY: Basic, 1978).
79 Kliebard, *The Struggle for the American Curriculum*; Filene, 'An Obituary for "The Progressive Movement,"' 20.
80 Kliebard, *The Struggle for the American Curriculum*, xi.
81 Herbert M. Kliebard, 'Keeping Out of Nature's Way: The Rise and Fall of Child-Study as the Basis for the Curriculum, 1880–1905,' in *Forging the American Curriculum: Essays in Curriculum History and Theory* (New York, NY: Routledge, 1992), 51.
82 G. Stanley Hall, 'Ideal School Based on Child Study,' *Journal of Proceedings and Addresses of the National Education Association* (1901): 474–88.
83 Kliebard, *The Struggle for the American Curriculum*, 76.

84 Ibid., 151–74.
85 The long quotation cited above is, perhaps, the most clear disavowal of pro-
    gressive education.
86 Herbert Kliebard, 'Education at the Turn of the Century: A Crucible for
    Curriculum Change,' *Educational Researcher* 9 (1989): 23.
87 As noted in the introduction, these domains – active learning, individual-
    ized instruction, relation of schools and society – taken together, are encom-
    passed by my working definition of progressive education.
88 Phillips, *College of Education, Toronto*, 102.
89 Ibid., 102.
90 The audiences were not mutually exclusive. Most telling, with regard to
    audience, is the content outside of the editorial articles. In *The School*, the
    non-editorial articles addressed issues of relevance to educators such as
    model lesson plans, book reviews and notices, teaching suggestions, cur-
    rent events, sample assessments or resources, and useful hints and sugges-
    tions for teachers. *Canadian School Journal*, outside of the editorials, reported
    on local trustee meetings, provided book lists for libraries and school
    administrators, gave account of appointments and promotions, described
    happenings at educational conferences, and responded to questions posed
    by taxpayers with regard to such issues as school organization or finance.
91 A notable limitation here is that the sources do not include many sources
    of oppositional discourses. Articles by socialists, Marxists, and separate
    school advocates are not evident. Editorials from educationists from uni-
    versities and private schools are rarely evident.
92 Kliebard, *The Struggle for the American Curriculum*, x.
93 Sol Cohen, *Challenging Orthodoxies: Toward a New Cultural History of Educa-
    tion* (New York, NY: Peter Lang, 1999), 108.
94 John L. Rury, 'Transformation in Perspective: Lawrence Cremin's *Transfor-
    mation of the School*,' *History of Education Quarterly* 31 (1991): 67–76; Cohen,
    Challenging Orthodoxies, 110.
95 David Labaree, 'Limits on the Impact of Educational Reform: The Case of
    Progressivism and U.S. Schools, 1900–1950,' paper presented at the Monte
    Verità conference, Ascona, Switzerland, September 2007, 2.
96 The remaining three levels are called the formal, the curriculum in use, and
    the received. See also, chapter 7 in David Labaree, *Education, Markets, and
    the Public Good* (London, UK: Routledge, 2007). Larry Cuban uses a similar
    framework to discuss levels of educational reform, which he calls rhetori-
    cal, intended, taught, and learned curricula. See, for example, Larry Cuban,
    'Curriculum Stability and Change,' in *Handbook of Research on Curriculum*,
    ed. Philip Jackson (New York, NY: Macmillan, 1992).

 97 Labaree, 'Limits on the Impact of Educational Reform,' 3.
 98 Ibid., 3. In the words of Labaree: 'The rhetorical level is the most open to reform efforts, since the actors are part of the same discourse community and thus are in tune with rhetorical currents running through this community.' *The School* and *The Canadian School Journal* were forums for a progressivist discourse community – although the community excluded a variety of oppositional discourses and communities emanating from, for example, communists, socialists, political groups, Catholic and Protestant organizations, and many academics or private school representatives.
 99 Ibid.
100 Rosa Bruno-Jofré, 'Manitoba Schooling in the Canadian Context and the Building of a Polity: 1919–1971,' *Canadian and International Education* 28, no. 2 (1999): 101.
101 Kliebard's title explicitly notes that he was concerned with *The Struggle for the Curriculum*, and his story is largely one of a competition for influence among prominent educationists, including Boyd Bode, George S. Counts, Harold Rugg, David Snedden, Arthur Bestor, Ralph Tyler, William Heard Kilpatrick, and George Stanley Hall.
102 See, for example, 'Two Sides to a Question: Is It Desirable that Pupils Should Always Be Required to Stand When Answering Questions?' *The School* (September 1941): 2–3. This article is an example of a piece in which the authors could have debated a pedagogical question. While divergent opinions are presented beside each other, neither author mentions the other. The respondents to the question argue their positions, and the source journal publishes these as parallels, allowing readers to compare the articles and agree or disagree with them.
103 The Ontario Educational Association, which published *Canadian School Journal*, for example, explicitly describes itself as a clearinghouse of educational ideas in many issues throughout the period.
104 Kliebard depicts Counts as a standard bearer of the social meliorist interest group and Snedden as a leading voice for the social efficiency movement.
105 Where possible or relevant, such details are noted, but it would be a Herculean task to trace the particulars of hundreds of voices in the preponderance of cases. Such an effort would not be worth the return, considering my particular research interest.
106 Daniel T. Rodgers, 'In Search of Progressivism,' *Reviews in American History* 10 (1982): 122. Rodgers denied that it was possible to derive a stable list or catalogue of progressive values in the political and social contexts,

but believed that constituencies were built on a faith in some common language or interest. The following paragraphs fill in what was only scantily sketched in the opening pages.

107 The curriculum, in particular, was a subject of discussion. See ch. 6.

108 These three domains, under the overarching theme of a rejection of traditional schools, constitute my operational definition of progressive education.

3. Progressive as Active Learning

1 The other two domains under consideration in this book – individualized instruction and correlation of school with society – are considered in chs. 5 and 6, respectively. The different orientations are heuristics for exploring the meanings of each domain of progressivist thought.

2 It was not only Ontarians who advocated for active, engaging learning experiences to supplant passive ones. John Dewey, most notably when establishing his progressive laboratory school at the University of Chicago, had the recollection noted in this chapter's epigraph.

3 See, for example, 'Education Now – And Then,' *Canadian School Journal* (January 1935): 24. This article presents a song written by Ontario teachers Irma H. Kaufmann and Truda T. Weil that could be sung to the tune 'Last Night on the Back Porch.' The text lacks musicality, but progressivist overtones are explicit: 'Yesterday: They taught them how to sit straight and fold their hands up tight; ... Today: They dote on self-expression and creative energy.'

4 G. Stanley Hall, 'Ideal School Based on Child Study,' *Journal of Proceedings and Addresses of the National Education Association* (1901): 474–88. The child study movement's vision for schooling was heavily influenced by educationists such as Jean-Jacques Rousseau, Johann Heinrich Pestalozzi, and Friedrich Froebel. Hall, regarded as the founder of child psychology in North America, had a strong influence on pioneering child study progressivists in Ontario, including William E. Blatz. On occasion, he is cited directly in Ontario's journal articles. Ryerson public school teacher M. Isabel Wilson, for example, quotes Hall at length when presenting a thesis that primary school activities should provoke creativity and active engagement. M. Isabel Wilson, 'Seat Work in the Primary Grades,' *The School* (November 1931): 237–41.

5 See, for an example of this very common theme in progressivist texts concerned with child study, 'Looking Ahead,' *Canadian School Journal* (March 1936): 95.

6 The Assistant Superintendent of Schools in London, Ontario, A.B. Lucas, provided one notable example of organic rhetoric in relation to children's activities when he noted: 'Every leaf differs from every other leaf; every flower differs from every other flower … To develop individuality and initiative it is necessary for the learner to be confronted with as many kinds of situations as possible, calling for initiative, under the personal guidance and personality of an expert teacher.' A.B. Lucas, 'Education for Democracy,' *Canadian School Journal* (April 1940): 139.

7 To read a comprehensive biography of William E. Blatz, see Jocelyn Motyer Raymond, *The Nursery World of Dr Blatz* (Toronto, ON: University of Toronto Press, 1991). Blatz, famous for his important role in the upbringing of the Dionne Quintuplets in Ontario, is considered here the architect of progressivist child study in the province. At the Thomas Fisher Rare Book Library archives, the Blatz collection includes fifty-three boxes in nine filing cabinets, covering his personal and professional correspondence between 1919 and 1966 (ms coll. 134).

8 E.A. Bott, 'Founding of the Institute of Child Study,' in *Twenty-five Years of Child Study: The Development of the Programme and Review of the Research at The Institute of Child Study, University of Toronto, 1926–1951*, ed. Karl S. Bernhardt, Margaret I. Fletcher, Frances L. Johnson, Dorothy A. Millichamp, and Mary L. Northway (Toronto: University of Toronto Press, 1951), 15–16. Bott, a University of Toronto psychologist, played a central role in bringing Blatz to the university and supporting the foundation of the Institute of Child Study.

9 W.G. Fleming, *Supporting Institutions and Services*, vol. 5, *Ontario's Educative Society* (Toronto, ON: University of Toronto Press, 1972), 187–8. Fleming comments on the connections among soldier rehabilitation, child study, and Blatz's research: 'While studies of child development were curtailed during the First World War, that period saw an intensification of interest in longitudinal psychological studies of individuals throughout life. Valuable findings resulted from attempts to improve rehabilitation treatment of disabled veterans. Among those who became interested in the broader implications of these findings was William E. Blatz. In order to prepare himself for further study of human development, particularly at the earlier stages of life, he undertook advanced studies in the University of Chicago in 1924. He returned to Toronto in time to participate in a study of mental hygiene problems in public school children.'

10 The staff of the Institute of Child Study, a centre for research into human development and education, co-published many books and articles explaining the relevance of child study to learning. See, for example, the

1951 anthology exploring different themes in child study that celebrated the institute's silver anniversary, which is cited numerous times in these opening pages: *Twenty-five Years of Child Study: The Development of the Programme and Review of the Research at The Institute of Child Study, University of Toronto, 1926–1951*, ed. Karl S. Bernhardt, Margaret I. Fletcher, Frances L. Johnson, Dorothy A. Millichamp, and Mary L. Northway (Toronto, ON: University of Toronto Press, 1951).

11 W.E. Blatz, 'Educational Frills,' *Canadian School Journal* (March 1936): 124.

12 Dorothy A. Millichamp and Margaret I. Fletcher, 'Goals and Growth of Nursery Education,' in *Twenty-Five Years of Child Study*, 26.

13 Raymond, *The Nursery World of Dr Blatz*, 90.

14 Ibid.

15 W.E. Blatz, 'The Saint George's School for Child Study,' *University of Toronto Monthly* (June 1926): 443.

16 N.S. MacDonald, 'Educational Value of the Kindergarten,' *Canadian School Board Journal* (May 1928): 7.

17 Dorothy A. Millichamp and Margaret I. Fletcher, 'Goals and Growth of Nursery Education,' 29. Millichamp and Fletcher were two of the teachers at the Institute of Child Study who actively and frequently published their findings in child study research.

18 Ibid.

19 T.A. Brough, 'Revising the Curriculum in British Columbia,' *The School* (October 1936): 101–5.

20 Millichamp and Fletcher, 'Goals and Growth of Nursery Education,' 30.

21 See, for example, 'The Alberta Activity-Programme,' *The School* (October 1936): 96. Emphasis in original text.

22 Ibid., 100–1.

23 Brough, 'Revising the Curriculum in British Columbia,' 101–2.

24 Ibid., 102. In Brough's terms: 'Knowledge should lead to action.'

25 See, for example, Blatz, 'Educational Frills.'

26 'Institute of Child Study,' *The School* (January 1941): 444–5. This article, which reviews educational research in Ontario, considers the implications of research done at the Institute of Child Study on the longitudinal development of children throughout life. The institute's research followed 109 children and considered their social adjustment and activity.

27 William E. Blatz, 'Security,' *The School* (February 1941): 499–503.

28 Ibid., 499.

29 Ibid., 500. Learning, according to Blatz, howsoever structured in schools, was instinctual, necessarily social, and persistent: 'Fortunately for our

peace of mind no system of education can entirely eradicate the influence of learning. The child will learn in spite of us.'

30 Millichamp and Fletcher, 'Goals and Growth of Nursery Education,' 35.

31 Ibid.

32 Mary L. Northway, 'Preface,' in W.E. Blatz, *Human Security: Some Reflections* (Toronto, ON: University of Toronto Press, 1967). Northway, one of Blatz's colleagues at the Institute of Child Study, refers to him as a provocative public speaker. Furthermore, in his own teaching, Blatz tried to engage his students in ways that would make them contradict him and express alternative views. In short, he 'stimulated thought, while his listeners responded by silently but actively contradicting his statements, supporting his thesis by extending his examples, interpreting or misinterpreting his implications, rebutting his arguments, and appreciating or depreciating his wit,' ix.

33 See, for example, John I. R. McKnight, 'The Teacher's Dilemma: Discovering New Ways of Teaching Old Material,' *The School* (January 1941): 398–9.

34 Blatz, 'Security,' 499.

35 See, for example, Henry Conn, 'The Unemployment Problem in Primary Classes,' *The School* (September 1929): 31–2. Conn's thesis in the article is that the most difficult task for any teacher is to motivate students to remain pleasantly and profitably engaged.

36 Ibid.

37 See, for example, Wilson, 'Seat Work in the Primary Grades,' 237.

38 Gordon Young, 'Optional Subjects,' *Canadian School Journal* (December 1933): 427.

39 Ibid.

40 J.D. Griffin, 'News and Comments,' *Canadian School Journal* (December 1933): 446.

41 Dickie earned her MA from Queen's University before moving to Alberta, where she instructed in all three of Calgary's normal schools. In 1940, Dickie wrote two articles in *The School* on the topic of enterprise education. She earned a PhD from the University of Toronto and a Governor General's Award for a children's history textbook titled *The Great Adventure*. Like most progressivist voices, she contrasted a new and progressive education with a traditional one that did not meet students' needs. While Dickie is not treated as a subject in the source journals, enterprise learning had an impact on Ontario's schools: 'After her involvement with the introduction of "The Enterprise," as the progressive education reforms in elementary schools were called in Alberta, she wrote *The Enterprise in Theory and Practice*. It became the standard text on progressive education used in teacher educa-

tion programs across Canada.' Amy von Von Heyking, *Creating Citizens: History and Identity in Alberta's Schools, 1905 to 1980* (Calgary, AB: University of Calgary Press, 2006), 64. See also Rebecca Priegert Coulter, 'Getting Things Done: Donalda J. Dickie and Leadership through Practice,' *Canadian Journal of Education* 28, no. 4 (2005): 667–98.
42 Donalda Dickie, 'Education via the Enterprise,' *The School* (March 1935): 4.
43 Ibid., 4.
44 In contemporary schooling contexts, the enterprise would best be described as a project method of teaching. Both integrate various subjects into learning tasks emphasizing some form of authentic activity. The learner is permitted space to pursue personal interests within the enabling constraints of a learning theme.
45 Donalda Dickie, 'Education via the Enterprise,' 4.
46 Correlation, in contemporary schools, is most commonly referred to as integration. Integration of subject matter might entail the use of, for example, mathematics, language, and social studies in one learning situation as opposed to treating these subjects separately. Correlation had a further inference involving a blurring of differences between subjects and contexts. I appeal to Dewey's description of this in the context of learning: 'We live in a world where all sides are bound together. All studies grow out of relations in the one great common world. When the child lives in varied but concrete and active relationship to this common world, his studies are naturally unified. It will no longer be a problem to correlate studies. The teacher will not have to resort to all sorts of devices to weave a little arithmetic into the history lesson, and the like.' Dewey, *The School and Society* (Chicago, IL: University of Chicago Press), 107.
47 See, for example, Donalda Dickie, 'Education via the Enterprise,' 103–7. In this article, the second of two parts, Dickie elaborates on the theme of enterprise education. She provides instruction for teachers on how to plan enterprises, including a sample project titled 'Down North: A Conducted Tour' that interrelates learning in the following subjects: flight, geography, weather, mining, freight, and Inuit peoples.
48 The issue of transfer of training will be discussed again in ch. 6 with regard to faculty psychology and the demise of humanistic study.
49 For further discussion on William James's study in relation to the transfer of training and faculty psychology, see ch. 6, which discusses humanistic rhetoric as a foil to progressivist ideas.
50 C.C. Goldring, 'The School and Business,' *Canadian School Journal* (January 1935): 11. The efficiency progressivist doubts regarding transferability of skills is discussed at length by Herbert Kliebard with regard to the US con-

text. See, in particular, Kliebard, *The Struggle for the American Curriculum*, 89–92.

51 In the U.S. context, Herbert Kliebard also reported that the collapse of mental discipline and the idea that experimental psychology had debunked faith in the transferability of learning was used as leverage for the dismantling of the classical, humanist curriculum. He hypothesized, however, that these justifications for reform need to be understood as a 'consequence of a changing social order, which brought with it a different conception of what knowledge was of most worth.' Herbert M. Kliebard, *The Struggle for the American Curriculum, 1893–1958*, 3rd ed. (New York, NY: RoutledgeFalmer, 2004), 6.

52 W.G. Martin, 'Education and Citizenship,' *Canadian School Journal* (May 1932): 194.

53 Ibid., 194.

54 Ibid., 194.

55 Robert M. Stamp, *The Schools of Ontario, 1876–1976* (Toronto, ON: University of Toronto Press, 1982), 166.

56 Goldring, 'The School and Business,' 10.

57 Ibid., 10.

58 A.M. Laird and J.E. Durrant, 'An Occupational Survey of a Small City,' *The School* (April 1939): 655. Occupational surveys of cities were undertaken in most urban cities during the interwar period, each resulting in a list of characteristics or traits desired of progressive young citizens entering the workforce. Laird and Durrant were concerned with the City of Guelph, Ontario.

59 Ibid., 655.

60 Ibid., 655.

61 C.C. Goldring, 'Educational News,' *Canadian School Journal* (November 1935): 325.

62 J.R. Littleproud, 'School Savings: A Project in Citizenship,' *Canadian School Journal* (January 1934): 9–10.

63 It is essentially this kind of prespecification of pedagogical objectives based on the precepts of activity analysis and behavioural objectives that, in the United States, characterized the idea of scientific curriculum design. For further reading on scientific curriculum making, see Werrett W. Charters, *Methods of Teaching: Developed from a Functional Standpoint* (Chicago, IL: Row, Peterson, 1909); *Curriculum Construction* (New York, NY: Macmillan, 1923); *Teaching the Common Branches* (Boston, MA: Houghton Mifflin, 1913); and Herbert M. Kliebard, 'Rise of Scientific Curriculum-Making,' in *Forging the American Curriculum: Essays in Curriculum History and Theory* (New York, NY: Routledge, 1992), 83–4.

64 The questioning of what personal traits or habits of mind schools could cultivate in order to facilitate efficient business practice in a progressive society was a continuous theme in the interwar years. On occasion, the notion that progressive schools should cultivate appropriate business habits was blatantly and explicitly stated. See, for example, W.J. Cairns, 'What To-Day's Business Man Asks of To-Day's Young Man,' *Canadian School Journal* (October 1936): 285. Cairns, manager of Bell Telephone's largest division, spoke to a group of Boy Scouts, informing them that dependability, loyalty, cheerfulness, enthusiasm, and initiative were, in order, the traits that he looked for when hiring employees. His speech was reproduced in the journal and sent to educationists across the province, reinforcing the importance of asking, 'What does the business man of today look for in young men?'

65 Littleproud, 'School Savings,' 9.

66 Ibid., 9.

67 Ibid. The following citation makes this point most clearly: Littleproud engages in a prolonged comparison between the 'old' and 'new' educational viewpoints: 'The old viewpoint was traditional; the new viewpoint is human. The old viewpoint was academic, the new viewpoint is citizenship. The aim of the school under the old viewpoint was to make scholars of all the children who attended its classes; the aim of the new viewpoint is to make good citizens of all who come under its influence.'

68 Ibid., 10.

69 Ibid.

70 Ibid.

71 C.R. Durrant, 'The Search for an Educational Ideal,' *Canadian School Journal* (April 1934): 123.

72 Charles F. Deeley, 'Two Thoughts on Projects,' *The School* (January 1941): 405.

73 Ibid., 405.

74 'Standards in the Middle School: A Discussion of Methods in Measurements in Matriculation Subjects,' *The School* (March 1941): 621.

75 Ibid. The editorial states: 'For the most part these pupils expect the school to play an important part in preparing them for vocational life, and we are justified in requiring standards which will make that preparation as nearly adequate as possible.'

76 Ibid., 622.

77 S.B. Sinclair, 'How Rural School Trustees Can Select an Efficient Teacher,' *Canadian School Journal* (March 1932): 94.

78 G.F. Rogers, 'Present Day Problems in Education,' *Canadian School Journal* (May 1933): 176.

79 Ibid., 176.

80 Ibid., 176.

81 'Conference vs. Debate,' *Canadian School Journal* (March 1932): 93.

82 Ibid.

83 Ibid., 93.

84 W.E. Gordon, 'A Guide to Young Canadians Seeking a Job,' *Canadian School Journal* (January 1937), 4. Another theme present in Gordon's article is the difficulty of finding work during the Depression and immediately afterwards. Progressive schools would provide their students with abilities that would facilitate vocational success.

85 G.F. Rogers, 'Present Day Problems in Education,' *Canadian School Journal* (May 1933): 173.

86 These surveys were, as noted above in relation to vocational surveys, common. Throughout the period studied, reports were made from surveys commissioned by different agencies and institutions, including the Department of Education, universities, the Ontario College of Education, and the teachers' federations.

87 J.E. Robertson, 'An Educational Survey,' *The Canadian School Journal* (March, 1932): 120. This survey was, of course, undertaken at the very moment when the Great Depression was most profoundly crunching school finances and grinding both building expansions and program revisions through the efficiency mill.

88 'Control of Expenditures for Education,' *Canadian School Journal* (October 1932): 339.

89 See, for example, R.D. Mess, 'Organizing the School Board for Efficiency,' *Canadian School Board Journal* (April 1928): 8. In this article, which reproduced an address delivered at the Urban Section of the Trustees' Department by the Reverend R.D. Mess in London, Ontario, one of the themes for progressivist reform is the idea that efficiency promotes stability and control when the world is in flux.

90 See, for example, 'The Challenge of Childhood,' *Canadian School Board Journal* (June 1928): 2.

91 'School Administration and School Finance in Ontario – Can They Be Improved?' *Canadian School Journal* (May 1932): 190.

92 'Control of Expenditures for Education,' 339.

93 Colonel E.E. Snider, 'How Shall We Achieve Greater Efficiency in Our Schools,' *Canadian School Journal* (September 1935): 253.

94 In March 1937, McCulley was identified as a notable figure in Ontario's educational scene, meriting a short biography in an article titled 'Who's Who,' *Canadian School Journal* (March 1937): 86. McCulley, a University of

Toronto graduate awarded the Massey Scholarship for graduate study in history at Oxford University, was described as being 'interested in progressive movements in education, being a member of the Executive and Chairman for two years of the Toronto Branch of the New Education Fellowship.' The New Education Fellowship was a UK-based organization promoting progressive education; it was in many respects the European counterpart to the U.S.-based Progressive Education Association. For further reading, see, for example, Margaret H. White, 'The New Education Fellowship: An International Community of Practice,' *New Era in Education* 82, no. 3 (2001); and Hermann Rohrs and Volker Lenhart, eds., *Progressive Education across the Continents: A Handbook* (New York, NY: Peter Lang, 1995).

95 Joseph McCulley, 'Education in a Changing Society,' *Canadian School Journal* (January 1932): 58.

96 Ibid., 58.

97 Ibid. In education, McCulley notes, this would require a paradigmatic shift, which would face opposition from entrenched ways of thinking: 'In all ages and in all places there has ever seemed to be among mankind a profound aversion to change. Particularly is this so when change necessitates a revision of mental concepts, – or a reconstruction of a philosophy of life.'

98 See, for example, 'The Educational Conventions,' *Canadian School Journal* (March 1937): 106. This article, summarizing conventions held across the province in the past months, presents a number of voices iterating the dominant theme in progressivist, social meliorist texts in the late 1930s: the necessity of fostering social cooperation. It reports, for instance, that Joseph McCulley held a convention on this same theme at Pickering College in Newmarket, Ontario. References were made to 'the emphasis placed on the knowledge of facts as not being of so great importance as the spirit in which the child uses the knowledge, and the development of the capacity of all pupils to live a socially useful life.'

99 W.G. Martin, 'Education for Citizenship,' *Canadian School Journal* (May 1932): 194.

100 Ibid.

101 'Editorial: Working Together,' *The School* (February 1941): 497. This was, of course, during the Second World War. Many articles during the early 1940s emphasized social meliorism and democratic government as necessary alternatives to fascism and Nazism. For a lengthier description of the meliorist ethos during the Second World War, see ch. 7.

102 Ibid., 497.

103 Ibid., 497.
104 John A. Cook, 'Co-operation in Education,' *Canadian School Journal* (November 1933): 406.
105 See, for example, R.H. Macklem, 'The Community School,' *The School* (April 1942): 656–9.
106 Ibid., 656.
107 Ibid., 656.
108 Ibid., 657.
109 F.J. McDonald, 'Character Training and Citizenship,' *Canadian School Journal* (June 1934): 238.
110 Ibid., 238.
111 Ibid., 238.
112 Ibid., 239–40.
113 B.C. Taylor, 'The Latin Society – I,' *The School* (September 1941): 41.
114 'Educational News: Democracy,' *The School* (November 1941): 260.
115 Watson shared the limelight with Thornton Mustard, principal of the Toronto Normal School. The two were co-chairs of the committee that drafted the 1937 revised Programme of Studies in Ontario. For a lengthier discussion, see ch. 7. See also Lynn S. Lemisko and Kurt W. Clausen, 'Connections, Contrarieties, and Convulsions: Curriculum and Pedagogical Reform in Alberta and Ontario, 1930–1955,' *Canadian Journal of Education* 29, no. 4 (2006): 1097–126.
116 Stanley Watson, 'Is the Role of the Teacher Changing,' *Canadian School Journal* (June 1937): 227–8.
117 Ibid., 228.
118 'Dr. Duncan McArthur, Deputy Minister of Education, Trustees' Department,' *Canadian School Journal* (April 1937): 135–40, 167.
119 Ibid., 140.
120 Ibid., 140.
121 See, for example, 'A Criticism of Our Educational System,' *Canadian School Journal* (September 1940): 321–2; Rene Lamoureux, 'The Training of Teachers,' *Canadian School Journal* (April 1940): 122–6; and A.B. Lucas, 'Education for Democracy,' 139, 162.
122 'A Criticism of Our Educational System,' 322. An editorial note at the article's head states the following: 'This report was given by a member of a Board of Education and an active member of the Ontario School Trustees' and Ratepayers' Association to the Board in one of the large cities in Ontario.'
123 See, for example, 'Teaching Democracy,' *Canadian School Journal* (September 1941): 271; and 'Democracy in Action,' *Canadian School Journal*

(November 1941): 345. Both articles argued the urgent need to develop school activities promoting democracy.

124 James Keillor, 'High School Civics,' *The School* (September 1926): 59.

125 Ibid., 59.

126 Ibid., 59.

127 James Keillor, 'High School Civics,' *The School* (January 1927): 492.

128 'Editorial Notes: New Approaches to the Social Studies,' *The School* (April 1937): 645.

129 Ibid., 645.

130 Ibid., 645.

131 See, for example, Joseph McCulley, 'Education in an Age of Insecurity,' *Canadian School Journal* (April 1937): 138–40. In this article, McCulley identified conflicts relating to religious surety, moral codes, financial stability, political faith, and the breakdown of a strong agricultural community as sources of profound anxiety among Ontarians. Furthermore, he argued that 'security in all these areas and many others has been shattered by our rapidly changing age … No longer is the classical and traditional curriculum carefully divided off into subject matter areas, sufficient to provide any understanding of the problems of modern life.' See also Lucy Dobson, 'Message of the President, O.E.A.,' *Canadian School Journal* (December 1940): 422. Dobson argues: 'We are living in a rapidly changing world. It is difficult to predict what sort of life our youth will live when they reach maturity, but it is essential that they be adequately equipped to take their place in the new world of tomorrow.'

132 Ibid. The article explains that L.C. Marshall and R.M. Goetz prepared the report on behalf of Ontario's Department of Education.

133 Students would be able to draw on their personal experiences and a range of different subjects to study – for example, inequities in public health and housing. They would also be able to develop their active participation in the improvement of community life for all.

134 'Editorial Notes: New Approaches to the Social Studies,' 645.

135 'Editorial Notes: The Social Sciences,' *The School* (January 1936): 363.

136 Ibid., 363. Many progressivist articles focus on a 'scientific' approach to education. Meliorist discourse shows concern for social science and, in a Deweyan sense, the development of scientific communities of learning. Efficiency discourse reveals a faith in mathematical science and the ability of objective intelligence testing to scientifically assess student ability. Developmentalist discourse often concerns science in biological spheres.

137 E.A. Corbett, 'Adult Education and the School,' *The School* (September 1938).

138 Ibid., 18. Radio, in particular, was frequently discussed as potentially exerting a unifying influence on Ontario's citizens, promoting national consciousness and operating as a defence mechanism for democratic thinking. See, for example, Gladstone Murray, 'Radio and Citizenship,' *Canadian School Journal* (April 1942): 113–14. The radio as an educational tool for promoting citizenship and democracy is discussed again in ch. 7.

139 The expansion of schooling and the effects of the Depression on schooling were discussed in ch. 1.

140 R.S. Lambert, 'Adult Education,' *The School* (June 1941): 883.

141 Ibid., 883. See ch. 7 for a more extended discussion of the democratic rhetoric that infused the source journals in Ontario between 1940 and 1942, when Canada's involvement in the Second World War thrust the topic of democracy into the limelight of progressivist discourse.

142 Ibid., 883.

143 See, for example, James S. Gordon, 'Adult Education in a Rural Community,' *Canadian School Journal* (December 1937): 428. This article is notable because it states quite plainly in the opening paragraph that citizenship training represents the core of adult education. Gordon's argument also follows a trope common to progressivist articles published in the context, in that it opens with an argument that condemns traditional schooling: 'Education, some time ago, was spoken in terms of 3 R's (readin', 'riting, 'rithmetic). Today it is considered in terms of 3 C's (character, culture, and citizenship). With the transition from the R's to the C's has come the realization that education is not confined to school and university years, but extends from the cradle to the grave.'

144 For example, 'Extension of Correspondence Courses,' *The School* (November 1935): 250.

145 E.A. Corbett, 'Can the Radio Be Used Effectively in University Extension Work?,' 93.

4. Progressive as Individualized Instruction

1 In the previous chapter, it was noted that William E. Blatz, founding director of the Institute of Child Study, began his medical career working in a rehabilitation program for injured soldiers in Toronto.

2 For further reading on the implications of increased professionalization and institutionalization of psychology in relation to the normalization of educational and family life, see Mona Gleason, *Normalizing the Ideal: Psychology, Schooling, and Family in Postwar Canada* (Toronto, ON: University

of Toronto Press, 1999). Gleason's text, which mostly concerns the context immediately following the period considered in this book, uses Michel Foucault's theoretical model to explain family life in Canada. Her analysis makes some rather broad generalizations regarding psychology as a normalizing discipline and, at points, has an ahistorical character.

3 Cynthia Commachio, *The Infinite Bonds of Family: Domesticity in Canada, 1850–1940* (Toronto, ON: University of Toronto Press, 1999), 134.

4 Ibid., 256.

5 William E. Blatz and Helen McMurchy Bott, *Parents and the Pre-School Child* (Toronto, ON: J.M. Dent, 1928), 14–15.

6 Ibid., 15.

7 Ibid., 16. Emphasis in original text.

8 Commacchio, *The Infinite Bonds of Family*, 96–7.

9 William E. Blatz, *Understanding the Young Child*, 240.

10 Dorothy A. Millichamp and Margaret I. Fletcher, 'Goals and Growth of Nursery Education,' in *Twenty-Five Years of Child Study*, 27.

11 Frederick Minkler, 'The Progressive Education Conferences at Hamilton and Windsor,' *The School* (January 1939): 378–84. The New Education Fellowship (NEF), introduced last chapter in the section on 'Criticality and Change,' was based out of Great Britain. The NEF was international in scope and aspired to promote a new and progressive education. The Hamilton conference was held on 17 November 1938, drawing eight hundred guests. Notably, the PEA conference occurred less than two months after Canada declared war on Germany. At the time, most progressivist articles in the Ontario journals were concerned with the active promotion of democratic citizenship and social meliorism.

12 Ibid.

13 Minkler attended fifteen sessions and admitted that his article was synthetic rather than descriptive.

14 Minkler, 'The Progressive Education Conferences,' 378. Emphasis in the original text.

15 See, for example, Helen Loy McDowell, 'Some Thoughts on Educating the Child of Pre-School Age,' *Canadian School Journal* (October 1936): 283, 305. McDowell, president of the Federated Women's Institutes of Ontario, asserts the individuality and uniqueness of each child, which requires careful, holistic study.

16 Minkler, 'The Progressive Education Conferences,' 379.

17 See, for example, S.R. Laycock, 'Extra-curricular Activities in the Modern School,' *The School* (October 1941): 93–7. Laycock, a Professor of Education,

explained that the progressive teacher 'thinks in terms of pupil development and pupil growth. Further, she conceives of her task as the all-round development of her pupils,' 93.

18 S.R. Laycock, 'The Diagnostic Approach to Problems of Pupil Adjustment,' *The School* (February 1939): 461. Emphasis in the original text.

19 Ibid., 461.

20 Ibid., 461.

21 Ibid., 461. Emphasis in the original text.

22 See, for example, Jocelyn M. Raymond, *The Nursery World of Dr Blatz* (Toronto, ON: University of Toronto Press, 1991); Mary L. Northway, 'Foreword,' in *Twenty-Five Years of Child Study;* and William E. Blatz, *Understanding the Young Child* (New York, NY: William Morrow, 1944).

23 See, for example, Charles A. Alexander, 'The Teacher's Place in the New Health Programme,' *Canadian School Journal* (January 1935).

24 The matter of IQ will be discussed at greater length below within the social efficiency orientation.

25 In fact, Blatz actually constructed an instrument for measuring parental intelligence, which addressed the 'duties and responsibilities of fathers to their children … and devised to stimulate thinking on the part of the fathers rather than to test their "knowledge about" children.' If it succeeded in stimulating discussion, Blatz believed, it would be justified. Parents would score the test themselves, and the knowledge garnered from its results would help them develop as parents. No one was expected 'to rate 100%, of course, for no one is a perfect parent.' William E. Blatz and Helen MacMurchy Bott, *An Intelligence Test for Fathers*, box 1, no. 43, William E. Blatz Fonds, Thomas Fisher Rare Book Library: 1.

26 Blatz conceded that an observational and anecdotal report by a 'trained psychologist is a far more reliable index to a child's educational needs than numerals marked on a written examination or the dictum of a single teacher's judgment.' Blatz, *Understanding the Young Child*, 234.

27 See, for example, Laycock, 'The Diagnostic Approach to Problems of Pupil Adjustment.' Blatz, for his part, believed that it was inconceivable to suggest that the IQ 'should be the only criterion for later selection and educational opportunities.' Blatz, *Understanding the Young Child*, 234.

28 William E. Blatz, 'Mental Hygiene and Education,' *The School* (January 1940): 378.

29 Ibid., 382.

30 See, for example, Samuel Farmer, 'The Aims of Education,' *Canadian School Journal* (February 1935): 41–2. Farmer, a school trustee from Port Perry, Ontario, lists as his first aim a concern for the development of individuals

through the natural stages of life and their happy coexistence with others: 'Education should be the development of the individual so that he [*sic*] may live happily and usefully with other people, making the best use of his native ability and life's opportunities. Every phase of life, its happiness and its sorrows, its comedies and its tragedies, and its final drama, all these educate.'

31 Blatz, 'Mental Hygiene and Education,' 377.

32 Minkler, 'The Progressive Education Conferences,' 378.

33 The 1937 curriculum reforms and their relationship to progressivist orientations are discussed at greater length in ch. 7.

34 'Dr. D. McArthur at the O.E.A.,' *The School* (June 1935): 834.

35 Ibid., 834.

36 D.S. Woods, 'Trends in the High School Curriculum,' *The School* (April 1940): 658.

37 Ibid., 658.

38 See, for example, W.C. Keirstead, 'Indoctrination in Education,' *The School* (May 1940): 743–8. Blatz explained that individual choice was necessary but that individuals were bound to accept responsibility for these choices. This was how responsibility was learned: 'At every moment of experience the individual must select a specific action pattern. From the beginning of his [*sic*] life there are situations in which a child may be taught to choose and accept the consequences of his choice. Responsibility may be defined as the habit of choosing, and accepting the consequences of the choice of behavior.' Blatz, *Understanding the Young Child*, 187.

39 W.C. Keirstead, 'Indoctrination in Education,' 743.

40 Ibid., 743.

41 Blatz wrote a great deal on the individual child's responsibility to self and to society. Most fully, he elaborated on this theme in *Understanding the Young Child*, in which he explained that to a certain extent, all people needed to learn to conform to societal expectations so they might 'feel comfortable in the community' even though the expectations might be nothing more than 'certain arbitrary and artificial rules of conduct.' Yet blind obedience to rules and dictates would ultimately lead to unhealthy resentment in the learner. Questioning regulations was necessary. In fact, the interest in promoting a progressive education was a necessary thing, for the members of any community – in this case the educational one – needed 'opportunities … to alter the rules or laws to fit changing conditions and ideas,' 57.

42 'The Institute of Child Study: The School Reporter Takes a Chance,' *The School* (April 1941): 692.

43 Fern Holland, 'To-morrow,' *Canadian School Journal* (September 1934): 316.

44 Ibid., 316.

45 In this discussion of social efficiency, the focus remains on the discourse and not on the authors. The aim here is not to develop a catalogue of 'advocates' enmeshed in rhetorical warfare or, in Kliebard's terms, conflicting interest groups waging war for the curriculum.

46 See, for example, Donald Peat, 'Two Sides to a Question: If Teachers Are to Devote More Time to Exceptional Children, to What Intelligence Group Should Most of the Additional Attention Be Given? To Below-Average Pupils,' *The School* (February 1942): 464.

47 Marion Goode Hodgins, 'Permanent Values in Education,' *The School* (May 1942): 760.

48 Ibid., 760–2. Although Goode's address was seen as primarily directed to teachers of commercial work in vocational schools, an editorial note reinforced the point that all schools should encourage the article's catalogued values because they were significant for all teachers.

49 Peat, 'Two Sides to a Question,' 464. Interestingly, the editor's introduction to Peat's article describes the author as a 'champion of the below-average children.'

50 Ibid., 464.

51 See, for example, Greer, 'Two Sides to a Question,' 465.

52 Peat, 'Two Sides to a Question,' 464.

53 See, for example, Colonel E.E. Snider, 'How Shall We Achieve Greater Efficiency in Our Schools,' *Canadian School Journal* (September 1935): 251–6. In this article, Snider argues that standardized tests measuring mental ability are so effective at promoting efficiency that they should be extended to each area in the province and country and used as global, comparative tools.

54 S.R. Laycock, 'Helping the Bright Pupil,' *The School* (March 1942): 561.

55 Ibid., 561.

56 Ibid., 561. For example, Laycock argues that a capable, progressive teacher 'knows that slightly above-average children have powers above the average in reasoning and analysis, and she [*sic*] sees that the classroom discussions and the pupils' written work bring out these powers. She encourages them to read and to look up additional material pertinent to lessons.'

57 Greer, 'Two Sides to a Question,' 465. An editorial note introducing Greer's article characterized the author as a 'protagonist of the brainy.' The context of the quotation was an Ontario farm where Greer worked as a young man. Apparently, the anecdote was a response to Greer, who asked his employer why he wanted to fertilize land that was already good, when the barren ten acres near a creek was in urgent need of improvement.

58 Ibid.

59 See, for example, R.S. Murray, 'The Problem of Teaching,' *Canadian School Journal* (December 1934): 415.

60 See, for example, 'Editorial: High Marks Still Count,' *The School* (March 1942): 557.

61 See, for example, Laycock, 'Helping the Bright Pupil,' 561.

62 See, for example, S.R. Laycock, 'Helping the Below-Average Pupil,' *The School* (February 1942), 467. Laycock qualifies the potential benefits of educating the 'dull child' by explaining that the field of potential study must be chosen carefully on the basis of good guidance.

63 Greer, 'Two Sides to a Question,' 465.

64 See, for example, Karl S. Bernhardt, 'Who Should Go to College,' *Canadian School Journal* (October 1936): 281–2. In this article, Bernhardt, Professor of Psychology at the University of Toronto, assesses the educational system in Ontario and finds it incredibly wasteful in terms of both time and money because it does not lead students to the correct courses that their lives should follow.

65 See, for example, S.B. Sinclair, 'Treatment of the Sub-Normal Child,' *Canadian School Journal* (July 1929): 18–19. Sinclair, former Inspector of Auxiliary Classes for the Province of Ontario, provides subcategories for describing children already identified as subnormal. Children with IQs below fifty are described as 'feeble-minded' and uneducable. 'Psychopathic children' with mental illness should be treated similarly. Individuals falling in the fifty to seventy-five range are 'dull and backward' and belong in ungraded school classes with special teachers.

66 See, for example, J.H. Putman, 'The Problem of Retarded Pupils,' *Canadian School Journal* (June 1939): 223–4. A gifted child, or one of normal intelligence, Putman argues, 'does not constitute a major problem in the modern school. He [*sic*] will look after himself.' A child who is 'retarded,' on the other hand, requires greater supports and needs, consequently, to be identified and given instruction at his level.

67 Laycock, 'Helping the Below-Average Pupil,' 467–8. The most common arguments for progressivist administrative reforms to schools between 1940 and 1942 included an assertion of democratic care for individuals in Ontario's schools by presenting Hitlerism, fascism, and Stalinism as brutish and oppressive by comparison.

68 See, for example, David H. Russell, 'Subject Matter Disabilities,' *The School* (February 1942): 471.

69 Ibid., 471.

70 Ibid., 471.

71 See, for example, 'Students Find Happiness,' *Canadian School Journal* (October 1929): 23. This article announces that the Inspector of Auxiliary Classes in Ontario, 'S.B. Sinclair, Ph.D. in a lecture in Toronto astonished his hearers by revealing a scientific system whereby boys and girls may be guided into their true account of service in the after life which follows vocational training. The fact that all pupils are not equally mentally equipped has been recognized for centuries, but it is only in recent years that a sane, sympathetic attitude has been taken towards those unfortunates who fall below the common standard.' Sinclair's system included mental intelligence testing and vocational guidance.

72 W.H.H. Green, 'The Vocational School and the Community,' *The School* (November 1940): 212. This conviction was one very frequently stated. See, for example, Marion E. Goode, 'The Methods of Guidance,' *The School* (December 1940): 288–91.

73 See, for example, H. Ruth Hooper and Edna Lancaster, 'Classes for More Intelligent Pupils,' *The School* (December 1940): 352–5. The authors, teachers at the Empress School in London, Ontario, were particularly concerned with gifted and intelligent children, whose education, they argued, should lead them most efficiently to leadership positions.

74 Goode, 'The Methods of Guidance,' 288.

75 Ibid., 289–90.

76 John A. Long, 'The Construction and Use of New-Type Tests,' *The School* (October 1940): 95. Long argued that reliability and consistency are evident in an assessment when 'repeated testing of the same candidates tend to give closely parallel results.'

77 Laycock, from the University of Saskatchewan, expressed this idea in the following terms: 'While the controversy still rages as to whether intelligence can be affected by environment or not, teachers had best be reconciled to the fact that, at present, so far as school children go, dull children cannot be made brilliant by any trick now known to educators.' Laycock, 'Helping the Below-Average Pupil,' 467.

78 Long, 'The Construction and Use of New-Type Tests,' 95. Long aimed to distinguish progressivist concerns for individual ability from traditionalist concerns for content mastery: 'It has been urged by critics of new-type tests that they *measure mere facts*. Usually this criticism comes from men of a philosophic turn of mind, for to the matter-of-fact scientist there is no such thing as a "mere fact": facts are to him [sic] the only basis for sure knowledge and are always matters of first importance. This criticism is frequently advanced by teachers of history, who argue that new-type devices give the examinee no scope to show his originality or to show his ability to organize

his knowledge in a logical matter. For the most part the argument is well founded, but often when new-type tests are singled out for this particular criticism, it is merely a matter of the pot calling the kettle black. If one examines our matriculation papers in history he will find little to show that the candidate is expected to do more than record legibly and grammatically certain facts which he is expected to have acquired from his teacher and his textbook.' Emphasis in the original text.

79 Ibid., 95. Long argues: 'In the essay-type examination the candidate is so slowed up by the mere mechanics of writing, that he [*sic*] manages to express surprisingly few ideas in a two- or three-hour period.' The teacher can also rejoice because 'objective examinations are *easily and quickly scored*,' 95. Emphasis in the original text.

80 The belief, based on Edward Thorndike's work, that transferability of training was not possible.

81 See, for example, Alfred E. Lavell, 'Abstract of an Address on 'Home, School, and the Prevention of Crime,' *Canadian School Journal* (April 1932): 148. Among the most desirable character traits was discipline.

82 Ibid.

83 Peat, 'Two Sides to a Question,' 464. Watson Kirkconnell, principal of Lindsay Collegiate Institute, presented a lecture in April 1927 titled 'Why Did They Go Astray?' in which he explained, in reference to the arrest of two local boys for 'banditry,' that if the system of education in Ontario 'could have given them a technical education instead of having to confine them to the regular matriculation course they would have been fitted to engage in work which suited them. I do not think I am going too far in laying the blame for their predicament to our present system of education.' Watson Kirkconnell, 'Puts Blame on the System,' *Canadian School Journal* (September 1927): 20.

84 See, for example, 'Education for Character,' *The School* (October 1934): 95. This article, which was followed by others during the 1934–5 school year, praised the U.S.-based National Education Association's publication of a report outlining character education as a process of integrated curriculum, guidance, and administration for the purpose of securing students' vocational adjustment. Certainly, it was not the only opinion on character education. For instance, as noted in the previous chapter, child study progressivists were explicitly on the side of fostering individuality and even nonconformity.

85 See, for example, Florence S. Dunlop, 'The School Psychologist,' *The School* (May 1940): 754.

86 C.L. Burton, 'Business as an Objective,' *Canadian School Journal* (October 1932): 341–2.

87 Ibid., 341.
88 Other reasons noted for classifying and separating schoolchildren according to ability included, to reiterate, the idea that slow children impede the progress of their peers, and the belief that each child's potential could best be realized by an education catered to his or her mental ability.
89 Harold W. Hill, 'Above-Average and Below-Average Students,' *The School* (December 1940): 327. In his terms, 'in mathematics, as in all other subjects, a problem is created by the existence of three main groups of students: the exceptionally bright, the exceptionally otherwise, and the great middle class between.'
90 Ibid.
91 Hooper and Lancaster, 'Classes for More Intelligent Pupils,' 352.
92 Ibid., 352.
93 Ibid., and, for example, Martin, 'Education and Citizenship,' 194.
94 For further reading on Harold Rugg, see Herbert M. Kliebard, *The Struggle for the American Curriculum, 1893–1958*, 3rd ed. (New York, NY: Routledge-Falmer, 2004), 170–73, and E.A. Winters, 'Harold Rugg and Education for Social Reconstruction' (PhD manuscript, University of Wisconsin, Madison, 1968). Like George S. Counts and Boyd Bode, Rugg had a profound impact on the terrain of social reconstructionism and social meliorism in the U.S. progressive education movement. He not only represented the PEA on the NEF but also developed the first social studies textbooks, titled *Man and His Changing Society*, in the United States. These texts, despite the economic collapse and financial cutbacks associated with the Depression, sold an astonishing 1,317,960 copies and 2,687,000 workbooks between 1929 and 1939. Rugg's textbooks, before being slandered and burned as subversive and socialist in the build-up to the Cold War, targeted social inequities, disparities between the rich and the poor, racial stereotypes, and changing gender roles in society.
95 'The N.E.F. Conference,' *The School* (May 1937): 741.
96 Ibid., 742.
97 For further discussion of the 1937 curriculum reforms in Ontario, see ch. 7.
98 'The N.E.F. Conference,' 743.
99 Ibid.
100 These are, incidentally, the themes that are considered in this section of the chapter.
101 'The N.E.F. Conference,' 742.
102 See, for example, 'Editorial: Government by the People,' *The School* (October 1940): 93. This article called on Ontario's educationists not to forget that 'the principle of democracy *is*, and should be present in the classroom

always, making the teacher conscious that his [*sic*] authority is a temporary trust to be used as little, but as effectively, as possible.' It cautions that
'democracy means "power of the people" and it can only be developed
by the people within themselves ... It is the right of people to make their
influence felt by free discussion and organization.' The war threatened to
repudiate democratic principles, posing a threat to the meliorist principles of progressive education: 'And the new education, designed to
make democracy more effective, will bear the first brunt of the attack,' 93.
Emphasis in the original text.

103 B.A. Fletcher, 'Some Principles of Education,' *The School* (January 1939):
372.

104 Ibid., 372–3.

105 See, for example, Martin, 'Education for Citizenship,' 194.

106 Duncan McArthur, 'Education for Citizenship,' *The School* (December
1934): 283–9.

107 Ibid., 284–5. Here, McArthur declared: 'Conditions have been created
which have encouraged, too greatly, the spirit of competition; the desire
to "come first" has provided, too frequently, a more powerful motive than
the ambition to master a particular field of knowledge. We have permitted, too frequently, the place in the procession to be considered of greater
consequence than the direction in which the procession is moving. The
good citizen recognizes the binding force of obligation to the community
and realizes that his own well-being cannot be separated from that of the
common-weal. The foundations on which alone the structure of good
citizenship may be erected must be laid in the schools.'

108 Ibid., 286. McArthur explained this aim in the following manner: 'The
objective which the schools must bear in mind is the creation of an understanding of the fundamental relationships subsisting between the individual and the community and the promotion of habits of mind which,
against this background of understanding, will make possible the exercise
of sound judgment in matters of public concern.'

109 Ibid., 284.

110 See, for example, 'The Importance of the School Today,' *Canadian School
Journal* (October 1942): 324. In this editorial note, individual children are
described as citizen units whose roles are vital in the maintenance and
integrity of a democratic community.

111 McArthur, 'Education for Citizenship,' 284. Among the targets of
McArthur's scorn were the annual departmental examinations in Ontario,
which, he felt, promoted a ruthless and competitive individualism.
The spirit of competition, he explained, crept 'into our schools through

practices designed originally to satisfy a thoroughly legitimate demand of parents to know the rate of progress of their children. Instead of measuring the extent of the development within the child of interest and initiative, of effort and appreciation, our system of gradation too frequently has become the means of self-glorification of the child or of its parent, and the creation of an attitude of mind which is fundamentally selfish and anti-social.'

112 'Editorial: Below Average,' *The School* (February 1942): 463. The editorial argued: 'The fact is that achievement marks are a much too facile instrument in education and are too often interpreted as indicating much more than they do.'

113 See, for example, 'What Others Are Saying,' *Canadian School Journal* (January 1936): 27. This article, attributed to J.G. Althouse, Dean of the Ontario College of Education, contains the following quotation: 'The rubbish heap should receive first the preference for a single, authorized text-book in a subject – instead the pupil should be encouraged to read all he [*sic*] could find on the prescribed subject. Second, the matriculation fetish, that is, the idea among business men and employers that none need apply unless they have a matriculation certificate. Third, the competitive report, which the child brings home, showing where he stands in comparison with the other pupils, instead of showing the child's attitude towards his work, or comparison with the best that he can do.'

114 Joseph McCulley, 'Education in an Age of Insecurity,' *Canadian School Journal* (April 1937): 138–40. His speech opened with the following thesis: 'This is indeed an age of insecurity. In fact this word describes conditions today just about as well as any word in the English language.'

115 Ibid.

116 Ibid., 140.

117 See, for example, H.P. Plumptre, 'Education for World Citizenship,' *Canadian School Journal* (September 1935): 247–50; Jessie L. Beattie, 'The New Education,' *Canadian School Journal* (May 1936): 158–60; and A.G. Larsson, 'Some Observations Regarding the Results of the Education Practised in the European Dictatorial Countries,' *Canadian School Journal* (March 1939): 79–81. Larsson's article is particularly memorable. He, a member of the Board of Education in St Marys, Ontario, reviews the educational programs in Germany, Italy, and Russia. He finds them narrow, false, debasing, and one-sided because they do not permit, let alone prepare, their students to challenge the maxims and principles of the ruling authority.

118 John Long, 'A Review of the Year, 1935,' *The School* (February 1936): 467.

119 See, for example, 'Changing the Educational Emphasis,' *Canadian School Journal* (March 1933): 84.

120 Critical intelligence and critical thought are most frequently referred to as freedom to be critical of the overarching demands of society and the power to pursue learning that is of personal interest, rather than that deemed necessary or relevant. See, for example, W.H. Fyfe, 'Message from the Principal of Queen's University,' *Canadian School Journal* (March 1936): 82.

121 'Changing the Educational Emphasis,' 83.

122 Ibid., 83.

123 See, for example, 'Vocational Training and Vocational Guidance,' *Canadian School Journal* (November 1932): 372.

124 'Editorial: As a Man Thinks,' *The School* (December 1939): 284.

125 See, for example, 'The Convention of 1933,' *Canadian School Journal* (May 1933): 163.

126 Ibid., 163. George S. Henry was, as noted in ch. 1, also the Minister of Education in Ontario between 1930 and 1934.

127 See, for example, 'Editorial: As a Man Thinks,' 283–4.

128 See, for example, 'The Work of Voluntary Agencies,' *The School* (November 1933): 188.

129 Ibid.

130 For example, 'President Butler and Democracy,' *The School* (October 1936): 95.

131 Ibid.

132 Ibid.

133 See, for example, 'Despair or Courage,' *Canadian School Journal* (January 1933): 5.

134 Henry Conn, 'Measuring Aptitude for School Work,' *The School* (April 1931): 717.

135 Watson Kirkconnell, 'Democracy for Canadians,' *The School* (June 1941): 881. Fittingly, Kirkconnell would subsequently become Canada's most prominent academic Cold Warrior. George S. Counts, an American progressivist concerned with social meliorism, first denounced the idea that the individual child should be seen as a cog to be fitted in some industrial order. Counts challenged educational reformers to abandon the principles of scientific management because these ideas inevitably led to a state where schools would perpetuate the existing social order rather than become creative forces for social justice. Counts rejected the progressivist concerns for testing and intelligence measuring, because these created false representations of human ability or limitations. For further reading on Counts, see George S. Counts, *The American Road to Culture: A Social Interpretation of Education in the United States* (New York, NY: John Day,

1930), and *Dare the School Build a New Social Order?* (New York, NY: John Day, 1932).

136 Joseph McCulley, 'Education and the War,' *The School* (February 1940): 473.

137 'Education for a Changing World,' *The School* (January 1935): 370.

138 G. Fred McNally, 'Curricula for Canadian High Schools,' *The School* (January 1935): 379. McNally would serve as Deputy Minister of Education in Alberta between 1935 and 1946. His publication in the Ontario journal concerned educational practices across Canada at the secondary level.

139 John A. Cook, 'Co-operation in Education,' *Canadian School Journal* (November 1933): 406.

5. Progressive as Contemporary

1 Mary L. Northway, 'Foreword,' in *Twenty-Five Years of Child Study: The Development of the Programme and Review of the Research at the Institute of Child Study, University of Toronto, 1926–1951*, ed. Karl S. Bernhardt, Margaret I. Fletcher, Frances L. Johnson, Dorothy A. Millichamp, and Mary L. Northway (Toronto, ON: University of Toronto Press), viii. In this foreword to a text commemorating the twenty-fifth year of the institute, Northway refers to it as a 'coordinating and unifying force' in education, standing apart from other models because of its freedom from any 'rigid departmental or faculty pattern.'

2 Ibid., vii. Northway believed that the institute's integrity emerged from its unity: 'So, if education is to preserve its real character, if it is to be an organism and not merely an organization, we must constantly be on our guard against the forces which tend to destroy its unity.'

3 Education via project and enterprise method was discussed in ch. 3.

4 These three aspects will be treated as themes for exploring the meanings of this progressivist domain from the child study orientation.

5 See, for example, both February 1939 and 1940.

6 Advocacy for medical and dental inspections as well as the presence of nurses in schools was the most common topic, spawning books and pamphlets on the subject. See, for example, 'Pickings,' *Canadian School Journal* (February 1941): 67.

7 'The Child's Health,' *Canadian School Journal* (February 1939): 35.

8 V.K. Greer, 'Appraisal of the New Programme of Studies,' *Canadian School Journal* (June 1938): 197.

9 Ibid.

10 See, for example, William M. Bellworth, 'Periodical Medical Examinations of School Children,' *Canadian School Journal* (February 1940): 37–8. Bellworth, a former patient and employee at the Toronto Hospital for Consumptives, relates health to happiness and sees both implicated in education.

11 In addition to being associated with the Toronto Boards of Education and Health, Phair was a member of the Executive Boards of a number of voluntary health agencies, including the Canadian Red Cross Society, the Victorian Order of Nurses, and the Canadian Welfare Council. He believed that social agencies and governmental institutions needed to work collaboratively to promote children's health. 'Dr. J. T. Phair,' *Canadian School Journal* (March 1937): 87.

12 'Health Service,' *Canadian School Journal* (March 1940): 110.

13 Edna L. Moore, 'School Health Service in Ontario,' *The School* (September 1940): 10. When Moore published this article, she was the Chief Public Health Nurse in Ontario. This article outlines the history of health services in the province. With reference to early developments, she said: 'In 1909 the City of Toronto took advantage of the existing legislation and established school health service under the auspices of the Board of Education. In 1917, following a plebiscite, the entire health service for the city was placed under the board of health and a generalized programme introduced.'

14 Ibid.

15 See, for example, 'Scholarship for Beautification,' *Canadian School Journal* (September 1940): 339. This particular article refers to the Carter Trophy, which was presented annually to a rural school in the Guelph region.

16 'Improvement of School Grounds,' *Canadian School Journal* (September 1940): 344.

17 Ibid.

18 See, for example, W.W. Tanner, 'A School Gardening Club,' *The School* (September 1938): 13–14. Tanner, Principal of the High and Vocational School in Timmins, saw such clubs that extended school activities as great successes in education.

19 See, for example, 'The School Board and Health,' *Canadian School Journal* (February 1939): 36.

20 'The Editor's Page,' *Canadian School Journal* (February 1936): 37.

21 O.T. Walker, 'Good Lighting in Our Schools,' *The School* (September 1938): 10–13.

22 Ibid., 12.

23 Ibid., 12–13.

24 'Looking Ahead,' *Canadian School Journal* (March 1936): 95.

25 Ibid., 95. Working with the analogy that heat expands and cold contracts, the article suggests that physical activity facilitates holistic growth and development: 'Greater activity will produce a more rounded life while coldness or inactivity will contract life.'

26 Jessie L. Beattie, 'The New Education,' *Canadian School Journal* (May 1936): 158.

27 Ibid., 160.

28 See, for example, 'Guard the Health of the Child,' *Canadian School Journal* (February 1940): 34.

29 See, for example, 'The Editor's Page,' *Canadian School Journal* (December 1942): 377. In this editorial, all aspects were seen as necessarily correlated to the holistic and healthy development of the child.

30 'Guard the Health of the Child,' 34.

31 'The New Course of Study,' *Canadian School Journal* (November 1937): 401–2.

32 Corbin A. Brown, 'Mental Health of School Children,' *Canadian School Journal* (February 1940): 36.

33 Ontario's home and school associations will be discussed in 'Home and School Movements, and the Promotion of Healthy Homes.'

34 Brown, 'Mental Health of School Children,' 36.

35 William E. Blatz, 'Security,' *The School* (February 1941): 499–503. Corbin Brown did not cite Blatz in his article, but security theory was referred to at the Institute of Child Study as 'the gospel according to Blatz.' Mary L. Northway, 'Postscript,' in *Human Security: Some Reflections* (Toronto, ON: University of Toronto Press, 1966), 123.

36 Blatz, 'Security,' 501. Blatz writes: 'Security may now be defined more fully. When an individual is willing to accept the consequences of his [sic] behaviour, not only known but unknown, not only predictable but unpredictable; when the thrill of adventure compensates for the intervening security which may ensue, then the individual is in a state of security. Thus, the acquisition of *any* skill, in the form of a habit, makes for security. The greater the number and the higher the degree of skill, the more secure is the individual. Competence makes for security, incompetence for insecurity. The insecure individual will compensate either by seeking some form of dependence or by spurring himself on to greater effort in order to obtain security.' Emphasis in the original text.

37 Ibid., 503.

38 'Editorial: A Dilemma,' *The School* (April 1941): 683.

39 Charles A. Alexander, 'The Teacher's Place in the New Health Programme,' *Canadian School Journal* (January 1935), 28.

40 R.H. Roberts, 'Health Education,' *The School* (October 1935): 99.
41 Ibid., 98–9.
42 A great number of brochures, articles, and manuals were published for parents by educationists. Between 1925 and 1940, the staff of the Institute of Child Study alone published 114 documents, including such titles as *Honesty* (1925), *The Importance of Failure* (1934), *How Children Learn* (1937), and *Social Work and Mr. Citizen* (1940).
43 This is particularly relevant to the work of Blatz and the Institute of Child Study, where a Parent Education Division was founded around the same time as the institute. Blatz published articles for parents and mothers in a number of popular magazines, in particular *Chatelaine, Childhood Education, Progressive Education, Child Welfare,* and *Child Study Magazine.* Government agencies were also involved in literature distribution. The most notable of these publications were the 'Little Blue Books' Mothers' Series written by Helen MacMurchy (later Helen MacMurchy Bott) and published by the Dominion of Canada's Department of Health in 1923. Titles included *The Canadian Mother's Book, How to Take Care of the Children,* and *How to Take Care of the Mother.* MacMurchy would eventually co-author a number of publications with Blatz and join the Institute of Child Study staff.
44 See, for example, 'The Editor's Page,' *Canadian School Journal* (February 1936): 38.
45 'The Home and School Movement,' *Canadian School Journal* (March 1933): 85.
46 Ibid.
47 'The Editor's Page,' *Canadian School Journal* (January 1935): 3.
48 'The Home and School Movement,' 85.
49 Nowhere was this truer than in relation to the work of William Blatz. As a second educational project, Blatz took over as Director of an educational experiment called the Progressive School, which had actually been founded in 1926 by a group of parents. These parents included many of Toronto's wealthiest families, including the Gundys and the Eatons. The parents decided to start a cooperative kindergarten that would pursue educational lines as outlined by John Dewey at his University of Chicago laboratory school. They hired a number of teachers from the United States who were familiar with progressive education to begin the program. In 1930, when Blatz assumed the school's leadership, he changed its name from the Progressive School to Windy Ridge. See Raymond, *The Nursery World of Dr Blatz.*
50 'Notes and News: Report of the Inspector of Manual Training and Household Science,' *The School* (June 1936): 56.

51 In many respects, they were the precursors to contemporary parent–teacher associations (PTAs). The increased interest in child study among parents led to the establishment of mothers' clubs, mothers' congresses, mothers' reading circles, art leagues, and young mothers' groups all across the province.

52 'Parents Are to Blame,' *Canadian School Journal* (October 1927): 24. This article, as an example, reports a speech by J.H. Putman, Senior Inspector of Ottawa's public schools, in which he accuses parents of meddling in the aims of education despite having very little scientific understanding of intelligence or ability.

53 See, for example, 'As the Press Viewed the O.E.A. Convention,' *Canadian School Journal* (April 1940): 154.

54 Ibid., 156. In this news piece, E.E. Reece of the Home and School Section questions the wisdom of the association's purchase of books for schools. Trustees, she explains, should handle this, instead of home and school groups.

55 See, for example, Helen Loy McDowell, 'Some Thoughts on Educating the Child of Pre-School Age,' *Canadian School Journal* (October 1936): 283.

56 'Child Study Institute,' *Canadian School Journal* (December 1939): 440.

57 'Editorial Notes: The School and Society,' *The School* (November 1934): 185.

58 Ibid.

59 G. Fred McNally, 'Curricula for Canadian High Schools,' *The School* (January 1935): 377.

60 See, for example, J.L. Jose, 'Is Business Practice Meeting the Community Needs?' *The School* (January 1941): 389.

61 Increasingly, high school programs were providing opportunities and facilities for full-time vocational study in day programs. See, for example, 'Vocational Education,' *The School* (January 1929): 425–6. The editorial notes: 'Twenty-five years ago the number of pupils attending day vocational schools was so small that they were not mentioned separately in the comparative statistics of the Department of Education; now more than a quarter of all the pupils in attendance at secondary schools in Ontario are enrolled in vocational schools and the proportion seems to be growing. It is not a phenomenon peculiar to Ontario.'

62 Jose, 'Is Business Practice Meeting the Community Needs?' 389–91.

63 J. Ferris David, 'Secondary Schools and Their Relation to Business,' *Canadian School Journal* (April 1933): 128. David was Chairman of the Ingersoll Board of Education as well as Vice-President, Urban Section, of the OSTRA.

64 Jose, 'Is Business Practice Meeting the Community Needs?' 391.

65 'Education of 90% of the Pupils for 10% of the Jobs,' *Canadian School Journal* (July 1929): 1.

66 F.G. Waide, 'Re-vamping Our Schools,' *Canadian School Journal* (September 1929): 11.
67 David, 'Secondary Schools and Their Relation to Business,' 128.
68 C.L. Burton, 'Business as an Objective,' *Canadian School Journal* (October 1932): 340.
69 Ibid. The depiction of schools as factories and children as resources is entirely consistent with many efficiency progressivists' characterizations of the educational process. Just as 'the earth's resources were progressively tapped to the world of trading,' Burton noted, children could be used to stimulate industrial development.
70 See, for example, W J. Cunningham, 'Efficiency, Unity, Economy,' *Canadian School Journal* (April 1937): 154–5. In this article, Cunningham, a member of the County Council Section of the OEA, argued that the promotion of efficiency was just as important to the successful progress of Ontario's educational system as any other factor.
71 B.A. Fletcher, 'Some General Principles of Education,' *The School* (January 1939): 371. This article reproduced a speech made at a Canada and New-foundland Education Association meeting. Emphasis in the original text.
72 David, 'Secondary Schools and Their Relation to Business,' 128.
73 M.A. Sorsoleil, 'Vocational Guidance,' *Canadian School Journal* (November 1937): 393–5, 412. The article reproduced Sorsoleil's essay. Curiously, while presenting guidance as a progressive reform in the province, he argued that the need and value of vocational counselling was as old as Plato's *Republic*, from which he cited the following passage: 'But as we caution the shoemaker you know against attempting to be an agriculturist or a weaver or a builder, besides with a view to our shoemaking being well done, and to every artisan we assigned in a like manner one occupation, namely, that for which he was naturally fitted, and in which, if he let other things alone and wrought at it all his time without neglecting his opportunities, he was likely to prove a successful workman,' 393.
74 Olive Russell, 'Is Vocational Guidance Feasible?' *The School* (March 1939): 565. Within a given range, admitted Russell, there could be various possible career paths.
75 Florence S. Dunlop, 'The School Psychologist,' *The School* (May 1940): 753.
76 W.G. Martin, 'Education for Citizenship,' *Canadian School Journal* (May 1932): 194. The article reproduced Martin's speech, which was delivered to the Trustees' and Ratepayers' Department of the OEA on 30 March 1932.
77 Burton, 'Business as an Objective,' 342.
78 'Vocational Training and Vocational Guidance,' *Canadian School Journal* (November 1932): 371.

202 Notes to pages 96–8

79 'Notes and News: Ontario,' *The School* (May 1935): 811.
80 Angus MacRae, *Talents and Temperaments* (London, UK: Nisbet, 1932), quoted in Marion E. Goode, 'The Need of Guidance,' *The School* (October 1940): 108.
81 Burton, 'Business as an Objective,' 342.
82 Goode, 'The Need of Guidance,' 108.
83 Ibid. Goode believed that a poor vocational choice led to many social ills: 'Again, the maladjusted worker must often fail to achieve material prosperity; and such failure, in addition to aggravating his mental discontent, may affect his physical well-being and that of his dependents, who, indeed, may suffer in more ways than one.'
84 Ibid., 108.
85 G.F. Rogers, 'Present Day Problems in Education,' *Canadian School Journal* (May 1933): 174. George Rogers was Chief Director of Education under both George S. Henry and Duncan McArthur. 'We are in the midst of an industrial revolution,' he declared, calling for a progressive revision of school curricula and management.
86 Electa Bissell, 'Developing a Sense of Responsibility in the Grade II Child,' *The School* (November 1929): 224.
87 See, for example, 'Editorial Notes: The School and Society,' *The School* (May 1933): 737.
88 See, for example, 'Editorial: The Coming Triumph of Humanity,' *The School* (December 1941): 275.
89 Joseph McCulley, 'Education in a Changing Society,' *Canadian School Journal* (January 1932): 58.
90 Ibid. McCulley describes the democratic ethos in terms of freedom to debate, challenge, and question. The schools, in his opinion, needed to foster criticality.
91 Martin, 'Education for Citizenship,' 199.
92 See, for example, John A. Cook, 'Co-operation in Education,' *Canadian School Journal* (November 1933): 406–7.
93 For further reading about the Depression and its impact on education, see ch. 1.
94 Cook, 'Co-operation in Education,' 406.
95 Ibid. Cook argued that students need to be constantly reminded of the principle of cooperation and how it has contributed to all aspects of their lives, including food, clothing, and transportation. Furthermore, Cook said, 'the pupil, after having been shown the particular value of this principle in the world about him [*sic*], should be placed in a position where he may take part in the actual demonstration of it.'

96 'Editorial Notes: The School and Society,' *The School* (May 1933): 737.
97 See, for example, George F. Rogers, 'Experiments in Education,' *Canadian School Journal* (May 1937): 232–3.
98 For a lengthier discussion of the 1937 to 1942 context, see ch. 7.
99 'Editorial: Schools and Democracy,' *The School* (February 1939): 459.
100 W.C. Keirstead, 'Indoctrination in Education,' *The School* (May 1940): 743.
101 Ibid., 743.
102 'Editorial: Schools and Democracy,' 459.
103 Ibid.
104 See, for example, 'Editorial Notes: The School and Society,' 737.
105 'Academic Freedom,' *The School* (September 1935): 2. The cited portion of the article from *The Times Educational Supplement* explored reasons for social reconstructionists' failure to affect meaningful educational reforms: 'The leaders of the movement, in their fervor for social reconstruction, appear to close their eyes to a large number of factors which stand in the way of their programme. They fail to realize that teacher and schools cannot move any faster than society is willing to approve. They assume that all teachers are ready to accept the same political, social, or economic programme ... The public response to this movement, as might have been expected, has been a virulent campaign on the part of the press ... It is doubtful whether such opposition would have been aroused, if the campaign had not concentrated on making teachers class-conscious, militant propagandists. A less vociferously conducted movement for a programme of educational enlightenment on crucial issues of the day, for a genuine training in intelligent citizenship, would have met with greater success.'
106 'Academic Freedom,' 2.
107 Cook, 'Co-operation in Education,' 406. Cook was President of the Rural School Section of the OEA.
108 Ibid. Cook asked his readers to consider the economy as an analogy for thinking about educational organization: 'Capitalism as long as there was a scarcity of the necessities of comfortable living, and as long as the employment of every individual who was able to work was required to produce sufficient goods to keep people living satisfactorily, was a great success. It may be as good an economic system as could be evolved to meet a situation where there was a scarcity of the necessities of life. However, when the time came that the machinery set up by the system was easily able, without the assistance of the whole working population, to produce more than could easily be consumed by the whole population, difficulties became apparent. Unemployment became general. And that piteous condition of maldistribution where poverty existed in the midst of plenty attacked us. What, since

then, has pure capitalism been able to do with respect to our difficulties? Nothing it would seem unless to aggravate them.'

109 See, for example, 'Neighbourliness – The Core of Progressive Education,' *Canadian School Journal* (February 1935): 55. The article, summarizing a lecture by Frederick L. Patry from the University of the State of New York, considers the promotion of community the hallmark of progressive schooling.

110 'Educational News: Ontario,' *The School* (April 1942): 723.

111 See, for example, Horace L. Brittain, 'Some Views of Administration of Public Education,' *Canadian School Journal* (December 1934): 406.

112 Joseph McCulley, 'Press Extracts from Addresses,' *Canadian School Journal* (March 1935): 87.

113 Frederick Minkler, 'The Progressive Education Conferences at Hamilton and Windsor,' *The School* (January 1939): 378. Minkler's article reported on the two PEA conferences held in the province. These were discussed at greater length in the previous chapter.

114 Ibid., 378.

115 'Editorial: Education Week,' 181.

116 Ibid. The author of the article did acknowledge a degree of incongruity between selling and teaching: 'Selling is not an activity congenial to teachers. To those who live in the academic calm, salesmanship connotes a glib and shameless sophistry with enthusiastic intent to deceive. Nevertheless we teach in a world where commodities survive on their publicized merits, in years when the demands on the public purse are heavy beyond precedent, and under conditions which will make people question the value of everything they paid for on trust before,' 181.

117 E.A. Corbett, 'Can the Radio Be Used Effectively in University Extension Work?' *The School* (October 1935): 94. Corbett was a pioneering adult educator who played an important role in the establishment of the Canadian Association for Adult Education in 1935.

118 See, for example, 'Pickering College, Newmarket, Ontario,' *Canadian School Journal* (November 1933): 404. The rest of the advertisement is equally telling: 'Teachers are aware that, in a time of crisis such as the present, education of our children should be the last economy. It is the purpose of this school to give to its students a rational appreciation of present day conditions and to fit them for the complex problems of the future.'

119 'News from Home and Abroad,' *Canadian School Journal* (June 1935): 196. The article reported that this branch included teachers in private and public schools, parents, and educationists interested in working on basic ideas of international cooperation and understanding.

120 'The Canadian Education Association,' *The School* (December, 1936), 283.

121 'Urban Trustees Association Annual Convention,' *Canadian School Journal* (June 1937): 236.

122 'Editorial Notes: Indoctrination,' *The School* (April 1936): 641.

123 A.S.H. Hill, 'Is Democracy Worth Fighting for?' *The School* (May 1940): 750. The theme of democratic education during the early 1940s will be discussed at greater length in ch. 7. Hill ran an article each month in *The School* that noted events happening during the war in Europe. He aimed to encourage teachers to engage their students with studies that reinforced the primacy of democracy.

124 'Editorial: School and Society,' *The School* (September 1941): 1.

125 David H. Russell, 'Education for Critical Thinking,' *The School* (November 1941): 188.

126 Angela A. Hannan, 'Canadian Leaders Deserve Respect,' *The School* (September 1941): 11. Hannan was a teacher at Forest High School in Forest, Ontario, whom the editors describe as having 'taken an active part in discussion groups on social and economic problems.'

6. Humanists as the Foil to Progressivists

1 In the context of this study, I use the term 'humanists' here as an alternative to 'anti-progressivists' or 'critics of progressive education.' I use it as an alternative to 'traditionalists,' 'conservatives,' or 'classicists.' By humanists, I mean the authors of those ideas that cannot be categorized as progressivist. Humanists defended the so-called traditional school models that progressive education sought to overthrow.

2 These were considered at length in ch. 1.

3 Bondy, 'The Present Situation in Modern Languages,' 120. The Reverend Bondy was the Superior of the Basilian Fathers at St Michael's College.

4 Ibid., 120.

5 See, for example, C.C. Goldring, 'Drifting towards Painless Education,' *Canadian School Journal* (May 1936): 153–7. Goldring, Superintendent of Schools in Toronto, argues in this article that school reforms and criticisms of educational systems are to be expected. Goldring, at length, cites William C. Bagley, Professor of Education at the Teachers College of Columbia University: 'Every generation discovers the school's shortcomings, especially its formalism and its preoccupation with symbols. Every generation demands realities and condemns symbols. And yet every attempt to revolutionize educational practice by discarding formal programs and dispensing with symbols has failed. The school is a very old institution. It is almost as old as civilization itself. In a sense it made the development of civilization possible.'

6 'Address by Sir Arthur W. Currie,' *Canadian School Journal* (January 1933): 6.
   This article reproduced an address that Currie gave at the Royal York Hotel
   in Toronto on 3 December 1932 at the Ridley College Old Boys' Association
   Banquet.
7 Ibid.
8 Maurice Hutton, quoted in S.E.D. Shortt, *The Search for an Ideal: Six Canadian
   Intellectuals and Their Convictions in an Age of Transition, 1890–1930* (Toronto,
   ON: University of Toronto Press, 1976), 92.
9 W.H. Fyfe, 'Science in Secondary Education,' *The School* (April 1934): 652.
10 A.B. McKillop, *Matters of Mind: The University in Ontario, 1791–1951*
   (Toronto, ON: University of Toronto Press, 1994), 463. McKillop's characterization of the diminished position of classics referred to the context of
   Ontario's universities, yet it is also fitting with reference to the educational
   discourse in the province's educational journals.
11 Ibid. McKillop summarizes the revised program of study's impact on Latin
   as follows: 'Students were allowed to choose between Latin and mathematics as the language of entry into university. Such reforms to the public
   school curriculum invariably undercut enrolment in classics programs
   throughout the province, even at the University of Toronto,' 463.
12 Henry Bowers, 'Guesswork,' *The School* (October 1939): 97.
13 Evangeline Lewis, 'What Pupils Think of the Activity Programme,' *The
   School* (October 1939): 101.
14 Bowers, 'Guesswork,' 97.
15 See, for example, 'Editorial: Fads and Frills in Education,' *Canadian School
   Journal* (February 1934): 43.
16 Ibid.
17 'Editorial Notes: Looking Backward,' *The School* (January 1934): 370.
18 Ibid., 370.
19 C.E. Mark, 'Some Educational Pitfalls,' *The School* (March 1940): 564.
20 Ibid., 564.
21 Bondy, 'The Present Situation in Modern Languages,' 120. Emphasis in the
   original text.
22 Ibid. Bondy devotes a paragraph to this thought, beginning: 'They call it
   progressive education and, since the term implies that we are going some-
   where, an attempt is made to define more or less accurately the intended
   destination. In its most radical form, its avowed aim is to train citizens in
   accordance with the average requirements of the local community. A long
   article would be needed to do justice to the loftiness of noble ideal.'
23 Fyfe, 'Science in Secondary Education,' 653.
24 R.B. Liddy, 'The School as a Factor in the Making of the Mind,' *Canadian
   School Journal* (June 1934): 233.

25 Ibid., 233.

26 Ibid., 233.

27 Ibid., 234.

28 See, for example, E.D. MacPhee, 'The Value of the Classics,' *The School* (October 1927): 111–20. A number of references to faculty psychology are made in the source journals, but MacPhee's article is by far the most comprehensive. He, an Associate Professor of Psychology at the University of Toronto, provides a thorough description of faculty psychology, explains why it proves inferior to experimental psychology, and includes a reference list for further reading.

29 See, for example, 'Original Papers in Relation to a Course of Liberal Education,' *American Journal of Science and Arts* 15, no. 2 (1829): 301–2. This article explains how each subject in the traditional, humanistic curriculum conveniently matches up with one of the human faculties: 'From the pure mathematics, he [*sic*] learns the art of demonstrable reasoning. In attending to the physical sciences, he becomes familiar with facts, with the process of induction, and the varieties of probable evidence. In ancient literature, he finds some of the most finished models of taste, by English reading he learns the powers of the language in which he is to speak and write. By logic and mental philosophy, he is taught the art of thinking; by rhetoric and oratory, the art of speaking. By frequent exercise on written composition, he acquires copiousness and accuracy of expression. By extemporaneous discussion, he becomes prompt, fluent, and animated.'

30 L.J. Crocker, 'What Are Our Objectives?,' *The School* (December 1940): 331.

31 In 1930, W.H. Fyfe's inauguration speech as Principal of Queen's University reinforced the message that the aim of education, particularly at the university, was 'to aid human beings in the growth of character, in the healthy development of all their faculties, physical, mental, moral, aesthetic, and spiritual.' W.H. Fyfe, 'Inaugural Address,' 24 October 1930, box 2, file 9, W.H. Fyfe Papers, Queen's University Archives.

32 A.J. Husband, 'The Teaching of History in the Secondary School,' *The School* (December 1931): 308. Husband explained that 'the training derived from study is one of the greatest importance. It helps to develop the logical faculties.'

33 J.H. Smith, 'Mere Knowledge Does Not Constitute an Education,' *Canadian School Journal* (January 1932): 38.

34 Ibid.

35 'Here and There: Mental Discipline,' *The School* (February 1935): 469.

36 See also W.H. Fyfe, 'The Objects of Education: Appreciation and Expression,' *Canadian School Journal* (April 1932): 132. In this address to students at Victoria University in Toronto, Fyfe treats education as an entity that

ennobles and civilizes the mind: 'There are many criteria of a good education. One of the best, I think, is appreciation. The uneducated man is unde-
veloped, and, therefore, largely insensate. There are pleasures to which
his sense is unawakened. He is blind to many forms of beauty; and deaf to
many kinds of truth. He moves through life with muted senses, and at the
same time pathetically exaggerates the few forms of pleasure which he can
appreciate.'

37 MacPhee, 'The Value of the Classics,' 112.

38 Peter Sandiford, 'Transfer of Training,' *The School* (October 1938): 94.

39 Ibid. Sandiford admitted that 'while the experiment cannot be defended
on scientific grounds, nevertheless it is important historically,' 94. See also
William James, *Principles of Psychology*, vol. I (New York, NY: Henry Holt,
1890): 666–7.

40 Ibid., 94–5. See also Edward Lee Thorndike and R.S. Woodworth, 'The
Influence of Improvement in One Mental Function upon the Efficiency of
Other Functions,' *Psychological Review* 8 (May 1901): 247–61.

41 MacPhee, 'The Value of the Classics,' 112–13.

42 This shift from a defence via mental discipline to one concerned with the
usefulness of the past for contemporary life mirrors the situation in the
United States. In that context, William Torrey Harris, Commissioner of
Education, argued that the classical curriculum composed of mathematics,
literature and art, grammar, history, and geography, 'five windows of the
soul,' best represented the culmination of human progress. Among Canadian humanists, years later, the scope of humanities' subjects was outlined
in similar terms, most notably by Watson Kirkconnell and A.S.P. Woodhouse, who included in their framework the study of language, literature,
fine arts, history, religion, and philosophy, to the exclusion of social sciences
and mathematics. For further reading, see William T. Harris, 'What Shall
the Public Schools Teach?,' *Forum* 4 (1888): 574; and Watson Kirkconnell
and A.S. Woodhouse, eds., *The Humanities in Canada* (Ottawa, ON: Humanities Research Council of Canada, 1947), 203.

43 Fyfe, 'Science in Secondary Education,' 656. See also Hilda Neatby, *So Little
for the Mind* (Toronto, ON: Clarke, Irwin, 1953).

44 Charles M. Ewing, 'The Case for Latin in the High Schools,' *The School*
(October 1934): 100.

45 Ibid., 101.

46 J.M. Paton, 'Better English,' *The School* (May 1936): 733.

47 Ibid., 733. Supporting the editorial's findings were scathing critiques of the
standard of written and oral English usage among Canadians by E.H.A.
Watson and Eric Duthie that had been published in *Queen's Quarterly*.

48 MacPhee, 'The Values of the Classics,' 113.

49 Ibid. He cited, for example, the research of L.V. Walker, who showed that 'the frequency of Latin words, phrases, and quotations in English shows merely that a Latin vocabulary may be of use in reading certain types of prose,' 113. He also cited V.A.C. Henmon's demonstrations of the effects of high school Latin on the ability to interpret phrases in modern languages.

50 'Here and There,' *The School* (November 1934): 189–90.

51 Ibid. The article actually described the latter approach as 'soul-destroying,' 189–90.

52 See, for example, B.C. Taylor, 'The Latin Society – I,' *The School* (September 1941): 41.

53 Ibid., 41.

54 Ibid. The editorial note reads as follows: 'Fifty years ago, nearly everyone said that Latin trained the mind for the business of living. Ten years ago, almost nobody believed it. Today, teachers like the author of this article are demonstrating that there can be a transfer of training when the teacher will make the transfer, instead of relying on a pious hope. The Latin club is one method of achieving this end. Mr. B. C. Taylor has had outstanding success in making Latin a rich and vital subject to high school pupils.'

55 R.H. King, 'Civics in Ancient History,' *The School* (February 1933): 515–21.

56 See, for example, 'Can the Present Courses of Study Be Adapted to Meet the Needs of Students Who Do Not Wish to Matriculate?' *Canadian School Journal* (August 1932): 270; and E.J. Transom, 'Time Off for Thinking,' *The School* (March 1941): 607.

57 'Editorial: Two Sides to a Question,' *The School* (October 1941): 91.

58 See, for example, 'The School Library Is an Educational Necessity,' *Canadian School Journal* (March 1928): 20.

59 L. Irene Cole, 'Elementary School Libraries,' *The School* (April 1931): 726–9.

60 Ibid., 726.

61 'Editorial Notes: Adult Education,' *The School* (March 1934): 559.

62 Ibid.

63 J.D. Campbell, 'The Elementary School Library of Ontario,' *Canadian School Journal* (April 1934): 131.

64 Ibid., 134. The reading opportunities provided by libraries, Campbell argued, were like 'the open sesame to the best thoughts and sentiments of all ages.'

65 See, for example, 'School Libraries Co-operation,' *Canadian School Journal* (July 1940): 265.

66 Arthur Slyfield, 'Establishing a School Library,' *The School* (September 1934): 13.

67 Ibid.
68 E. Lillian Morley, 'The Rural School Library,' *Canadian School Journal* (March 1932): 76.
69 See, for example, J.E. Montague, 'County Libraries,' *Canadian School Journal* (July 1940): 270.
70 'Books for Information, Inspiration, and Pleasure,' *Canadian School Journal* (February 1933): 44.
71 James B. Conant, quoted in George F. Rogers, 'President's Address: Canadian Education Association,' *The School* (January 1937): 384.
72 Ibid.
73 'The Editor's Page,' *Canadian School Journal* (July 1935): 205. Capitalization in the original text.
74 See, for example, Wilfred Bovey, 'The Educational Value of Handicrafts,' *The School* (November 1935): 183–8. Bovey, President of the Canadian Handicrafts Guild and Vice-President of the Association for Adult Education, saw the liberal arts as wonderful things that many students could not necessarily afford to pursue in school or work; however, 'if we turn to the other point of view, if we think of education as a process which teaches us to get the most out of life, to live the best and the fullest way that we can, to spend our leisure that we may not only gain a return but gain happiness, a process which helps us to observe and to enjoy the things around us,' 183.
75 W.E.M. Aitken, 'The Use of a High School Library,' *The School* (March 1931): 614.
76 Rogers, 'President's Address,' 385. See also 'Reflections from the O.E.A. Convention,' *Canadian School Journal* (April 1937): 158. Canada's Governor General, Lord Tweedsmuir, who attended that OEA convention in 1937, noted that systems of education should avoid the tendency to be overly concerned with efficiency and utility, ideals better suited to machinery than to education.
77 See, for example, Arthur A. Lowther, 'A Vocational School Literature Course,' *The School* (September 1926): 53. Lowther was concerned with how to develop a love of literature and classics in the context of a vocational school.
78 See, for example, J.W. Brown, 'The School Library,' *Canadian School Journal* (January 1934): 8. Brown, a librarian, treated the theme of book selection. For him, the choice of text was as important as the ability to read.
79 Mae Locklin, 'The Senior Library in the Rotary School,' *The School* (March 1930): 363.
80 See, for example, Isabel M. Thomas, 'Getting Students to Do Home Reading,' *The School* (September 1933): 58–9; and 'The Editor's Page,' *Canadian School Journal* (July 1938): 241.

81 'Educational News,' *Canadian School Journal* (January 1935): 23. This thought is attributed to Lyman Abbott, who said that 'the home ought to be no more without a library than without a dining-room and kitchen. If you have but one room, and it is lighted by the wood fire in the flaming fireplace as Abraham Lincoln's was, do as Abraham Lincoln did, pick out one corner for a library and use it. Every man ought to provide for the brain as well as the stomach.'

82 M. Isabel Wilson, 'Silent Reading,' *The School* (May 1931): 852. Wilson also said that 'happy is the child whose young mind is stored with beautiful thoughts and beautiful expressions.'

83 See, for example, Doris M. Gill, 'History Teaching through Great Lives: Alexander the Great,' *The School* (October 1929): 231; and Archer Wallace, 'A Boy and His Reading,' *Canadian School Journal* (February 1932): 56.

84 See, for example, Lillian H. Smith, 'Fifty Essential Books for Boys and Girls,' *Canadian School Journal* (March 1934): 91.

85 M.A. Campbell, 'The Public School Library,' *Canadian School Journal* (January 1932): 45.

86 See, for example, S. Silcox, 'The Teacher's Book Shelf,' *The School* (March 1930): 470.

87 See, for example, Kathleen M. Crosby, 'The School and Library Boards Co-operate,' *Canadian School Journal* (July 1938): 244–5. Crosby, a school librarian in the Orillia Public Library, provides a testimonial for how public librarians, working closely with schoolteachers, can promote the development of children's reading tastes, introduce students to the classics of literature, and bring history alive.

88 'Co-operating for Good Reading,' *Canadian School Journal* (July 1939): 253.

89 See, for example, 'More Books for More Children,' *Canadian School Journal* (July 1941): 221.

90 Ewing, 'The Case for Latin in the High Schools,' 100.

91 Ibid.

92 'Educationists Face Their Problems,' *The School* (May 1935): 741.

93 Ibid., 741–2.

94 Ibid., 742.

95 'Editorial Notes: The Place of Latin in the Schools,' *The School* (December 1936): 274.

96 Committee of the Classical Section of the OEA, 'The Report on Latin,' *The School* (June 1935): 865–71.

97 Ibid.

98 'Notes and News: Ontario,' *The School* (June 1935): 895.

99 Ibid., 897.

100 The 1937 and 1938 curriculum revisions are considered in greater length in the following chapter. For further reading on the decline of classics, see McKillop, *Matters of Mind*. For a debate between Duncan McArthur, Minister of Education, and J.F. Macdonald, Classics Professor at the University of Toronto, at the OEA conference, see 'McArthur Would Cut Language Requirement,' *Globe and Mail*, 30 March 1940: 5. Among the reasons that McArthur gave to Macdonald for removing Latin as a mandatory subject were the antiquated thinking related to mental discipline and the unpleasant teaching methods associated with the classical language.

101 See, for example, McKillop, *Matters of Mind*, 463. McKillop notes, with a hint of irony, that a former student in classics played a pivotal role in the subject's diminished status: 'In 1934, with the election of the Liberal government of Mitchell Hepburn in Ontario, Duncan McArthur became deputy minister (and later minister) of education. McArthur, a 1912 graduate in "honour classics" from the University of Toronto, championed French as opposed to Latin in the province's high schools, possibly for political reasons.'

102 'As the Press Viewed the O.E.A. Convention,' *Canadian School Journal* (April 1940): 155.

103 Ibid.

7. Continuities and Change

1 In fact, the source journals generally heaped praise on McArthur. Particularly after his appointment as minister following the death of Leo Simpson, the journals reiterated McArthur's credentials, experience, and commitment to Ontario's schools. See, for example, 'The New Minister of Education,' *Canadian School Journal* (September 1940): 319; 'The New Education,' *The School* (October 1940): 172; and 'Personal,' *The School* (October 1940): 174. Having reported, in 'The New Education,' that 'a revision of the *Programme of Studies* has just been published,' the following commentary in 'Personal' extols the virtues of the minister, arguing that 'the province is fortunate in having a distinguished educationist in the cabinet post charged with the administration of the schools.' *Canadian School Journal*, likewise, praised McArthur and expressed confidence that he would 'vitally affect the youth of Ontario and influence the critical period which will follow the war. Ontario looks forward to still greater progress in the field of education and recognizes the valuable service which Dr. McArthur will contribute as a member of the Cabinet in all matters affecting public interest.'

2 See, for example, 'Education Criticism,' *The Globe*, 5 June 1934: 5.

3 See, for example, 'Notes and News: Ontario,' *The School* (September 1934): 65–8. Simpson was a medical doctor as opposed to an academic, like McArthur.

4 Robert M. Stamp, *The Schools of Ontario, 1876–1976.* (Toronto, ON: University of Toronto Press, 1982), 155.

5 'Notes and News: Ontario,' 66–8. The committee struck by McArthur to review the curriculum as well as the work of Thornton Mustard and Stanley Watson in the composition of a revised program of study were discussed briefly in ch. 3.

6 E.J. Transom, 'Time Off for Thinking,' *The School* (February 1941): 507. Transom believed that the new, progressive schools drew their principles from the study of contemporary society: 'The work of the teacher, principal, or supervisor now is to study society, ascertain modern trends and movements, learn the fundamentals of personality, child development, and child psychology.'

7 These concerns, on the whole, are dominated by those espoused by meliorist and developmentalist journal articles. The Department of Education's concern for efficiency was directed primarily at reforming the system of taxation and consolidating school boards. See, for example, 'Summary of Dr. McArthur's Address,' *Canadian School Journal* (May 1940): 192–3.

8 John Seath, *Education for Industrial Purposes* (Toronto, ON: King's Printer, 1911).

9 Ibid., 263. Seath actually noted seven domains for study in Ontario's schools: courses leading to university matriculation, courses leading to normal schools or Faculties of Education, household science courses, commercial courses, agricultural courses, manual training courses, and middle school art courses.

10 W.G. Fleming, *Schools, Pupils, and Teachers*, vol. 3 of *Ontario's Educative Society* (Toronto, ON: University of Toronto Press, 1972), 129.

11 Ibid., 130.

12 Ibid., 123.

13 Stamp, *The Schools of Ontario*, 167.

14 The preparation of students for an uncertain future, and overall concerns about managing or controlling education in a mutable and unpredictable world, were common themes in progressivist texts, including John Dewey's. See, for example, Richard D. Mosier, 'Progressivism in Education,' *Peabody Journal of Education* 29, no. 5 (1951): 274–81.

15 *Programme of Studies for Grades I to VI of the Public and Separate Schools, 1937* (Toronto, ON: Department of Education, 1937). The British publications are most commonly referred to as the Hadow Reports.

16 *Health: A Handbook of Suggestions for Teachers in Public and Separate Schools* (Toronto, ON: Ryerson, 1938).
17 Ibid., v. In the foreword, the handbook is described as having taken shape following experiments on the teaching of health in elementary schools in Ontario. The experiments were initiated by the Department of Health, supervised by the Department of Education, and implemented by progressivist educators: 'This experiment was initiated by Dr. J. T. Phair, Chief Medical Officer of Health for the Province. Through the offices of Mr. V. K. Greer, Chief Inspector of Public and Separate Schools, the co-operation of six inspectors was obtained. These Inspectors, in turn, enlisted the services of a number of progressive and interested teachers who were prepared to undertake the work.'
18 Ibid., vii–viii.
19 Ibid., 6–16.
20 Ibid., 15.
21 Ibid., 28.
22 Ibid. In the handbook's discussion on 'The Individual Child,' the focus on health is described as a means of enabling a flexible curriculum. The traditional program is described as having set up arbitrary academic levels of achievement and insisting that they be met by every child: 'The inevitable result has been rigidity and inflexibility of the school programme. There has been over-emphasis on arbitrary academic standards. The neglect or inadequate consideration given to the physical, emotional, and social development of the individual child has resulted in the adoption of classroom procedures which too frequently are inelastic and ineffective in developing a well-balanced personality,' 28.
23 Ibid. The text's foreword states: 'The Handbook is submitted for use in schools, not as a final guide, but as an experimental and tentative outline of procedure. It is hoped that the teachers will accept it as such, record their observations and suggestions, and forward them to the Department of Education. Such observations and suggestions should prove of great value in future revisions,' vi.
24 See, for example, 'Dr. McArthur's Views on Youth,' *Toronto Daily Star*, 30 July 1943: 6. The article, incidentally, praises McArthur's 'progressive views on education.'
25 Ibid., 6.
26 *Programme of Studies for Grades I to VI … 1937*, 25.
27 Ibid., 25.
28 Ibid., 35.
29 Ibid., 35.

30 'Editorial Notes: New Approaches to the Social Studies,' *The School* (April 1937): 645.

31 'Ontario's Educational System,' *Toronto Daily Star*, 19 July 1943: 6.

32 *Programme of Studies for Grades I to VI ... 1937*, 71.

33 Ibid., 71.

34 Ibid., 73.

35 Ibid., 87.

36 Ibid., 87.

37 Ibid., 87.

38 Ibid., 101.

39 Ibid., 127. Emphasis in the original text.

40 See, for example, 'New School Course to Discourage Exams, Abolish Homework,' *Toronto Daily Star*, 14 September 1937: 1. This front page article in the newspaper summarized the spirit of the 164-page curriculum document as leading to 'less stress on factual type of teaching.'

41 Duncan McArthur, 'Education for Citizenship,' *The School*, December 1934, 286.

42 Robin S. Harris, *Quiet Evolution: A Study of the Educational System of Ontario* (Toronto, ON: University of Toronto Press, 1967). The high school entrance examinations were not withdrawn until 1949.

43 McArthur, 'Education for Citizenship,' 288.

44 Ibid., 288.

45 Ibid. McArthur explained the relationship between examinations and textbooks as follows: 'The presumed necessities of examinations, again, encourage the teacher to attempt to satisfy the requirements of education by demanding that the pupil make himself [*sic*] familiar with the information contained within the authorized text. Instruction in such cases is degraded to the mere reciting of facts set forth on the pages of the text. Such a process, by no stretch of the imagination, can be found to have any relation to education,' 288.

46 Ibid., 288.

47 'Supplement: Reports on Educational Progress in Canada and Newfoundland, 1940–1941,' *The School* (June 1941): 919.

48 See, for example, 'New School Course to Discourage Exams, Abolish Homework.' Recall, also, the cliché about French education, which postulated that at any given moment of the schoolday all children of the same age were having exactly the same lesson. This vision of a standardized and centralized educational system reflected how entrenched *le programme* – the national curriculum, dating from Napoleonic times – had become in the country's educational system.

49 See, for example, Julian Nundy, 'Education: Teachers as Lone Wolves: France, 750,000 Children Sit Down to Be Tested on the Same Day,' *The Independent*, 10 June 1993.
50 'Optional French and Latin Urged by Deputy Minister,' *Toronto Daily Star*, 30 March 1940: 27.
51 These were discussed at length in ch. 6.
52 'Optional French and Latin,' 27. *The Globe* attributes a slightly different quotation to McArthur: 'It does not matter what you teach, as long as it is unpleasant. That educational psychology is absolutely antiquated.' 'McArthur Would Cut Language Requirement,' *The Globe*, 30 March 1940: 5.
53 'Optional French and Latin,' 27.
54 'Latin,' *Canadian School Journal* (April 1940): 155.
55 Ibid., 155.
56 Patrice Milewski, '"The Little Gray Book": Pedagogy, Discourse, and Rupture in 1937,' *History of Education* 37, no. 1 (2008): 92.
57 Ibid., 92. Emphasis in original text.
58 Ibid., 92. My emphasis. The parallels that Milewski draws between the educational rhetoric and medical discourse seem to go too far, and it seems a further stretch to assert that 'this discourse formed a body of knowledge that intervened in the experience of teaching and learning to shape or define normal child development, teaching, learning and schooling,' 92.
59 Stamp, *The Schools of Ontario*, 175.
60 Fleming, *Schools, Pupils, and Teachers*, 9.
61 V.K. Greer, 'Appraisal of the New Programme of Studies,' *Canadian School Journal* (June 1938): 194.
62 Ibid., 231. Greer's article is spread over seven pages in *Canadian School Journal*.
63 *Programme of Studies for Grades VII and VIII of the Public and Separate Schools*, 6.
64 Ibid., 7.
65 Greer, 'Appraisal.' Greer boasted: 'The new courses and the new textbooks in arithmetic will make the work more interesting and will delay complex processes until they are more readily understood by the pupils,' 198. See also 'The Aim of the Course' in the *Programme of Studies for Grades VII and VIII*, which states: 'The teacher should endeavour to lead his [sic] pupils at each stage of their growth to explain for themselves, in terms that are intelligible to them at the time, the social world in which they are a part,' 26.
66 Greer, 'Appraisal.' Greer argued that the new curriculum offered a more holistic view of learners, focusing attention on the individual's development and not merely on academic achievement: 'No doubt the authors of

the new courses intended that less emphasis should be put upon the annual external examination used solely as a basis for the promotion of pupils. It would be an equally faulty extreme, however, to promote all pupils on the basis of age. The best procedure will be the careful study for the work being done by pupils when they first begin to show retardation. Individual attention will then be given, and there is no doubt that by doing this we shall avoid demotions and failures to a much greater extent than we have done in the past,' 199.

67 See, for example, the section 'Activity and Interest' in the *Programme of Studies for Grades VII and VIII of the Public and Separate Schools, 1942*, which states the following: 'All learning involves activity and effort on the part of the learner. "Learning is an active process." "We learn to do by doing." "The child develops through his own activity." In applying these precepts one must remember that the term "activity" does not refer to physical movement only. It must be borne in mind that mental processes – thinking, reflecting, planning – are as truly "activities" as conducting an experiment or acting in a play,' 9.

68 Ibid., 9.

69 Ibid., 9.

70 Ibid., 9.

71 Ibid., 105.

72 Ibid., 116.

73 Ibid., 116.

74 The value of home economics extended from the cultivation of girls' 'standards of good taste in clothing and home-furnishings' to the fostering of 'an appreciation of scrupulous cleanliness in person, dress, and surroundings,' 116. The content of the course included particular activities that each girl needed to learn, including needlework, familiarity with various textiles and sewing equipment, cooking, laundering, and furnishings.

75 *Programme of Studies for Grades VII and VIII … 1942*, 26.

76 Ibid. The document states: 'Every event occurs in a geographical setting, has roots in the past, has implications for the present and may have repercussions in the future,' 29.

77 Ibid., 29.

78 Ibid., 29. Emphasis in original text.

79 *Programme of Studies for Grades VII and VIII … 1942*, 29.

80 Ibid., 40.

81 Ibid., 43. See also Greer, 'Appraisal.' Greer argues for the importance of libraries in schools to support academic work: 'The course places strong emphasis on the advantages of supplementary reading, and again the success of the

course will depend largely on an ample and well-chosen library and on the ability of the teacher to inspire the pupils to read good books,' 197–8.

82 *Programme of Studies for Grades VII and VIII … 1942,* 40.

83 Greer, 'Appraisal of the New Programme of Studies,' 196.

84 Ibid., 196.

85 Ibid., 197. Greer's use of Eliot is all the more interesting in light of Herbert Kliebard's identification of Eliot as standing 'in the forefront of the *humanist* interest group … Eliot, a humanist in his general orientation, was also a mental disciplinarian, but, although this thinking affected his thinking on curriculum matters to a large extent, he was not exactly a defender of the status quo in curriculum matters.' Herbert M. Kliebard, *The Struggle for the American Curriculum, 1893–1958,* 3rd ed. (New York, NY: RoutledgeFalmer, 2004), 9. Emphasis in original text.

86 Greer, 'Appraisal,' 197. Incidentally, L.J. Bondy, seen in the previous chapter, writing in the same year as Greer, wondered how long English would be deemed useful by progressivists. The humanities had lost ground with the demise of classics, and they would continue to be marginalized in the face of ongoing reforms: 'It is enough for my purpose that, in a scheme of this kind, it is only by mere accident that modern languages will be found *useful,* and their defenders will find it increasingly difficult to explain why they should be retained … For a brief moment a few of the more thoughtless among the defenders of modern languages seemed to welcome the change. The loss of the Ancients would be the gain of the Moderns. Now it is becoming more and more evident that the forces that have achieved such success in ostracizing Greek and Latin are being arrayed with the same deadly purpose against the modern languages. The success of these efforts is already being felt. Italian and Spanish have practically disappeared from our high schools; German is slowly yielding ground. For reasons that are largely extraneous to education, French has not suffered so much in this province. However, unless something is done to improve its position, we may confidently expect that it will join its vanishing companions. And all this in the magic name of progress.' L.J. Bondy, 'The Present Situation in Modern Languages in Our Schools,' *The School* (October 1938): 121. Emphasis in the original text.

87 Ibid., 128.

88 *Programme of Studies for Grades VII and VIII … 1942,* 5.

89 Ibid., 6.

90 Ibid., 13–21. The section provided Ontario's teachers with directions regarding how to use enterprise activities to foster purposeful activity, natural ways of learning, integrated subject matter, self-direction, and fundamental skills.

91 Fleming, *Schools, Pupils, and Teachers,* 128–30.

92 Ibid. These themes, Fleming noted, dealt more with contemporary social problems and issues. Increasingly, they concerned Canada's growing relationship with the United States and its role in the North Atlantic.

93 This theme is discussed at greater length in ch. 3 in relation to social meliorism and active learning.

94 See, for example, the following by McArthur: 'Education for Democracy,' *Canadian School Journal* (January 1941): 13; 'Education and the Empire,' *The Empire Club of Canada Speeches* (Toronto, ON: Empire Club of Canada, 1941); and 'Message from the Minister of Education,' *Canadian School Journal* (December 1942): 373.

95 McArthur, 'Education for Democracy,' 13.

96 Ibid., 13.

97 'Message from the Minister of Education,' 373.

98 Ibid., 373.

99 'Schools and the War,' *Canadian School Journal* (June 1942): 174.

100 'Notes and News: Teaching as a War Profession,' *Canadian School Journal* (October 1942): 324.

101 Gladstone Murray, 'Radio and Citizenship,' *Canadian School Journal* (April 1942): 113.

102 Ibid., 113.

103 Ibid., 113. Murray argued that 'radio listening has become a part of the defence mechanism of democratic society,' 113.

104 Murray, 'Radio and Citizenship,' 114.

105 A.S.H. Hill, 'Towards Victory: A Current Events Notebook,' *The School* (September 1940): 7. It was in this same edition that Phillips published the controversial editorial 'Declaration of Faith,' which was discussed in ch. 1 of this book.

106 Hill, 'Towards Victory: A Current Events Notebook,' 7.

107 H.E. Smith, 'The New Education in Alberta,' *The School* (November 1940): 187–8.

108 Ibid., 188.

109 See, for example, Charles Phillips, 'Editorial: School and Society' *The School* (September 1941): 1. Phillips then informed readers of *The School* that 'many articles on a variety of subjects will be found to refer repeatedly to education for democratic citizenship. Beginning with this issue, emphasis will be placed on a particular monthly theme.' These themes were all related to classroom practice. In September 1941, for example, the theme was classroom management.

110 See, for example, C.C. Goldring, 'Some Educational Gaps,' *Canadian School Journal* (April 1942): 140–1.

111 Peter A. Baskerville, *Ontario: Image, Identity, and Power* (Toronto, ON:

Oxford University Press, 2002), 204. Hepburn, Ontario's premier, bitterly opposed labour unions and refused to allow the Congress of Industrial Organizations (CIO) to form unions in the province. He not only took the side of General Motors when a CIO-led strike began in Oshawa on 8 April 1937, but also formed a volunteer police force to suppress the striking workers. At the same time, the CCF supported the strike.

112 Stamp, *The Schools of Ontario*, 180.
113 Baskerville, *Ontario*, 205.
114 Stamp, *The Schools of Ontario*, 174.
115 The social meliorist concerns for social justice, international cooperation, and active citizenship were persistent throughout the interwar period and survived the demise of the League.
116 Baskerville, *Ontario*, 205.
117 'Notes and Comment,' *Toronto Daily Star*, 16 March 1943: 6.
118 Ibid., 6. In fact, when critiquing democratic, progressivist education, Drew had argued that 'firm measures supported by the mandate of the strap still have an important place.'
119 Robert D. Gidney, *From Hope to Harris: The Reshaping of Ontario's Schools* (Toronto, ON: University of Toronto Press, 1999), 10.
120 Ibid., 10.
121 Stamp, *The Schools of Ontario*, 177.
122 'Dr. Duncan McArthur,' *Canadian School Journal* (April 1937): 126. This article reproduced a speech that McArthur, then Deputy Minister of Education, delivered to the Trustees' Department at the OEA conference in 1937.
123 Ibid., 126. McArthur depicted grade nine, which provided opportunities for students to sample different topics and programs, as the core of modern schools: 'That year, I say without any hesitation, will be the most important year for the boys and girls of our Collegiate Institutes. The decisions likely to be made during the course of that year, discussions with parents and teachers, will have a most important bearing on the future of our boys and girls.'

Conclusion

1 In 2010, *Antistasis: A New Brunswick Education Journal* was established at the University of New Brunswick. As founding editor, I have modelled the journal on *The School* and *The Canadian School Journal*, framing educational discussions as public, not merely academic, goods.
2 John Dewey, *Experience and Education* (New York, NY: Collier, 1938), 90. Emphasis in the original text.

References

Primary Sources

Archival Sources

ARCHIVES OF ONTARIO (TORONTO, ON)
Department of Education Central Registry Files, 1906–68
Education Collection, 1829–1976
George S. Henry Family Fonds, 1817–1989
Howard Ferguson Fonds, 1907–39
Mitchell F. Hepburn Fonds, 1893–1945
Ontario Educational Association Fonds, 1860–1946
Ontario Federation of Home and School Association Fonds, 1916–85
Premier Mitchell F. Hepburn Private Correspondence, 1934–42
Premier Mitchell F. Hepburn Public Correspondence Records, 1934–42
Programme of Studies for Grades I to VI of the Public and Separate Schools, 1937
Reports of the Minister of Education to the Province of Ontario, 1917–45
Revised Programme of Studies for Grades VII to VIII of the Public and Separate Schools, 1938

QUEEN'S UNIVERSITY ARCHIVES (KINGSTON, ON)
Adam Shortt Fonds, 1879–1931
Duncan McArthur Fonds, 1929–40
George Monro Grant Fonds, 1860–1902
John Watson Fonds, 1872–1939
McKim's Directory of Canadian Publications, 1918–42
Queen's Quarterly Fonds, 1893–1955
William Hamilton Fyfe Fonds, 1919–67

THOMAS FISHER RARE BOOK LIBRARY (UNIVERSITY OF TORONTO, TORONTO, ON)
William Emet Blatz Fonds, 1895–1964

ONTARIO INSTITUTE FOR STUDIES IN EDUCATION LIBRARY (UNIVERSITY OF
TORONTO, TORONTO, ON)
The Canadian School Journal
The Canadian School Board Journal
The School

DUNCAN MCARTHUR HALL EDUCATION LIBRARY (QUEEN'S UNIVERSITY,
KINGSTON, ON)
The School

Newspapers/Newsletters/Periodicals

Bulletin (Toronto, ON: Federation of Women Teachers' Associations of
    Ontario)
The Bulletin (Toronto, ON: Ontario Secondary School Teachers' Federation)
The Globe and Mail (Toronto, ON)
The Ottawa Citizen (Ottawa, ON)
Queen's Quarterly (Kingston, ON: Queen's University)
Saturday Night (Toronto, ON)
The Toronto Star (Toronto, ON)
University of Toronto Monthly (Toronto, ON: University of Toronto)

Secondary Sources

Altenbaugh, Richard T. 1994. Whither Progressive Education? *Educational
    Researcher* 23(5): 35–6.
Althouse, J.G. 1958. *Addresses*. Toronto, ON: W. G. Gage.
Anchor, Robert. 2001. On How to Kick the History Habit and Discover That
    Every Day in Every Way, Things Are Getting Meta and Meta and Meta …
    History and Theory 40(1): 104–16.
Anderson, L.W. 1993. Recurrent Problems in Teacher Education. In *Teacher
    Educators Annual Handbook 1993*, ed. T.A. Simpson, 50–61. Red Hill, Aus-
    tralia: Queensland University of Technology.
Andrews, J. 1984. Alternative Futures for Faculties of Education. *Canadian
    Journal of Education* 9: 261–75.
Apple, Michael. 1986. *Teachers and Texts: A Political Economy of Class and Gender
    Relations in Education*. New York, NY: Routledge & Kegan Paul.
– 1990. *Ideology and Curriculum*. New York, NY: Routledge.

Ash, Maurice. 1969. *Who Are the Progressives Now? An Account of an Educational Confrontation*. London, UK: Routledge & Kegan Paul.

Axelrod, Paul. 1997. *The Promise of Schooling: Education in Canada, 1800–1914*. Toronto, ON: University of Toronto Press.

– 2005. Beyond the Progressive Education Debate: A Profile of Toronto Schooling in the 1950s. *Historical Studies in Education* 17(2): 227–41.

Bailyn, Bernard. 1960. *Education in the Forming of American Society*. New York, NY: Vintage.

Ballantine, Jeanne H., and Floyd M. Hammack. 2009. *The Sociology of Education: A Systematic Analysis*. 6th ed. Englewood Cliifs, NJ: Pearson Prentice Hall.

Barton, Angela Calabrese, and Margery D. Osborne. 1998. Marginalized Discourses and Pedagogies: Constructively Confronting Science for All. *Journal of Research in Science Teaching* 35(4) (1998): 339–40.

Baskerville, Peter A. 2002. *Ontario: Image, Identity, and Power*. Toronto, ON: Oxford University Press.

Benford, Robert D., and David A. Snow. 2000. Framing Processes and Social Movements: An Overview and Assessment. *Annual Review of Sociology* 26: 611–39.

Bernhardt, Karl S., Margaret I. Fletcher, Frances L. Johnson, Dorothy A. Millichamp, and Mary L. Northway, eds. 1951. *Twenty-Five Years of Child Study: The Development of the Programme and Review of the Research at the Institute of Child Study, University of Toronto, 1926–1951*. Toronto, ON: University of Toronto Press.

Bernstein, Richard J. 1991. *The New Constellation: The Ethical–Political Horizons of Modernity/Postmodernity*. Oxford, UK: Polity.

Bhaskar, Roy. 1997. *A Realist Theory of Science*. New York, NY: Verso.

– 1998. Facts and Values: Theory and Practice/Reason and the Dialectic of Human Emancipation/Depth, Rationality, and Change. In *Critical Realism: Essential Readings*, ed. M. Archer, R. Bhaskar, A. Collier, T. Lawson, and A. Norrie, 409–43. London, UK: Routledge.

– 1998. *The Possibility of Naturalism: A Philosophical Critique of the Contemporary Human Sciences*. London, UK: Routledge.

– 1998. *Reclaiming Reality: A Critical Introduction to Contemporary Philosophy*. New York, NY: Verso.

Biesta, Gert J.J., and Siebren Miedema. 1996. Dewey in Europe: A Case Study on the International Dimensions of the Turn-of-the-Century Educational Reform. *American Journal of Education* 105: 1–26.

Blatz, William E. 1926. The Saint George's School for Child Study, *University of Toronto Monthly* (June), 443–5.

– 1940. *Hostages to Peace: Parents and the Children of Democracy*. New York, NY: William Morrow.

– 1944. *Understanding the Young Child*. New York, NY: William Morrow.

– 1967. *Human Security: Some Reflections*. Toronto, ON: University of Toronto Press.

Blatz, William E., and Helen M. Bott. 1928. *Parents and the Pre-School Child*. Toronto, ON: J.M. Dent and Sons.

Bledstein, B. 1976. *The Culture of Professionalism: The Middle Class and the Development of Higher Education in America*. New York, NY: Norton.

Bobbitt, Franklin. 1918. Scientific Method in Curriculum-Making. In *The Curriculum*, Preface and ch. 6. Cambridge, MA: Riverside.

Bothwell, Robert. 2006. *The Penguin History of Canada*. Toronto, ON: Penguin Canada.

Bott, E.A. 1951. Founding of the Institute of Child Study. In *Twenty-five Years of Child Study: The Development of the Programme and Review of the Research at the Institute of Child Study, University of Toronto, 1926–1951*, ed. Karl S. Bernhardt, Margaret I. Fletcher, Frances L. Johnson, Dorothy A. Millichamp, and Mary L. Northway. Toronto, ON: University of Toronto Press, 15–17

Bowers, C.A. 1964. The Social Frontier: A Historical Sketch. *History of Education Quarterly* 4(3): 167–80.

Bowles, Samuel, and Harry Gintis. 1976. *Schooling in Capitalist America*. New York, NY: Basic.

Boyd, William, and Wyatt Rawson. 1965. *The Story of the New Education*. London, UK: Heinemann.

Breed, Frederick S. 1933. What Is Progressive Education? *Elementary School Journal* 34(2): 111–17.

Brehony, Kevin J. 2004. A New Education for a New Era: The Contribution of the Conferences of the New Education Fellowship to the Disciplinary Field of Education, 1921–38. *Paedagogica Historica* 40(5): 733–55.

Brickman, William W. 1964. Revisionism and the Study of the History of Education. *History of Education Quarterly* 4(4): 209–23.

Bruno-Jofré, Rosa. 1998–9. Citizenship and Schooling in Manitoba: 1918–1945. *Manitoba History* 36: 26–36.

– 1999. Manitoba Schooling in the Canadian Context and the Building of a Polity: 1919–1971. *Canadian and International Education* 28(2): 99–129.

– 2000. Public Schooling in English Canada: Addressing Difference in the Context of Globalization. *Canadian Ethnic Studies* 32(1): 38–53.

– 2007. To Those in 'Heathen Darkness': Deweyan Democracy and Education in the American Interdenominational Configuration. Paper presented at the International Standing Conference for the History of Education, Hamburg, 25 July 2007.

Bruno-Jofré, Rosa, and Martin Schiralli. 2002. Teaching History: A Discussion of Contemporary Challenges. *Encounters on Education* 3: 117–27.

Buenker, J.D., J.C. Burnham, and R.M. Crunden. 1977. *Progressivism.* Cambridge, MA: Schenkman.

Bury, J.B. 1920. *The Idea of Progress: An Inquiry into Its Origin and Growth.* New York, NY: Dover.

Butin, Dan W. 2005. Diversity, Democracy, and Definitions: Contested Positions for the Future of the Social Foundations. In *Teaching Social Foundations of Education,* ed. Dan W. Butin, 191–200. Mahwah, NJ: Lawrence Erlbaum Associates.

Butts, Freeman R. 1967. Civilization-Building and the Modernization Process: A Framework for the Reinterpretation of the History of Education. *History of Education Quarterly* 7(2): 147–74.

– 1973. *In the First Person Singular: The Foundations of Education.* San Francisco, CA: Caddo Gap.

Callahan, R. 1962. *Education and the Culture of Efficiency: A Study of the Social Forces That Have Shaped the Administration of Public Schools.* Chicago, IL: University of Chicago Press.

Canadian Teachers' Federation. 1957. *Trends in the Economic Status of Teachers, 1910–1955.* Ottawa, ON: Canadian Teachers Federation.

Charters, Werrett W. 1909. *Methods of Teaching: Developed from a Functional Standpoint.* Chicago, IL: Row, Peterson.

– 1913. *Teaching the Common Branches.* Boston, MA: Houghton Mifflin.

– 1923. *Curriculum Construction.* New York, NY: Macmillan.

Cohen, David K. 1998. Dewey's Problem. *Elementary School Journal* 98(1): 427–46.

Cohen, Sol. 1973. The History of the History of Education, 1900–1976: The Uses of the Past. *Harvard Educational Review* 46(3): 298–330.

– 1995. The Influence of Progressive Education on School Reform in the USA. In *Progressive Education across the Continents,* ed. Hermann Rohrs and Volker Lenhart, 321–31. Frankfurt, Germany: Peter Lang.

– *Challenging Orthodoxies: Toward a New Cultural History of Education.* New York, NY: Peter Lang.

Collier, Andres. 1994. *Critical Realism: An Introduction to Roy Bhaskar's Philosophy.* New York, NY: Verso.

Commachio, Cynthia. 1993. *Nations Are Built of Babies.* Montreal, QC, and Kingston, ON: McGill–Queen's University Press.

– 1997. 'A Postscript for Father': Defining a New Fatherhood in Interwar Canada. *Canadian Historical Review* 78(3): 385–408.

– 1999. *The Infinite Bonds of Family: Domesticity in Canada, 1850–1940.* Toronto, ON: University of Toronto Press.

– 2006. *The Dominion of Youth: Adolescence and the Making of a Modern Canada, 1920–1950.* Waterloo, ON: Wilfrid Laurier University Press.

Committee on Teacher Education. 1971. *Teacher Education: Perseverance or Professionalism?* Charlottetown, PEI: University of Prince Edward Island.

Coulter, Rebecca P. 2005. Getting Things Done: Donalda J. Dickie and Leadership through Practice. *Canadian Journal of Education* 28(4): 667–98.

Counts, George S. 1930. *The American Road to Culture: A Social Interpretation of Education in the United States.* New York, NY: John Day.

– 1932. *Dare the School Build a New Social Order?* New York, NY: John Day, 1932.

– 1934. *The Social Foundations of Education.* New York, NY: Charles Scribner's Sons.

Cremin, Lawrence. 1961. John Dewey and the Progressive Education Movement, 1915–1952. In *Dewey on Education*, ed. Reginald D. Archambault. New York, NY: Random House.

– 1961. *The Transformation of the School: Progressivism in American Education, 1876–1957.* New York, NY: Alfred A. Knopf.

– 1965. *The Wonderful World of Ellwood Patterson Cubberley: An Essay on the Historiography of American Education.* New York, NY: Teachers College Press.

– 1988. *American Education: The Metropolitan Experience, 1876–1980.* New York, NY: Harper & Row.

Cross, Wilbur. 1934. *Twenty-Five Years After: Sidelights on the Mental Hygiene Movement and Its Founder.* New York, NY: Doubleday.

Cuban, Larry. 1992. Curriculum Stability and Change. In *Handbook of Research on Curriculum*, ed. P.W. Jackson, 216–47. New York, NY: Macmillan.

– 2001. Can Historians Help School Reformers? *Curriculum Inquiry* 31(4): 453–67.

Cubberley, Ellwood. 1919. *Public Education in the United States.* Cambridge, MA: Riverside.

Cunningham, Peter. 2001. Innovators, Networks, and Structures: Towards a Prosopography of Progressivism. *History of Education* 30(5): 433–51.

Curtis, Bruce. 1988. *Building the Educational State: Canada West, 1836–1871.* London, ON: Althouse.

– 2000. *The Politics of Population: State Formation, Statistics, and the Census of Canada, 1840–1875.* Toronto, ON: University of Toronto Press.

Curtis, Bruce, D.W. Livingstone, and Harry Smaller. 1992. *Stacking the Deck: The Streaming of Working-Class Kids in Ontario Schools.* Toronto, ON: Our Schools / Our Selves Education Foundation.

Dain, Norman. 1980. *Clifford W. Beers: Advocate for the Insane.* Pittsburgh, PA: University of Pittsburgh Press.

Davies, Scott. 2002. The Paradox of Progressive Education: A Frame Analysis. *Sociology of Education* 75: 269–86.

Dewey, John. 1897. My Pedagogic Creed. *The School Journal* 54(3): 77–80.

– 1904. The Relation of Theory to Practice in Education. In *The Third Yearbook,* pt 1. *National Society for the Scientific Study of Education,* ed. C. Murray, 9–30. Chicago, IL: University of Chicago Press.

– 1907. *The School and Society.* Chicago, IL: University of Chicago Press.

– 1912. *Cyclopedia of Education,* ed. Paul Monroe. I:572. New York, NY: Macmillan Company.

– 1916. *Democracy and Education.* New York, NY: Free Press.

– 1929. *The Sources of a Science of Education.* New York, NY: Horace Liveright.

– 1930. Whither Humanism? *The Thinker* 2: 9–12.

– 1934. Education for a Changing Social Order. *Peabody Reflector and Alumni News* 7: 123–4.

– 1938. *Experience and Education.* New York, NY: Touchstone.

– 1960. *The Quest for Certainty.* New York, NY: Capricorn.

– 1966. *Lectures in the Philosophy of Education: 1899,* ed. Reginald D. Archambault. New York, NY: Random House.

– 1991. *How We Think.* Buffalo, NY: Prometheus.

Drummond, Ian M. 1987. *Progress without Planning: The Economic History of Ontario from Confederation to the Second World War.* Toronto, ON: University of Toronto Press.

Easterbrook, W.T., and H.G.J. Aitken. 1990. *Canadian Economic History.* Toronto, ON: University of Toronto Press.

Edmonson, Henry T. 2006. *John Dewey and the Decline of American Education: How the Patron Saint of Schools Has Corrupted Teaching and Learning.* Wilmington, DE: ISI.

Egan, Kieran. 1999. Clashing Armies in the Curriculum Wars. In *Children's Minds, Talking Rabbits, and Clockwork Oranges: Essays on Education.* New York, NY: Teachers College Press.

– 2002. *Getting It Wrong from the Beginning: Our Progressive Inheritance from Herbert Spencer, John Dewey, and Jean Piaget.* New Haven, CT: Yale University Press.

– 2005. Students' Development in Theory and Practice: The Doubtful Role of Research. *Harvard Educational Review* 75(1): 25–41.

Fay, Brian. 1998. Introduction: The Linguistic Turn and Beyond in Contemporary Theory of History. In *History and Theory: Contemporary Readings,* ed. Brian Fay, Philip Pomper, and Richard T. Vann, 1–12. Oxford, UK: Blackwell.

Filene, Peter G. 1970. An Obituary for 'The Progressive Movement.' *American Quarterly* 22(1): (Spring): 20–34.

Fish, Stanley. 1990. Rhetoric. In *Critical Terms for Literary Study*, ed. F. Lentricchia and T. Mclaughlin. Chicago, IL: University of Chicago Press.

Fleming, W.G. 1971. *The Expansion of the Educational System*. Vol. 1 of *Ontario's Educative Society*. Toronto, ON: University of Toronto Press, 1971),

– 1972. *The Administrative Structure*. Vol. 2 of *Ontario's Educative Society*. Toronto, ON: University of Toronto Press.

– 1972. *Schools, Pupils, and Teachers*. Vol. 3 of *Ontario's Educative Society*. Toronto, ON: University of Toronto Press.

– 1972. *Supporting Institutions and Services*. Vol. 5 of *Ontario's Educative Society*. Toronto, ON: University of Toronto Press.

– 1972. *Educational Contributions of Associations*. Vol. 7 of *Ontario's Educative Society*. Toronto, ON: University of Toronto Press.

Fraser, James W. 1988. Who Were the Progressive Educators Anyway? A Case Study of the Progressive Education Movement in Boston, 1905–1925. *Educational Foundations* 2(1): 4–30.

Gamson, David A. 2003. District Progressivism: Rethinking Reform in Urban School Systems, 1900–1928. *Paedagogica Historica* 39(4): 417–34.

Gardiner, Patrick. 1952. *The Nature of Historical Explanation*. London, UK: Oxford University Press.

Gersman, Elinor M. 1972. A Bibliography for Historians of Education. *History of Education Quarterly* 12(1): 81–8.

– 1977. A Selected Bibliography of Periodicals in Educational History. *History of Education Quarterly* 17(3): 275–96.

– 1972. A Bibliography for Historians of Education. *History of Education Quarterly* 12(4): 531–41.

Giddens, Anthony. 1984. *The Constitution of Society*. Cambridge, UK: Polity.

– 1990. *The Consequence of Modernity*. Cambridge, UK: Polity.

Gidney, Robert D. 1999. *From Hope to Harris: The Reshaping of Ontario's Schools*. Toronto, ON: University of Toronto Press.

Giroux, Henry A. 1983. *Theory and Resistance in Education: A Pedagogy for the Opposition*. South Hadley, MA: Bergin and Garvey.

– 1993. *Living Dangerously: Multiculturalism and the Politics of Difference*. New York, NY: Peter Lang.

Gleason, Mona. 1999. *Normalizing the Ideal: Psychology, Schooling, and the Family in Postwar Canada*. Toronto, ON: University of Toronto Press.

Goldring, C.C. 1937. *We Are Canadian Citizens*. Toronto, ON: J.M. Dent.

Goodman, Joyce, and Jane Martin. 2004. Editorial: History of Education — Defining a Field. *History of Education* 33(1): 1–10.

Grosvenor, Ian. 2007. 'Seen But Not Heard': City Childhoods from the Past into the Present. *Paedagogica Historica* 43(3): 405–29.

Guillet, Edwin C. 1960. *In the Cause of Education: Centennial History of the Ontario Educational Association, 1861–1960*. Toronto, ON: University of Toronto Press.

Hall, G. Stanley. 1901. Ideal School Based on Child Study. In *Journal of Proceedings and Addresses of the National Education Association*, 474–88. Washington, DC: National Education Association.

Hall-Quest, Alfred L. *Editorial Foreword: Experience and Education*. New York, NY: Collier.

Harris, Robin S. 1967. *Quiet Evolution: A Study of the Educational System of Ontario*. Toronto, ON: University of Toronto Press.

Harris, William T. 1888. What Shall the Public Schools Teach? *Forum* 4: 573–81.

Hayes, William. 2006. *The Progressive Education Movement: Is It Still a Factor in Today's Schools?* New York, NY: Rowman & Littlefield Education.

Heap, Ruby, and Alison Prentice, eds. 1991. *Gender and Education in Ontario: An Historical Reader*. Toronto, ON: Canadian Scholars' Press.

Hébert, Y.H., and L. Wilkinson. 2002. The Citizenship Debates: Conceptual, Policy, Experiential, and Educational Issues. In *Citizenship in Transformation in Canada*, ed. Y.H. Hébert, 3–36. Toronto, ON: University of Toronto Press.

Heron, Craig. 1998. *The Workers' Revolt in Canada, 1917–1925*. Toronto, ON: University of Toronto Press.

Himmelfarb, Gertrude. 1997. Telling It as You Like It: Postmodernist History and the Flight from Fact. In *The Postmodern History Reader*, ed. Keith Jenkins, 158–74. New York, NY: Routledge.

Hlebowitsh, Peter S., and William G. Wraga. 1995. Social Class Analysis and the Early Progressive Tradition. *Curriculum Inquiry* 25(1): 7–21.

Iacovetta, Franca, and Wendy Mitchinson. 1998. *On the Case: Explorations in Social History*. Toronto, ON: University of Toronto Press.

James, William. 1890. *Principles of Psychology*. Vol. 1. New York, NY: Henry Holt.

Jay, Martin. 1990. Fieldwork and Theorizing in Intellectual History. *Theory and Society* 19: 311–21.

Jenkins, Keith. 1999. *Why History? Ethics and Postmodernity*. New York, NY: Routledge.

Kaestle, Carl F. 1972. Social Reform and the Urban School. *History of Education Quarterly* 12(1): 211–28.

Katz, Michael B. 1968. *The Irony of Early School Reform: Educational Innovation in Mid-Nineteenth Century Massachusetts*. Boston, MA: Beacon.

– 1976. The Origins of Public Education: A Reassessment. *History of Education Quarterly* 16(4): 381–407.

Kirkconnell, Watson, and A.S. Woodhouse, eds. 1947. *The Humanities in Canada*. Ottawa, ON: Humanities Research Council of Canada.

Kliebard, Herbert. 1989. Education at the Turn of the Century: A Crucible for Curriculum Change,' *Educational Researcher* 9: 16–24.

– 1992. *Forging the American Curriculum: Essays in Curriculum History and Theory.* London, UK: Routledge.

– 1992. The Decline of Humanistic Studies in the American School Curriculum. In *Forging the American Curriculum: Essays in Curriculum History and Theory,* ed. Herbert Kliebard, 3–16. London, UK: Routledge.

– 1992. Keeping Out of Nature's Way: The Rise and Fall of Child-Study as the Basis for Curriculum, 1880–1905. In *Forging the American Curriculum: Essays in Curriculum History and Theory,* ed. Herbert M. Kliebard, 61–7. London, UK: Routledge.

– 1992. The Liberal Arts Curriculum and Its Enemies: The Effort to Redefine General Education. In *Forging the American Curriculum: Essays in Curriculum History and Theory,* ed. Herbert M. Kliebard, 27–50. London, UK: Routledge.

– 1992. Vocational Education as Symbolic Action: Connecting Schooling with the Workplace. In *Forging the American Curriculum: Essays in Curriculum History and Theory,* ed. Herbert M. Kliebard, 183–201. London, UK: Routledge.

– 1995. Why History of Education? *Journal of Educational Research* 88(4): 194–9.

– 2004. *The Struggle for the American Curriculum, 1893–1958.* 3rd ed. New York, NY: RoutledgeFalmer.

Kloppenberg, James T. 1986. *Social Democracy and Progressivism in European and American Thought, 1870–1920.* New York, NY: Oxford University Press.

– 1996. Pragmatism: An Old Name for Some New Ways of Thinking? *Journal of American History* 83(1): 100–38.

Kneller, George. 1983. 'The Proper Study of Education.' *Journal of Teacher Education* 48: 177–84.

Krug, E.A. 1964. *The Shaping of the American High School, 1880–1920.* New York, NY: Harper & Row.

– 1972. *The Shaping of the American High School, 1920–1941.* Madison, WI: University of Wisconsin Press.

Labaree, David. 2005. Progressivism, Schools, and Schools of Education: An American Romance. *Paedagogica Historica* 41(1–2): 275–88.

– 2006. Innovation, Nostalgia, and the Politics of Educational Change. *Education Administration Quarterly* 42(1): 157–64.

– 2007. *Education, Markets, and the Public Good.* London, UK: Routledge.

– 2007. 'Limits on the Impact of Educational Reform: The Case of Progressivism and U.S. Schools, 1900–1950. Paper presented at Monte Verità conference, Ascona, Switzerland.

Lagemann, Ellen C. 1989. *The Politics of Knowledge: The Carnegie Corporation, Philanthropy, and Public Policy.* Middleton, CT: Wesleyan University Press.

– 2005. Does History Matter in Educational Research? A Brief for the Humanities in the Age of Science. *Harvard Educational Review* 75(1): 9–24.

Lawn, Martin. 1996. *Modern Times? Work, Professionalism, and Citizenship in Teaching*. London, UK: Falmer.

Lawr, Douglas A., and Robert D. Gidney, eds. 1973. *Educating Canadians: A Documentary History of Public Education*. Toronto, ON: Van Nostrand Reinhold.

Lemisko, Lynn S., and Kurt W. Clausen. 2006. Connections, Contrarieties, and Convolutions: Curriculum and Pedagogical Reform in Alberta and Ontario, 1930–1955. *Canadian Journal of Education* 29(4): 1097–126.

Levin, Ben. 1996. Moving Away from the Common School? In *Monographs in Education, 23; Papers on Contemporary Issues in Education Policy and Administration in Canada: A Foundations Perspective*, ed. R. Bruno-Jofré and L. Grieger, 33–54. Winnipeg, MB: University of Manitoba.

Levin, Robert A. 1991. Debate over Schooling: Influences of Dewey and Thorndike. *Childhood Education* 68(2): 71–5.

Levine, Arthur. 2005. *Educating School Leaders*. New York, NY: Education Schools Project.

Levine, David. 1964. *Varieties of Reform Thought*. Madison, WI: State Historical Society of Wisconsin.

Lorenz, Chris. 1994. Historical Knowledge and Historical Reality: A Plea for 'Internal Realism.' *History and Theory* 33: 342–76.

– 1998. Can Histories Be True? Narrativism, Positivism, and the 'Metaphorical Turn.' *History and Theory* 37(1): 309–30.

– 1999. You Got Your History, I Got Mine. *Österreichische Zeitschrift für Geschichtswissenschaften* 10(4): 563–84.

– 2000. Some Afterthoughts on Culture and Explanation in Historical Inquiry. *History and Theory* 39: 348–63.

Massolin, Philip. 2001. *Canadian Intellectuals, the Tory Tradition, and the Challenge of Modernity, 1939–1970*. Toronto, ON: University of Toronto Press.

McArthur, Duncan. 1927. *History of Canada for High Schools*. Toronto, ON: W.G. Gage.

– 1941. Education and the Empire. In *The Empire Club of Canada Speeches*, 212–24. Toronto, ON: Empire Club of Canada.

McKay, Ian. 2000. The Liberal Order Framework: A Prospectus for a Reconnaissance of Canadian History. *Canadian Historical Review* 81(4): 617–45.

– 2005. *Rebels, Reds, Radicals: Rethinking Canada's Left History*. Toronto, ON: Between the Lines.

McKenty, Neil. 1967. *Mitch Hepburn*. Toronto, ON: McClelland and Stewart.

McKey, Alan. 2003. *Textual Analysis: A Beginner's Guide*. London, UK: Sage.

McKillop, A.B. 1994. *Matters of Mind: The University in Ontario, 1791–1951*. Toronto, ON: University of Toronto Press.

Milewski, Patrice. 2008. 'The Little Gray Book': Pedagogy, Discourse, and Rupture in 1937. *History of Education* 37(1): 91–111.

Mirel, Jeffrey E. 1990. Progressive School Reform in Comparative Perspective. In *Southern Cities, Southern Schools: Public Education in the Urban South*, ed. D.N. Plank and R. Ginsberg. New York, NY: Greenwood.

– 2003. Old Educational Ideas, New American Schools: Progressivism and the Rhetoric of Educational Revolution. *Paedagogica Historica* 39(4): 477–97.

Mitchell, Tom. 1996–7. The Manufacture of Souls of Good Quality: Winnipeg's 1919 National Conference on Canadian Citizenship, English-Canadian Nationalism, and the New Order after the Great War. *Journal of Canadian Studies* 31(4): 5–29.

Morrison, Keith. 1989. Bringing Progressivism into a Critical Theory of Education. *British Journal of Sociology of Education* 10(1): 3–18.

Mosier, Richard D. 1951. Progressivism in Education. *Peabody Journal of Education* 29(5): 274–81.

Mulvany, C. Pelham. 1884. *Toronto: Past and Present, A Handbook of the City*. Toronto, ON: W.E. Caiger.

Murphy, Madonna M. 2006. *The History and Philosophy of Education: Voices of Educational Pioneers*. Upper Saddle River, NJ: Pearson Education.

Nash, Paul. 1962. Historical versus Geographical Factors in Canadian Education. *International Review of Education* 8(1): 13–22.

Naylor, James. 1991. *The New Democracy: Challenging the Social Order in Industrial Ontario, 1914–1925*. Toronto, ON: University of Toronto Press.

Neatby, Hilda. 1953. *So Little for the Mind*. Toronto, ON: Clarke, Irwin.

Nelles, Henry V. 1974. *The Politics of Development: Forests, Mines, and Hydro-Electric Power in Ontario, 1849–1941*. Hamden, CT: Archon.

Newnham, W.T., and A.S. Nease. 1970. *The Professional Teacher in Ontario: The Heritage, Responsibilities, and Practices*. 3rd ed. Toronto, ON: Ryerson.

Nichols, Roy F. 1963. The Genealogy of Historical Generalizations. In *Generalizations in the Writing of History*, ed. L. Gottschalk. Chicago, IL: University of Chicago Press.

Nisbet, Roger. 1969. *History and Social Change: Aspects of the Western Theory of Development*. New York, NY: Oxford University Press.

Osborne, Ken. 1986–7. Archives in the Classroom. *Archivaria* 23: 16–40.

. 2000. 'Our History Syllabus Leaves Us Gasping': History in Canadian Schools – Past, Present, and Future. *Canadian Historical Review* 81(3): 404–35.

2003. Teaching History in Schools: A Canadian Debate. *Journal of Curriculum Studies* 35, no. 5 (2003): 585–626.

Owram, Doug. 1986. *The Government Generation: Canadian Intellectuals and the State, 1900–1945*. Toronto, ON: University of Toronto Press.

Ozmon, Howard. 1965. Progressive Education: And Some of Its Critics. *Peabody Journal of Education* 43(3): 169–74.

Palmer, Howard. 1984. Reluctant Hosts: Anglo-Canadian Views of Multiculturalism in the Twentieth Century. In *Cultural Diversity and Canadian Education: Issues and Innovations*, ed. J.R. Mallea and J. Young, 21–40. Ottawa, ON: Carleton University Press.

Patterson, Robert S. 1986. The Implementation of Progressive Education in Canada, 1930–1945. In *Essays in Canadian Education*, ed. N. Kach, K. Mazurek, R.S. Patterson, and I. Defavery, 79–96. Calgary, AB: Detselig.

– 1986. Society and Education during the Wars and Their Interlude. In *Canadian Education: A History*, ed. J.D. Wilson, T. Stamp, and L.P. Audet, 360–84. Toronto, ON: Prentice Hall of Canada.

– 1974. *Profiles of Canadian Educators*. Toronto, ON: D.C. Heath.

– 1990. The Canadian Experience with Progressive Education. In *Canadian Education: Historical Themes and Contemporary Issues*, ed. E.B. Titley, 95–110. Calgary, AB: Detselig.

Pepper, Stephen C. 1942. *World Hypotheses: A Study in Evidence*. Berkeley, CA: University of California Press.

Phillips, Charles E. 1957. *The Development of Education in Canada*. Toronto, ON: W.J. Gage.

– 1977. *College of Education, Toronto: Memories of OCE*. Toronto, ON: University of Toronto Press.

Popkewitz, Thomas S. 1984. *Paradigm and Ideology in Educational Research: Social Functions of the Intellectual*. New York, NY: Falmer.

– 2005. An Introduction. In *Inventing the Modern Self and John Dewey: Modernities and the Traveling of Pragmatism in Education*, ed. Thomas S. Popkewitz, 3–38. New York, NY: Palgrave Macmillan.

Potter, Garry, and José Lópéz. 2001. After Postmodernism: The Millennium. In *After Postmodernism: An Introduction to Critical Realism*, ed. Garry Potter and José Lópéz. New York, NY: Althone.

Provincial Committee on Aims and Objectives of Education in the Schools of Ontario. 1968. *Living and Learning*. Toronto, ON: Newton.

Ravitch, Diane. 1978. *The Revisionists Revised: A Critique of the Radical Attack on the Schools*. New York, NY: Basic.

– 2000. *Left Back: A Century of School Reforms*. New York, NY: Simon and Schuster.

Raymond, Jocelyn M. 1991. *The Nursery World of Dr Blatz*. Toronto, ON: University of Toronto Press.

Reese, William J. 1982. *Power and the Promise of School Reform: Grass-Roots Movements during the Progressive Era*. Boston, MA: Routledge & Kegan Paul.

Richardson, Theresa. 2006. Rethinking Progressive High School Reform in the 1930s: Youth, Mental Hygiene, and General Education. *American Educational History Journal* 33(1): 77–87.

Ridenour, Nina. 1961. *Mental Health in the United States: A Fifty-Year History*. Cambridge, MA: Harvard University Press.

Rodgers, Daniel T. 1982. In Search of Progressivism. *Reviews in American History* 10 (December): 113–32.

– 1998. *Atlantic Crossings: Social Politics in a Progressive Age*. Cambridge, MA: Belknap.

Rohrs, Hermann. 1995. Internationalism in Progressive Education and Initial Steps toward a World Education Movement. In *Progressive Education across the Continents*, ed. Hermann Rohrs and Volker Lenhart, 11–30. Frankfurt, Germany: Peter Lang.

Rohrs, Hermann, and Volker Lenhart, eds. 1995. *Progressive Education across the Continents: A Handbook*. New York, NY: Peter Lang.

Roman, Fredrick William. 1923. *The New Education in Europe: An Account of Recent Fundamental Changes in the Educational Philosophy of Great Britain, France, and Germany*. London, UK: George Routledge.

Rugg, Harold. 1947. *The Foundations of American Education*. New York, NY: World Book.

– 1952. *The Teacher of Teachers*. New York, NY: Harper and Brothers.

Rugg, Harold, and William Withers. 1955. *Social Foundations of Education*. New York, NY: Harper and Brothers.

Rury, John L. 1991. Transformation in Perspective: Lawrence Cremin's *Transformation of the School*. *History of Education Quarterly* 31: 67–76.

Sack, Saul. 1962. Liberal Education: What Was It? What Is It? *History of Education Quarterly* 2(4): 210–24.

Schwab, Joseph J. 1959. The 'Impossible' Role of the Teacher in Progressive Education. *School Review* 67(2): 139–59.

Seath, John. 1911. *Education for Industrial Purposes*. Toronto, ON: King's Printer.

Selleck, Richard. 1968. *The New Education, 1870–1914*. London, UK: Pitman.

– 1972. *English Primary Education and the Progressives, 1914–1939*. London, UK: Routledge & Kegan Paul.

Shortt, Samuel E.D. 1976. *The Search for an Ideal: Six Canadian Intellectuals and Their Convictions in an Age of Transition, 1890–1930*. Toronto, ON: University of Toronto Press.

Solomon, Lawrence. 2007. *Toronto Sprawls: A History*. Toronto, ON: University of Toronto Press.

Southgate, Beverly. 2001. *History: What and Why? Ancient, Modern, and Post-modern Perspectives*. London, UK: Routledge.

Spelt, James. 1955. *The Urban Development in South-Central Ontario*. Assen, Netherlands: Koninklijke Van Gorcum.

Spencer, Herbert. 1963. *Education: Intellectual, Moral, and Physical*. Patterson, NJ: Littlefield, Adams.

Spring, Joel. 1972. *Education and the Rise of the Corporate State*. Boston, MA: Beacon.

– 1994. *The American School, 1642–1993*. New York, NY: McGraw-Hill.

Stamp, Robert M. 1982. *The Schools of Ontario, 1876–1976*. Toronto, ON: University of Toronto Press.

– 1985. *The Historical Background to Separate Schools in Ontario*. Toronto, ON: Queen's Printer for Ontario.

– 1988. *Ontario Secondary School Program Innovations and Student Retention Rates, 1920s–1970s: A Report to the Ontario Study of the Relevance of Education and the Issue of Dropouts*. Toronto, ON: Queen's Printer for Ontario.

– 2005. Growing up Progressive. *Historical Studies in Education* 17(1): 187–98.

Stevenson, Hugh A., Robert Stamp, and Donald Wilson, eds. 1972. *The Best of Times, The Worst of Times: Contemporary Issues in Canadian Education*. Toronto, ON: Holt, Rinehart, and Winston of Canada.

Stewart, W.A. Campbell. 1979. Progressive Education – Past, Present, and Future. *British Journal of Educational Studies* 27(2): 103–10.

Sutherland, Neil. 1975. 'To Create a Strong and Healthy Race': School Children in the Public Health Movement, 1880–1914. In *Education and Social Change: Themes from Ontario's Past*, ed. Michael B. Katz, 133–66. New York, NY: NYU Press.

– 1976. *Children in English-Canadian Society: Framing the Twentieth-Century Consensus*. Toronto, ON: University of Toronto Press.

Talburt, Susan. 2001. Dewey, Identity Politics, and the Parvenue: Some Questions Facing the Social Foundations of Education. *Educational Foundations* 15(3): 47–62.

Taylor, Charles. 1985. *Philosophy and the Human Sciences*. Cambridge, MA: Cambridge University Press.

Taylor, Frederick W. 1911. *The Principles of Scientific Management*. New York, NY: Harper and Brothers.

Thompson, John H., and Allen Seager. 1985. *Canada, 1922–1939: Decades of Discord*. Toronto, ON: McClelland and Stewart.

Thorndike, Edwards, and Robert S. Woodworth. 1901. The Influence of Improvement in One Mental Function upon the Efficiency of Other Functions. *Psychological Review* 8: 247–61.

Titley, Brian E., ed. 1990. *Canadian Education: Historical Themes and Contemporary Issues*. Calgary, AB: Detselig.

– 1996. Reclaiming a Heritage: First Nations Education in the Late Twentieth Century. In *Monographs in Education, 23; Papers on Contemporary Issues in Education Policy and Administration in Canada: A Foundations Perspective*, ed. Rosa Bruno-Jofré and Lisa Grieger, 55–68. Winnipeg, MB: University of Manitoba Press.

Tomkins, George S. 1981. Foreign Influences on Curriculum and Curriculum Policy Making in Canada: Some Impressions in Historical and Contemporary Perspective. *Curriculum Inquiry* 11(2): 157–66.

– 2008. *A Common Countenance: Stability and Change in the Canadian Curriculum*. Vancouver, BC: Pacific Educational Press.

Tyack, David. 1965. The History of Education and the Preparation of Teachers. A Reappraisal. *Journal of Teacher Education* 16(4): 427–31.

– 1967. *Turning Points in American Educational History*. Waltham, MA: Blaisdell.

– 1974. *The One Best System: A History of American Urban Education*. Cambridge, MA: Harvard University Press.

Tyack, David B., and Larry Cuban. 1995. *Tinkering towards Utopia*. Cambridge, MA: Harvard University Press.

Tyler, Ralph W. 1949. *Basic Principles of Curriculum and Instruction*. Chicago, IL: University of Chicago Press.

Tyler, Ralph W., and Richard M. Wolf, eds. 1974. *Critical Issues in Testing*. Berkeley, CA: McCutchan.

Von Heyking, Amy. 2006. *Creating Citizens: History and Identity in Alberta's Schools, 1905 to 1980*. Calgary, AB: University of Calgary Press.

White, Margaret H. 2001. The New Education Fellowship: An International Community of Practice. *New Era in Education* 82(3): 71–5.

Whitehead, Kay and Judith Peppard. Transnational Innovations, Local Conditions, and Disruptive Teachers and Students in Interwar Education. *Paedagogica Historica* 42(1–2): 177–89.

Whiteside, Tom. 1978. *The Sociology of Educational Innovation*. London, UK: Methuen.

Williams, Raymond. 1975. *The Long Revolution*. Harmondsworth, UK: Penguin.

Wright, Frank W. 1930. The Evolution of Normal Schools. *Elementary School Journal* 30(5): 363–71.

Wrigley, Julia. 1982. *Class Politics and the Public Schools: Chicago, 1900–1950*. New Brunswick, NJ: Rutgers University Press.

Zilversmit, Arthur. 1993. *Changing Schools: Progressive Education Theory and Practice, 1930–1960*. Chicago, IL: University of Chicago Press.

Index